THEN SINGS MY SOUL

BOOK 3

ROBERT J. MORGAN

THOMAS NELSON

Since 1798

NASHVILLE   DALLAS   MEXICO CITY   RIO DE JANEIRO

Published in Nashville, Tennessee, by Thomas Nelson. Thomas Nelson is a registered trademark of Thomas Nelson, Inc.

Thomas Nelson, Inc., titles may be purchased in bulk for educational, business, fund-raising, or sales promotional use. For information, please e-mail SpecialMarkets@ThomasNelson.com.

Library of Congress Cataloging-in-Publication Data is available

ISBN-13: 978-0-8499-4713-1

Printed in the United States of America

13 14 15 LB 6 5 4

TO
Miranda

Contents

Part 3: Six Hymn Stories I Love to Tell

Part 4: Hymning in Private and in Public

Epilogue

Ye who long pain and sorrow bear,
Praise God and on Him cast your care!
Alleluia! Alleluia!

Introduction

The largest creatures known to have inhabited our planet—the size of Boeing jets with hearts as big as Volkswagens—are still prowling our globe today. Bigger than the dinosaurs of old, these monsters weigh about 150 tons each. That's comparable to twenty-three elephants glued together; and, in fact, just the tongue of one of these creatures weighs as much as a grown elephant. Fifty people could line up on it.

Though endangered, about ten thousand of these creatures—Giant Blue Whales—still roam the oceanic lanes of earth. And they are always hungry. Each of these leviathans eats five tons of fish a day (they love shrimp). They glide open-mouthed through the seas, taking in as much as fifty tons of water in a single gulp.

Since whales are mammals, Giant Blues give birth to their young; and one newborn will guzzle about fifty gallons of mother's milk a day. During the first several weeks of life, these little balls of blubber gain ten pounds an hour.

And you thought your child was growing fast!

Most amazing to me, these denizens of the sea are the operatic super-stars of the oceans. Just as birds fill the skies with their songs, Giant Blues do the same in the deep. I recently listened to an almost-giddy scientist who unexpectedly "eavesdropped" on Blue Whales singing off the coast of New York City. He could hardly describe the thrill of hearing them through his sonar equipment. Giant Blue Whales have a unique series of very low, very long notes, and their voices reverberate mysteriously through the ocean. They sing with greater decibels than a jetliner taking off, and the sound of their voice travels up to five hundred miles through the water.

Learning that, I couldn't help thinking of Psalm 148:7, which says:

All Creatures of Our God and King

St. Francis of Assisi

Geistliche Kirchengesänge Cologne

1. All crea-tures of our God and King, Lift up your voice and with us sing, Al-le-lu-ia! Al-le-lu-ia! Thou burn-ing sun with gold-en beam, Thou sil-ver moon with soft-er gleam, O praise Him O praise Him! Al-le-lu-ia! Al-le-lu-ia! Al-le-lu-ia!

2. Let all things their Cre-a-tor bless, And wor-ship Him in hum-ble-ness. O praise Him! Al-le-lu-ia! Praise, praise the Fa-ther, praise the Son, And praise the spir-it, Three in One! O praise Him

Praise the LORD from the earth,
you great sea creatures and all ocean depths.

Psalm 148 is one of my favorite passages because it calls on all creation to sing praises to the Lord—in the air, on the land, beneath the seas. The angels are commanded to sing. The sun and moon, the stars of light, fire and hail, snow and clouds—all are made for God's glory. Mountains and hills, fruitful trees and cedars; beasts and cattle; creeping things and flying fowl—let them praise the name of the Lord.

And us too!

Kings of the earth and all peoples;
Princes and all judges of the earth;
Both young men and maidens;
Old men and children.
Let them praise the name of the LORD,
For His name alone is exalted;
His glory is above the earth and
heaven. (verses 11–13 NKJV)

This is the psalm that inspired Saint Francis of Assisi to compose his great poem "Canticle to Brother Son" (*Cantico Di Frater Sole*) which is paraphrased into English as "All Creatures of Our God and King." It's among my favorite hymns, because, like the psalmist, St. Francis exuberantly calls on all creation to sing God's praise:

All creatures of our God and King
Lift up your voice and with us sing,
Alleluia! Alleluia!

Thou burning sun with golden beam,
Thou silver moon with softer gleam!
O praise Him . . . !

Thou rushing wind that art so strong
Ye clouds that sail in Heaven along,
O praise Him . . . !

Thou flowing water, pure and clear,
Make music for thy Lord to hear,
O praise Him . . . !

Dear mother earth, who day by day
Unfoldest blessings on our way,
O praise Him . . . !

Let all things their Creator bless,
And worship Him in humbleness,
O praise Him . . . !

What St. Francis could not have realized in his medieval era is that scientists have now catalogued approximately 5,400 species of singing animals. Some creatures even show the capacity of learning songs, improvising melodies, and composing new tunes.

There's an unusual strain of wild dog in New Guinea famous for its singing. The "New Guinea Singing Dogs," one of the rarest breeds on earth, weren't discovered until the 1950s. They're noted for their unique howling vocalizations. When they sing, they do so with different tones and pitches, filling our ears with harmonies like a barbershop quartet.

God created this universe with a capacity for song, from the tiny cricket to the massive Blue Whale, and all creation is designed to sing His praises. I don't want to be left out; and I don't want us to leave out the great hymns of the faith—that vast two-thousand-year repertoire of music that reverberates through the ages, for God inhabits the praises of His people.

This book—the last in the *Then Sings My Soul* trilogy—is designed to keep the story and the songs of our Christian hymnody alive for the next generation. The first two installments, *Then Sings My Soul* and

Then Sings My Soul Book 2, contain the stories of our timeless and best-loved hymns. This volume provides an overarching span across the centuries of Christian song. Here you'll find the rest of the story—how God has kept us singing from the Red Sea to the return of Christ. (The first biblical hymn is in Exodus 15, when the Israelites were delivered from Egypt; the last is in Revelation 19, at the moment of Christ's second coming.)

My deepest thanks goes to all the hymn-lovers who have paved the way for this volume—and to Thomas Nelson Publishers. I've had a publishing relationship with Nelson since 1996. Few authors are privileged with such a long history with the same company; and I've had nothing but happy relations with all my friends and colleagues there. Matt Baugher at Nelson conceived the idea for this edition of *Then Sings*, and I'm honored to work with him and his blue-ribbon team. The senior editor for this project, Adria Haley, is the best!

My literary agent, Chris Ferebee, is a dear friend and wise counselor. I don't know what I'd do without him. Nor could I do without my assistant, Sherry Anderson, who pours her heart into her work for the Lord and His people.

My creative team at Clearly Media consists of dear friends Joshua Rowe, Michael Walker, and Stephen Fox. They maintain my website at www.robertjmorgan.com, where you can contact me and also find additional resources related to this and other books. That's where you can also find a free planning guide I've prepared for churches who want to use this book to celebrate the story of the hymns in a special worship service designed to worship through the hymnal, from ancient to modern times.

My Nashville congregation, the Donelson Fellowship, is a unique group of devoted Christ-followers and music-lovers who have allowed me to preach and write among them for well over thirty years. I'd like to also tip my hat to Dr. Don Ellsworth for his personal encouragement and puissant insights on this project.

And finally, there's no one like Katrina! Thank you, dear encourager and faithful friend, for all your wifely smiles and songs.

May the Lord give us all smiles. And may He give us songs, both ancient and modern, both now and forevermore, so we can continuously . . .

Praise, praise the Father, praise the Son,
And praise the Spirit, Three in One!
O praise Him! O praise Him!
Alleluia! Alleluia! Alleuia!

PART 1

THE
HISTORY
OF
HYMNODY

"Teach Me Some Melodious Sonnet"

About a year into our marriage, Katrina told me she might be pregnant. There were no home tests in those days, and it took awhile to get definitive answers from the doctor. He suggested we come back for the results in a few days. For reasons I can't remember, Katrina didn't accompany me on the return trip to the doctor's office; I went to hear the news by myself. Yes, the nurse said, we were expecting. Yes, we were going to be parents.

Though excited by the prospects, I drove home in a state of nerves. I didn't have a job. I didn't have health insurance. I had no idea how to support my family. We had been trying to find a church to pastor, but had been turned down a dozen times. How would we get by? Absently I switched on the car radio and heard these words suddenly wafting through the speakers:

> *Be not dismayed whate'er betide,*
> *God will take care of you!*
> *Beneath His wings of love abide,*
> *God will take care of you!*
>
> *God will take care of you,*
> *Through every day o'er all the way;*
> *He will take care of you;*
> *God will take care of you.*

Civilla Martin wrote that hymn at the beginning of the twentieth century (as well as the words to "The Blood Will Never Lose Its Power" and "His Eye Is on the Sparrow"). She died four years before I was born;

3

God Will Take Care of You

Civilla D. Martin

W. Stillman Martin

1. Be not dis-mayed what - e'er be - tide, God will take care of you;
2. Thro' days of toil, when heart doth fail, God will take care of you;
3. All you may need He will pro - vide, God will take care of you;
4. No mat - ter what may be the test, God will take care of you;

Be - neath His wings of love a - bide, God will take care of you.
When dan - gers fierce your path as - sail, God will take care of you.
Noth - ing you ask will be de - nied, God will take care of you.
Lean, wea - ry one, up - on His breast, God will take care of you.

God will take care of you. Thro' ev - ery day, o'er all the way,

He will take care of you; God will take care of you.

but her song lived on to calm my spirits on that springtime day in 1977. Listening to the words of that hymn, I knew everything would be fine.

Have you ever had a similar experience? When in the grip of nervous tension, nothing soothes the soul like the words and melody of one of our beloved hymns. Many such testimonies from around the world fill my filing cabinets, sent in response to the first two volumes of *Then Sings My Soul.* Nothing can do for us what hymns can, for there's a part of our spirits that only responds to God's truth in musical form. Psalm 92:1–4 exhorts us:

It is good to say, "Thank you" to the Lord, to sing praises to the God who is above all gods. Every morning tell him, "Thank you for your kindness," and every evening rejoice in all his faithfulness. Sing his praises, accompanied by music from the harp and lute and lyre. You have done so much for me, O Lord. No wonder I am glad! I sing for joy. (TLB)

As I wrote in my book of hymn devotions, *Near to the Heart of God*: "Hymns are distillations of the richest truths of God, versified, emotionalized, set to music, and released in the mind and from the mouth. They're miniature Bible studies that lead us effortlessly to worship, testimony, exhortation, prayer, and praise. They're bursts of devotional richness with rhyme and rhythm. They clear our minds, soothe our nerves, verbalize our worship, summarize our faith, and sing our great Redeemer's praise."[1]

The eminent church historian Philip Schaff wrote, "The hymn is a popular spiritual song, presenting a healthful Christian sentiment in a noble, simple, and universally intelligible form, and adapted to be read and sung with edification by the whole congregation of the faithful. . . . They resound in all pious hearts, and have, like the daily rising sun and the yearly returning spring, an indestructible freshness and power. . . . Next to the Holy Scripture, a good hymn-book is the richest fountain of edification."[2]

Once upon a time, English-speaking Christians owned their own hymnals just as most believers today own their own Bibles. In the 1700s and 1800s, these were small volumes without musical notes, giving stanzas of hymn texts in tiny print. I have quite a few of these little tan volumes in my possession, bound in leather, pages brittle. Worshippers carried these under-sized hymnbooks to church each Sunday, then took them home and sang from them in personal or family devotions the rest of the week. Hymnals were, as someone put it, the ordinary person's systematic theology books—their Bibles in one hand; their hymnals in the other.

For us today, hymns are portable units of praise, capable of being sung in the heart and with the voice, as needed by the soul, seven days a week. In the words of the apostle Paul: "Let the word of Christ dwell in you richly as you teach and admonish one another with all wisdom, and as you sing psalms, hymns and spiritual songs with gratitude in your hearts to God" (Colossians 3:16).

Our appreciation for Christian music skyrockets when we understand the heritage of our hymnody. Studying the annals of our hymnals is like sinking a shaft through the layers of church history until we come to the very core of praise in biblical truth and in biblical times.

In the prior two volumes of *Then Sings My Soul*, I've told the stories of hymns without providing much historical context. In this final volume, I want to devote a few pages to sharing in simple fashion the overarching history of worship and praise from biblical times to our own. Think of it as standing on a scenic overlook and viewing a panorama of praise that stretches back nearly four thousand years and that extends forward to the very throne of God in heaven.

I'm convinced that ordinary, pew-sitting, churchgoing Christians like me need to understand the history of our hymnody. Rather than a chore, it's an enthralling study, acquainting us with thousands of years of rich legacies, brave heroes, and astounding stories of the faith being passed down by Spirit-filled witnesses from one era to the next. We're largely unaware of our heritage, of the valor and victories of the great cloud of witnesses who have preceded us. But without knowing the heritage of our past, we'll leave no legacy for the future.

I believe the history of the church is encoded in her hymns, and the story of Christianity is enfolded in its songs. If you know the hymns of the ages, you'll know the history of the church. If we lose the hymns, we'll lose a priceless legacy; and we'll be the first generation of Christians to ever do so. Every other generation of believers has added its songs to the hymnal without discarding the contributions of earlier eras.

There are some great advantages to the modern technologies that allow us to project words to giant screens. We do it in our church and it enables us to sing tapestries of songs and hymns, both ancient and modern, without having to stop and turn to different pages in a book. But there are some disadvantages too. Without holding these old hymns in our hands, we're more likely to forget them. Without flipping through the pages of a hymnal, we're apt to forget its contents.

I think we need to teach, emphasize, and celebrate hymns in our public gatherings; and I'm also an advocate for keeping a hymnbook by our devotional materials for daily singing and personal use. Just today during my morning devotions, I found a much-needed prayer in the stanzas of that old hymn that says, "Breathe on me, breathe on me, Holy Spirit, breathe on me. / Take Thou my heart, cleanse every part. Holy Spirit, breathe on me."

A good hymn combines prayer with praise, keen theology with vivid imagery, and the majesty of God with our daily needs.

And to think—there are thousands of hymns ripe for rediscovery, and that's what this book aims to do. *Then Sings My Soul Book 3* isn't designed to provide an in-depth or academic approach to the history of hymnody. Instead, I'd like to tell a generalized (yes, and oversimplified) story to help you better understand and appreciate the wonderful heritage of our hymnal. The hymnbook is one of the richest treasure troves we have for biographical, theological, historical, and personal enrichment.

For our purposes, I'm going to divide the story of Western hymnody into seven segments:

- Biblical Hymns
- Ancient Hymns
- Medieval Hymns
- German Hymns
- English Hymns
- Gospel Songs and American Hymns
- Contemporary Praise and Worship Music

Charles Wesley exclaimed: "O for a thousand tongues to sing my great Redeemer's praise!" You may not have a thousand tongues, but you do have thousands of hymns and thousands of years of hymn stories. As we turn the page to get started, why not take a moment to pray:

Come, Thou Fount of every blessing,
Tune my heart to sing Thy grace;
Streams of mercy, never ceasing,
Call for songs of loudest praise.
Teach me some melodious sonnet,
Sung by flaming tongues above,
Praise the mount! I'm fixed upon it,
Mount of Thy redeeming love.

Biblical Hymns

My friend Frank Fortunato, international music director for OM (Operation Mobilisation) International, recently gave me an account of what happened when three teams of national Christians tried to take the gospel into the towns and villages of a restrictive African nation. Braving bumpy roads and uncertain receptions, they lugged around portable 16 mm projection equipment sets. Each team showed the JESUS film every night for a month, which amounted to ninety presentations of the gospel in thirty days.

Just as they finished, civil war broke out in the area. The workers had to flee. They were extremely disappointed because they felt their presentations had paved the way for conversions to occur and churches to be planted. But the war made further contact impossible. For six years they prayed and wondered if anything had come from their efforts.

One day a man showed up in the capital asking to see the staff person who had overseen the JESUS film project. He had exciting news. "You know," he said, "I was with you that month [when] you and your team showed the JESUS film. I watched it every night. In fact, I memorized it."

The man pulled from his pocket a collection of eighteen dog-eared sheets of paper. It was a song he'd written from the words of the film. He had set the life of Christ to music. His ballad covered the birth, life, teachings, miracles, death, and resurrection of Jesus. Since this African culture was an oral society, his song was well received in the towns and villages where the film had originally been shown.

The man said, "I first taught the song to a few of my people—all eighteen pages. They learned it, and then they taught it to others; it went from person to person and from heart to heart." As a result, forty-eight new churches were planted as the story of Jesus was sung across cultural barriers and through the isolation of a remote and restrictive region.[3]

That story gives us insight into biblical times. In the ancient world of the Bible, much of the collecting, preserving, and spreading of truth was done through song. The great hymns of the Bible—including the short ones like Psalm 117 and the long ones like Psalm 119—were meant to be learned by heart and circulated through singing, from person to person. Biblical hymns give us the singable version of God's good news. This is, in fact, why so much of the Old Testament (even many of the sermons of the prophets) is given in poetical form.

The first reference to music in the Bible goes back to a man named Jubal, who is described as the "father" of all who play the harp and flute (Genesis 4:21).

The first recorded hymn in the Bible is found in Exodus 15, after the Israelites escaped Egypt through the parted waters of the Red Sea. Moses and the Israelites quickly drew up the story in the form of a song that could be easily learned and spread abroad. It began: "I will sing to the LORD, for he is highly exalted. The horse and its rider he has hurled into the sea" (v. 1).

Exodus 15:20 describes the exuberance of the moment, saying: "Then Miriam the prophetess, Aaron's sister, took a tambourine in her hand, and all the women followed her, with tambourines and dancing."

The parting of the Red Sea was the greatest miracle in the Old Testament, a story to be told and retold as long as time endures.[4] By setting it to music, Moses provided a vehicle of praise to spread the news from person to person, from nation to nation, and from one generation to the next. (See Psalm 90 for another of our oldest hymns, also penned by Moses.)

Unfortunately the next time we see the Israelites in song, it's in sensuous idolatry around a golden calf. Leaving the Red Sea, the mass of Israelites traveled to Mount Sinai where Moses hiked to the mountaintop to seek God's guidance. During his prolonged absence, the people grew anxious and impatient. They compelled Aaron to craft an idol of gold similar to those they had seen in Egypt, and the desert erupted with the sounds of singing and partying and revelry. Moses heard the strains of music in the distance, descended from the mountain, and broke the Ten Commandments on the rocks.

But by the time we get to the book of Deuteronomy, the old Law Giver is again teaching the Israelites the songs of Jehovah. We read in Deuteronomy 31:30–32:3: "And Moses recited the words of this song from beginning to end in the hearing of the whole assembly of Israel:

> *Listen, O heavens, and I will speak;*
> *hear, O earth, the words of my mouth.*
> *Let my teaching fall like rain,*
> *and my words descend like dew,*
> *like showers on new grace,*
> *like abundant rain on tender plants.*
> *I will proclaim the name of the LORD.*
> *Oh, praise the greatness of our God!*

Ending his song, Moses advised the Israelites to take the words to heart. "They are not just idle words for you," he said. "They are your life" (Deuteronomy 32:47). He was describing not only the nature of God's Word but the character of his hymn, which represented God's Word crafted for singing.

As we turn the page to the book of Joshua and read the rest of the historical books of the Old Testament, we find a few poems, hymns, and ballads sprinkled throughout the text, such as Deborah's song in Judges 5. Then we come to the story of David—shepherd, poet, musician, king. It was this iconic man—one of the greatest musicians in history—who launched and formalized the ministry of music in about the year 1000 BC.

David determined to establish Jerusalem as the spiritual center as well as the political and military capital of Israel. He employed thousands of musicians (both vocal and instrumental) for the great worship convocations in Jerusalem, and he personally wrote many of the hymns for them to sing and play. Scores of them are preserved in our book of Psalms—the Hebrew Hymnal.

Of the thirty-eight thousand Levites chosen by David for the service in the tabernacle, four thousand of them were musicians, appointed to lead the nation in praise (1 Chronicles 23:3–5). They were to "sing joyful songs, accompanied by musical instruments: lyres, harps and cymbals" (1 Chronicles 15:16).

When the temple was later built and dedicated by King Solomon, we read that all the musicians were dressed in fine linen and playing cymbals, harps, and lyres. They were accompanied by 120 priests sounding trumpets. The trumpeters and singers joined in unison, as with one voice, to give praise and thanks to the Lord. Accompanied by trumpets, cymbals, and other instruments, they raised their voices in praise to God and sang: "He is good; his love endures forever" (2 Chronicles 5:12–13).

David and Solomon ordained great choirs to lead the nation in worship. This is important for anyone who believes in the power of the ministry of music in a local church. I have a friend who laments the dearth of choirs in many American churches. Only about half of all churches—and only a small number of contemporary, cutting-edge congregations—have choirs. Many worship leaders believe that modern praise-and-worship music can't be effectively conveyed through the medium of singing choirs. But as my friend points out, choirs are God's idea. We see them in the pages of the Old Testament, and we read of vast choirs of men and angels in the nativity accounts of the New Testament and in prophecies about our Lord's return in the book of Revelation. Vast groups of singers joining their God-given voices to proclaim God's truth through the harmony of song . . . well, that's a potent force.

Continuing through the Old Testament, the writings of the prophets are filled with singable poems. You can easily spot this in newer translations by the way the text appears in the columns. It's centered or indented in a way to make it stand out from the narrative. This gives us a visual sign we are reading psalms and canticles. The literary pattern of Hebrew parallelism tells us the same. Notice, for example, the great Song of the Suffering Servant in Isaiah 53:

Surely he took up our infirmities
  and carried our sorrows,
yet we considered him stricken by God,
  smitten by him, and afflicted.
But he was pierced for our transgressions,
  he was crushed for our iniquities;
the punishment that brought us peace was upon him,
  and by his wounds we are healed. (verses 4–6)

I can tell this is a hymn as I scan the words in my Bible because every other line is indented, and because every second line restates and amplifies the first. God devised a form of poetry in His Word that doesn't depend on rhyme or rhythm, since He wanted it translated into every language and dialect on earth. Rhyme and rhythm seldom carry over from one language to the next. But the rhythm of parallel thoughts (the patterned repetition of content) is another matter. God's hymns are translation-friendly; and the repetition of ideas makes them easier to memorize and sing.

The biblical writers knew, as our friends at OM International discovered, that epic songs are a powerful way of preserving and proclaiming truth in a rudimentary society as well as in our own.

Turning to the New Testament, we run into hymns right off the bat: the Nativity Canticles, connected with the birth of Christ. We revel in them: the songs of Mary and Zechariah in Luke 1 (the Magnificat and the Benedictus); the anthem of the angels over Shepherd's Field in Bethlehem in Luke 2 (Gloria in Excelsis Deo); and the praise of Simeon (Nunc Dimittis) in Luke 2:29–32.

Jesus Himself undoubtedly sang the Hebrew psalms throughout His life, but only once does the Bible specifically mention it, when His disciples sung a hymn in the Upper Room (Matthew 26:30).

In the New Testament letters, Paul included a number of hymn stanzas. For example, consider this hymn recorded in 1 Timothy 3:16. We don't know whether Paul wrote it himself or whether he was quoting a song being sung in the churches he visited, but it sums up the entire life and mission of Christ:

He appeared in a body,
was vindicated by the Spirit,
was seen by angels,
was preached among the nations,
was believed on in the world,
was taken up in glory.

In his second letter to Timothy, Paul again provided us with the words of a hymn, which he endorses by calling it a "trustworthy" verse. It's in 2 Timothy 2:11–13:

If we died with him,
we will also live with him;
if we endure,
we will also reign with him.
if we disown him,
he will also disown us;
if we are faithless,
he will remain faithful,
for he cannot disown himself.

Thumb through the New Testament epistles in a newer translation and notice how often hymns and poems are incorporated into the writing. This tells us the apostle Paul was either a great hymn-writer who composed songs for the early church, or a great hymn-singer who relished spicing up his letters with the words of the newest contemporary songs being sung among the congregations. Because of this, we have such classic New Testament hymns, such as "Jesus Christ is Lord," the words of which are recorded in Philippians 2:6–11.

. . . Who, being in very nature God,
did not consider equality with God
something to be grasped,

but made himself nothing,
taking the very nature of a servant,
being made in human likeness.
And being found in appearance as a man, he humbled himself
and became obedient to death—even death on a cross!
Therefore God exalted him to the highest place
and gave him the name that is above every name,
that at the name of Jesus every knee should bow,
in heaven and on earth and under the earth,
and every tongue confess that Jesus Christ is Lord,
to the glory of God the father.

Paul told the Colossians to let the Word of God dwell in us richly as we teach and admonish one another by singing psalms, hymns, and spiritual songs with gratitude in our hearts (Colossians 3:16). The apostle himself gave us a timeless example in Acts 16 when, following their flogging and imprisonment, he and Silas burst into song in the prison at midnight—an early example of music being used evangelistically.

The last book of the Bible—Revelation—is full of hymns, even revealing to us some of the lyrics of songs being sung by angels around the heavenly throne: "Holy, holy, holy is the Lord God Almighty, who was, and is, and is to come" (Revelation 4:8).

The final hymn in recorded Scripture is in Revelation 19. It anticipates the words that will peal forth as Jesus prepares to return to earth at the time of the Second Coming. It's been called the real "Hallelujah Chorus!" because of the fourfold occurrence of a word that is rarely used in Scripture and saved for only the most special occasions: "Hallelujah!"

Hallelujah!
Salvation and glory and power belong to our God . . .
Hallelujah! . . .
Amen, Hallelujah! . . .
Praise our God,

all you his servants,
you who fear him,
both small and great!
Hallelujah!
For our Lord God Almighty reigns.
Let us rejoice and be glad and give him glory!
For the wedding of the Lamb has come. . . . (verses 1–7)

The rich foundation of hymnody that stretches throughout the Bible from Exodus 15 to Revelation 19 tells us:

- God loves music—He put so much of it in His book. According to my friend Don Ellsworth, there are over 550 references to music in the Bible.
- He loves when His people sing His praises.
- He enjoys the music of each succeeding generation—the old songs coupled with the new.
- He understands the power of song in preserving, emotionalizing, and proclaiming His truth.
- His Word lays a foundation for the succeeding hymnody of all Christian history, and as we sing today we're continuing the great traditions of God's method and His message as revealed in His Word.
- He gifts men and women in every age with the ability to write words and music that bring Him glory and spread His name abroad.

Years ago, I was speaking at Cedarville College in Ohio, and Warren W. Wiersbe was also on the program. The students had sung passionately, and when Dr. Wiersbe rose to speak he commented that music began with the Trinity, and that according to the Bible every member of the Trinity sings.

God the Father sings, for Zephaniah 3:17 says, "The LORD your God is with you, he is mighty to save. He will take great delight in you, he will quiet you with his love, he will rejoice over you with singing."

God the Son sings, for Matthew 26:30 says about Him and His disciples, "When they had sung a hymn, they went out to the Mount of Olives."

But how does God the Holy Spirit sing? He sings through His church. Ephesians 5:18–19 commands: "Be filled with the Spirit. Speak to one another with psalms, hymns and spiritual songs. Sing and make music in your heart to the Lord."

When we sing to the Lord, it's the Holy Spirit welling up and over-flowing in our hearts!

> *Come, we that love the Lord*
> *And let our joys be known;*
> *Join in a song with sweet accord*
> *And thus surround the throne.*

Ancient Hymns

H ymn-singing passed from the New Testament into the age of the church fathers without missing a note, so to speak. Our earliest description of Christian worship after the days of the apostles comes from an unlikely source—a pagan Roman governor named Gaius Plinius Caecilius Secundus, better known as Pliny the Younger. Born into a powerful family in northern Italy about the time the apostle Paul was executed, Pliny was mentored by his uncle, Pliny the Elder.

Interestingly, both uncle and nephew observed the eruption of Mount Vesuvius on August 24, AD 79, and the elder Pliny died while trying to rescue survivors. The younger Pliny inherited his uncle's estate and went on to become a powerful political leader and the governor of Bithynia (modern Turkey). We know a lot about him because he was a prodigious letter writer, and many of his epistles have been preserved in history.

About the year AD 110, Pliny wrote to Emperor Trajan about the perplexing growth of Christianity in his territories. His letter gives us one of our earliest descriptions of Christian worship as it was practiced not long after the death of the last apostle, John. Pliny wrote that the Christians were in the habit of meeting before dawn on Sunday mornings and "singing hymns to Christ as to God." They pledged themselves to avoid theft, robbery, adultery, infidelity, and other evil works. They dismissed for their day's labors, but they gathered again in the evening to share meals in one another's homes.

We don't know exactly what hymns these believers sang in AD 110, but it was undoubtedly a mixture of Old Testament psalms, New Testament hymns, and more contemporary expressions of praise. Every generation of true believers, after all, writes its own music. The early church historian Eusebius, quoting a treatise in his possession in the early 300s, wrote:

"Who does not know . . . all the earliest psalms and hymns that sing of Christ as the Word of God and regard Him as God?"[5]

We have a few of these early hymns. One of our oldest extant Christian hymns is *Phos Hilaron*, often called the "Lamplighting Hymn," evidently intended as a song for twilight. Written in Greek and perhaps dating to the second century, it's still sung today under the title "O Gladsome Light," based on a translation into English by Robert S. Bridges in 1899. It's one of the oldest-known Christian hymns still being sung today. The words say, in part:

> *O gladsome light, O grace of our Creator's face,*
> *The eternal splendor wearing; celestial, holy blessed,*
> *Our Savior Jesus Christ, joyful in Your appearing!*
>
> *As fades the day's last light we see the lamps of night,*
> *Our common hymn outpouring, O God of might unknown,*
> *You, the incarnate Son, and Spirit blessed adoring.*

Another ancient hymn is "Shepherd of Eager Youth," the oldest Christian hymn of a known author, Clement of Alexandria (AD 160–215), though he himself attributes it to an earlier writer. It can be sung to the tune of "My Faith Looks Up to Thee." The words, as translated by Dr. Henry Martyn Dexter in 1846, say, in part:

> *Shepherd of tender youth, guiding in love and truth*
> *Through devious (various) ways; Christ our triumphant King,*
> *We come Thy Name to sing and here our children bring*
> *To join Thy praise.*

Perhaps the most famous ancient hymn is "Gloria in Excelsis Deo," which is Latin for "Glory to God in the Highest." Inspired by the song the angels sang at the birth of Christ, this hymn kept growing longer as more and more verses were added until it formed a very early doxology, which, by the 300s, was often used in morning prayers. Its author or authors are unknown, but it's traditionally attributed to Saint Hilary of Poitiers who was born about the year AD 300. The words, translated from Latin into English, say, in part:

> *Glory to God in the highest,*
> *and on earth peace to people of good will.*
> *We praise you.*
> *We bless you.*
> *We adore you.*
> *We glorify you.*
> *We give thanks to you for your great glory.*

The oldest hymn still widely sung today is the Gloria Patri, sometimes called the "Lesser Doxology." St. Basil the Great says this anonymous hymn was in use in both the Eastern and Western churches during the days of St. Clement in Rome, who lived until about AD 100. It simply says: "Glory be to the Father and to the Son and to the Holy Ghost." Later a closing portion was added: "As it was in the beginning, is now, and ever shall be world without end. Amen! Amen!"

The *Odes of Solomon*, often called the first Christian hymnal, is a collection of forty-two poems or hymns that date to the early years of Christian history. A biblical scholar named James Rendel Harris discovered these songs in 1908 as he sorted through a pile of old Syriac manuscripts that had landed in his office. They were evidently composed in Antioch around the year AD 100.

About a dozen years after Harris published the *Odes of Solomon*, archaeologists in Oxyrhynchus (Oxy-reen'-kus), a site about one hundred miles south of Cairo, uncovered another treasure. It was a papyrus containing the words and a few musical notations for a Christian hymn, dating from the late AD 400s. It is our earliest extant hymn with both words and music. Called the Oxyrhynchus Hymn, this papyrus is now housed in the Sackler Library in Oxford. You can find online recordings of the music, as interpreted by various artists. The words, as translated from the Greek, say, in part:

Let it be silent
Let the luminous stars not shine,
Let the winds and all the noisy rivers die down;
And as we hymn the Father, the Son, and the Holy Spirit,
Let all the powers add "Amen! Amen!"

This isn't an exhaustive study of our earliest hymns, just a sampling to show the nature of the church's inceptive hymnody. But anyone who has been around church life for very long knows that the devil sometimes has a heyday with its music ministries. In those early years of the church, it didn't take long for controversy to erupt around the singing of hymns. It wasn't a matter of musical styles or changing forms. At issue was the content of the hymns, especially the doctrines associated with the identity of Christ.

In those days, the vital truths of the Person of Christ became a subject of dispute. A parish priest in Alexandria named Arius (born about AD 250) began to teach that Jesus Christ was not God the Son but a created being. Poets wrote hymns on the subject and spread his heresy. "There was a time when He was not," said one of the songs.

Athanasius, the great bishop of Alexandria, rebuked Arius and criticized the Arian hymns that were spreading the false doctrine. Biblical preachers composed hymns ringing with true theology regarding the authority of Christ and the Word of God. They sometimes even mimicked the Arian tunes.

In Milan, the great bishop Ambrose (c. 340–397) wrote a number of hymns on this and other subjects. He was a champion of congregational singing; and he's the one who for the first time started providing the church with lyrics featuring meter, rhythm, and even some rhyming. Saint Augustine wrote famously in his *Confessions* of how deeply he was moved by the songs he learned in the church where Ambrose preached.

"Those strains flowed into mine ears," wrote Augustine, "and the truth distilled into my heart. My feelings of piety were enkindled, and tears fell from my eyes."

Ambrose's Christmas carol "Come, Thou Redeemer of the Earth" is still sung. Translated by John M. Neale, it says:

> *Come, Thou Redeemer of the earth,*
> *And manifest Thy virgin birth;*
> *Let every age adoring fall;*
> *Such birth befits the God of all.*

Hilary, bishop of Poitiers, also reacted to the heretical Arian hymns by composing orthodox hymns, and thus became known as the Father of Latin Hymnody.

My favorite ancient hymnist, Aurelius Clemens Prudentius (348–413), also weighed in on this subject. Prudentius was a lawyer who retired from his profession at age fifty-seven to write sacred verse and whose hymns are full of poignancy and fervor. Perhaps his greatest hymn—still a favorite today—is the hauntingly beautiful hymn "Of the Father's Love Begotten," extolling the sacredness of Jesus Christ. Something about this ancient song creates a holy hush in the hearts of believers, especially when sung with its nearly thousand-year-old melody, "Divinum Mysterium."

> *Of the Father's love begotten, ere the worlds began to be,*
> *He is Alpha and Omega, He the source, the ending He,*
> *Of the things that are, that have been,*
> *And that future years shall see,*
> *Evermore and evermore . . .*

Still, hymn controversies rattled church leaders. At the Council of Laodicea, which convened sometime between the years of AD 343 and 381 (the most commonly accepted date is in the mid-360s), a series of decrees of canons were issued. The Fifteenth Canon decreed: "No others shall sing in the Church, save only the canonical singers, who go up into the ambo (the platform containing the lectern) and sing from a book."

This obviously had a devastating effect on congregational singing, and the ministry of music was increasingly left in the hands of tuneless priests and professional singers. Gregory the Great, who dominated the last half of the sixth century and served as pope from 590 to 604, was a great advocate for reforming Christian music. It's difficult to uncover his exact innovations, though he's remembered primarily for the "Gregorian Chant" named in his memory. Many scholars now date the Gregorian Chant to a later era, but Gregory did establish liturgical patterns that codified church song and shaped church worship for a millennium. Unfortunately, church music was left in the hands of the priests and trained choirs. For a thousand years, Christians gathered in churches and cathedrals to hear the chants of the priests and choirs of the professionals. Church music died out among the masses and was heard only at the Mass. Specialized musical forms, formal choral groups, and liturgical patterns took over. Congregational singing withered and wasted away for ten sad and silent centuries.

Medieval Hymns

fter the Council of Laodicea published its Fifteenth Canon, congregational singing fell out of favor, and for a thousand years the church in the West lost its song. Christians still sang, of course, but not often at church during worship services. True Christians can't keep from singing. Every generation of believers has written their own songs of praise, and we have samples from every era.

Some of the hymns found in our hymnbooks today hail from medieval days, largely thanks to the diligent work of nineteenth-century translators like John Mason Neale. We owe Neale an enormous debt of gratitude. Yes, he did harbor an intense dislike for Isaac Watts and the popularization of the newfangled English hymn. But that simply motivated Neale to uncover and translate the hymns of the Latin church, which he found superior to the evolving evangelical music around him. About the only still-popular hymn Neale wrote with originality is the Christmas carol "Good King Wenceslas." His other enduring songs are primarily translations rendered from various segments of long Latin poems written in the medieval monasteries of Europe and the Middle East.

A good example is "All Glory, Laud, and Honor," a Palm Sunday hymn dating from about AD 821. Theodulph of Orleans originally composed it in Latin while reportedly imprisoned for his faith in Angers by King Louis I. It Says:

All glory, laud and honor
To Thee, Redeemer, King,
To Whom the lips of children
Made sweet hosannas ring.

All Glory, Laud, and Honor

Theodulph of Orleans

Melchior Teschner

1. All glo - ry, laud, and hon - or To Thee, Re - deem - er, King.
2. The com - pa - ny of an - gels Are prais - ing Thee on high,
3. To Thee, be - fore Thy pas - sion, They sang their hymns of praise;

To whom the lips of chil - dren Made sweet ho - san - nas ring.
And mor - tal men and all things Cre - a - ted make re - ply.
To Thee, now high ex - alt - ed, Our mel - o - dy we raise.

Thou art the King of Is - ra - el, Thou Da - vid's roy - al Son,
The peo - ple of the He - brews With palms be - fore Thee went;
Thou didst ac - cept their prais - es; Ac - cept the praise we bring,

Who in the Lord's name com - est, The King and Bless - ed One.
Our praise and prayer and an - thems Be - fore Thee we pre - sent.
Who in all good de - light - est, Thou good and gra - cious King.

Another hymnist from the 800s is Joseph the Hymnographer. As a young man, Joseph had been captured by pirates and enslaved on the island of Crete. After his release, he traveled to Constantinople and became one of the most prolific of the Greek hymnists. Some scholars think he wrote as many as a thousand hymns. John Neale translated Joseph's hymn honoring martyrs and set it to the same tune as his aforementioned "Good King Wenceslas."

> *Let us now our voices raise,*
> *Wake the day with gladness;*
> *God Himself to joy and praise*
> *Turns our human sadness;*
> *Joy that martyrs won their crown,*
> *Opened heav'ns bright portal,*
> *When they laid the mortal down,*
> *For the life immortal.*

Perhaps the most famous medieval hymnists are two Bernards.

Bernard of Cluny lived in the first half of the twelfth century, but we have little biographical information about his life. He was born in the west of France to English parents, devoted himself to monastic life, and wrote one great poem of three thousand lines from which his subsequent hymns are taken. His original poem "De Contemptu Mundi" (On Contempt for the World) was full of condemnation and judgment for the world of his day. Secular society and much of the church—including priests, nuns, and even the pope—were filled with corruption. The world was overwhelmed with evil, and only the sweetness of the God-fearing life could sustain the soul in the Last Days. Bernard's poem is full of warnings about the judgment of God, but he also bursts into glorious language when describing the hope of heaven. It was from one of the "heaven" passages that John M. Neale developed this hymn, which he adapted and translated in 1858, "Jerusalem the Golden."

O Sacred Head, Now Wounded

Based on Medieval Latin poem
Ascribed to Bernard of Clairvaux

Hans Leo Hassler
Harm. by J.S. Bach

1. O sa - cred Head now wound - ed, With grief and shame weighed down,
2. What Thou, my Lord hast suf - fered Was all for sin - ners' gain:
3. What lan - guage shall I bor - row To thank thee, dear - est Friend,

Now scorn - ful - ly sur - round - ed With thorns, Thine on - ly crown;
Mine, mine was the trans - gres - sion, But Thine the dead - ly pain;
For this thy dy - ing sor - row, Thy pit - y with - out end?

How pale thou art with an - guish, with sore a - buse and scorn!
Lo, here I fall, my Sav - ior! 'Tis I de - serve Thy place;
O make me thine for - ev - er, And should I faint - ing be,

How does that vis - age lan - guish Which once was bright as morn!
Look on me with Thy fa - vor, Vouch - safe to me Thy grace.
Lord, let me nev - er, nev - er Out - live my love to thee.

Jerusalem the golden, with milk and honey blest,
Beneath thy contemplation sink heart and voice oppressed.
I know not, O I know not, what joys await me there,
What radiancy of glory, what bliss beyond compare.

The other Bernard is Saint Bernard of Clairvaux, who was born in or near 1091. He founded a famous monastery in France, whence Christian scholarship, ministry, training, and work progressed amid the chaos of medieval Europe. Archbishop Richard Trench said of him, "Probably no man during his lifetime ever exercised a personal influence in Christendom equal to his."[6]

There are two well-known hymns based on Bernard's writing. His "O Sacred Head, Now Wounded" is a deeply moving portrayal of Calvary. His other famous hymn, "De Nomine Jesu," has been sung for almost a thousand years. Crusading soldiers sang it while keeping guard over the holy sepulcher in Jerusalem. It's been translated again and again throughout history. Edward Caswall gave it to us in English in 1849:

Jesus, the very thought of Thee
With sweetness fills the breast;
But sweeter far Thy face to see,
And in Thy presence rest.

But lest we stray too far from John Neale, don't forget that he's the one who gave us the great Christmas carol "O Come, O Come, Emmanuel." He rendered it into English from a series of Latin antiphons and set the song to the music of a fifteenth-century French funeral melody.

I'll close this section with a hymn that I love so much I traveled to Italy to visit the spot where it was penned by St. Francis of Assisi in about 1225: "All Creatures of our God and King." Just outside the hillside town of Assisi, almost in the exact middle of Italy, is the little church and orchard where St. Francis reportedly wrote his great hymn "Canticle to Brother Sun." Undoubtedly influenced by Psalm 148, it calls on all the elements of creation—men and angels and animals and natural wonders—to praise the Lord with shouts of "Alleluia!" William H. Draper paraphrased it into our famous English hymn in 1919 for a children's festival in Leeds, England.

All creatures of our God and King,
Lift up your voice and with us sing,
Alleluia! Allulia!

Nevertheless, many of God's creatures did not lift up their voices and sing—at least not in Europe's medieval congregations on Sundays. Despite flashes of hymns and the personal songs of pious believers, congregational singing remained at low ebb for centuries.

But that was about to change.

German Hymns

ecently I traveled to Prague, drawn there in part by the magnetism of Jan Hus, the early Reformer whose towering statue dominates the Old Town Square. Influenced by England's John Wycliffe, Hus was a professor and preacher who railed against the moral and theological scandals of the church of his day. For his efforts he was burned at the stake in 1415, and his followers were warned against singing hymns. But the Hussites and Bohemian Brethren disregarded the advice, and pockets of hymn-singing Christians began appearing in Bavaria and Moravia. (Today these areas are mostly in southern Germany and the Czech Republic.)

One of these preachers, Bishop Luke of Prague, was so enthused about revitalizing congregational hymns that he helped spearhead the publication of a landmark book on the newfangled printing presses of Europe. On January 13, 1501, Bishop Luke and his Moravian Brethren published the first modern-day hymnal designed for congregational use. It contained eighty-nine hymns in the Bohemian (Czech) tongue. Some were translations of ancient hymns or chants, but others were compositions from Jan Hus and other Hussite leaders. In a world in which only the priests chanted and only in Latin, suddenly a few churches began singing again in their own tongue.

One of the oldest "Protestant" hymns was written by Jan Hus himself, and is still occasionally found in some of the Lutheran hymnals. It begins, "Jesus Christ, our blessed Savior, / Turned away God's wrath forever."

All this set the stage for a revolution in congregational worship—the rediscovery of congregational singing and church hymns. By and large, it was Martin Luther who got the church singing again. As God would have it, Luther was not only a great theologian, but also a musician who knew that when people are on fire for Christ they can't help but sing their

A Mighty Fortress Is Our God

Martin Luther   Martin Luther

1. A might-y for-tress is our God. A bul-wark nev-er fail - ing;
2. Did we in our own strength con-fide, Our striv-ing wouldbe los - ing,
3. And though this world with dev - ils filled, Should threat-en to un-do us,
4. That word a-bove all earth-ly powers, No thanks to them, a-bid - eth;

Our helper He a-mid the flood Of mor-tal ills pre - vail - ing.
Were not the right man on our side, The man of God's own choos - ing.
We will not fear, for God hath willed, His truth to tri-umph through us.
The Spir-it and the gifts are ours Through Him who with us sid - eth.

For still our an-cient foe Doth seek to work us woe- His craft and power are
Dost ask who that may be? Christ Je-sus, it is He- Lord Sab-a - oth His
The prince of dark-ness grim, We trem-ble not for him- His rage we can en-
Let goods and kin-dred go, This mor-tal life al - so- The bo-dy they may

great, And, armed with cru - el hate, On earth is not His e - qual.
name, From age to age the same, And He must win the bat - tle.
dure, For lo, his doom is sure: One lit - tle word shall fell him.
kill; God's truth a - bid-eth still: His king-dom is for - ev - er.

beliefs. Because he taught the "priesthood of all believers," he advocated full involvement in the church's music ministries—everyone should sing.

As Luther wrote in a preface to a collection of hymns, God is "praised and honored, and we are made better and stronger in faith, when His holy Word is impressed on our hearts by sweet music."

"I intend to make German Psalms for the people," he said, "spiritual songs so that the Word of God even by means of song may lie among the people." One historian said that Luther gave the German people both the Bible in their own language, and the German hymnbook. As a result, the people were able to listen to God though His Word and respond back to Him in their songs.

The event that sparked Luther's commitment to hymns was the martyrdom of two young Augustinian monks, Heinrich Voes and Johann Esch. They were burned at the stake in Brussels on July 1, 1523, the first martyrs of the Reformation. In response, Luther expressed his grief by writing a ballad about them entitled (translated) "A New Song Here Shall Be Begun," the first lines of which say:

> *A new song here shall be begun—*
> *The Lord God help our singing!—*
> *Of what our God Himself hath done,*
> *Praise, honor to Him bringing. . . .*

Within a year, Luther, who was forty at the time, had about two dozen compositions for his church in Wittenberg and would slowly add to their number. The first Lutheran hymnal appeared the next year, and in it was the famous Battle Hymn of the Reformation: *Ein' Feste Burg ist unser Gott*—"A Mighty Fortress Is Our God," based on Psalm 46. It is almost certain that Luther composed not only the words but also the regal music to which it's still sung.

Later he wrote a few more hymns, but he was primarily concerned with getting the ball rolling. After introducing his twenty-three hymns, he encouraged

33

Jesus, Thy Blood and Righteousness

Nickolaus von Zinzendorf

William Gardiner

1. Je - sus, Thy blood and righ - teous - ness
2. Bold shall I stand in Thy great day,
3. Lord, I be - lieve Thy pre - cious blood,
4. Lord, I be - lieve were sin - ners more

My beau - ty are, my glo - rious dress; 'Midst
For who aught to my charge shall lay? Ful -
Which, at the mer - cy seat of God, For -
Than sands up - on the o - cean shore, Thou

flam - ing worlds, in these ar - rayed, With
ly ab - solved through these I am, From
ev - er doth for sin - ners plead, For
hast for all a ran - som paid, For

joy shall I lift up my head.
sin and fear, from guilt and shame.
me, e'en for my soul, was shed.
all a full a - tone - ment made.

German poets to compose evangelical hymns—and they did! Writing to one musician, Spalatin, Luther said: "Grace and peace. I am willing to make German Psalms for the people, after the example of the Prophets and the ancient fathers; that is, spiritual hymns whereby the Word of God, through singing, may conserve itself among the people. We are therefore seeking everywhere for poets. Since you are endowed with versatility and good taste in German expression, and since, through abundant effort, you have cultivated both these gifts, I beg you to join hands with us and make the attempt to transform a Psalm into a hymn, after the pattern I enclose. I desire, however, that newfangled words, and courtly expressions, be omitted in order that the language may be the simplest and most familiar to the people."[7]

Enflamed by the fires of Reformation, congregations began singing again, and during the first one hundred years of the Reformation, scholars reckon that twenty-five thousand hymns were written in Germany alone.[8] Hymnists such as Luther's young friend Johann Walter and, a generation later, Michael Praetorius, kept the German people hymning. Even during the Thirty Years' War (1618–1648), new hymns appeared, including Martin Rinkart's famous "Now Thank We All Our God."

One young man who grew up during the horrors of the Thirty Years' War became a famous church musician in Germany, and today we consider him among the greatest hymnists who ever lived—Paul Gerhardt. His hymns are more introspective and subjective than Luther's, more personal and pietistic. My favorite Gerhardt hymns are "We Sing, Emmanuel, Thy Praise" and "Commit Whatever Grieves Thee."

Another pietistic hymnist of the seventeenth century was Joachim Neander, author of the rousing anthem "Praise to the Lord, the Almighty."

Out of the Pietistic movement came the Moravians, who were great congregational singers. Under persecution, they fled Bohemia and sought refuge on the estate of a godly nobleman, Count Nicolaus Ludwig von Zinzendorf. Their community was called Herrnhut, meaning "Under the Lord's Watch."

Several years ago, I visited Herrnhut. Zinzendorf's great manor house was in a state of disrepair, but the village of Herrnhut was going strong, and in the middle of it was the simple white Meeting House that still serves as the center for their community. Zinzendorf himself was a prolific writer whose best-known hymn is "Jesus, Thy Blood and Righteousness."

The most famous German composer of this era was Johann Sebastian Bach (1685–1750), who, rather than composing new hymn tunes, usually took music that had already been written for church use and developed it into ingenious settings. If you visit the British Museum, you can see many of his original scores, and at the end of them are the initials SDG, which stand for *Soli Deo Gloria*, "To God alone be the glory." For a tranquil moment of joy, listen to Bach's arrangement of "Jesu, Joy of Man's Desiring," a melody originally composed by Johann Schop in the seventeenth century but arranged and popularized by Bach in 1723.

But a curious thing happened to Reformation congregational singing. As Luther's movement spread westward, all the new Protestant churches adopted his revival of congregational singing, but not everyone embraced the singing of humanly composed hymns. The followers of John Calvin in Switzerland, France, Holland, Scotland, and England tended to believe that only *biblical* hymns should be sung, specifically the psalms of David (and this opinion spread throughout the American colonies).

This set the stage for a new series of worship wars and threatened to unravel the unity of the church in the fifteenth and sixteenth centuries.

English Hymns

fter pastoring the same church for over three decades, I know the challenge of trying to satisfy everyone's musical tastes. Sometimes I feel like the rope in a tug of war between my younger members and my older congregants, or between my drum lovers and my organ fans. In our case, we've found that a balanced approach is best (as I'll explain later in this book). But all along the way, I've derived much encouragement and loads of insight from the similar conflicts that tugged at the church—especially in England—in the days leading up to Isaac Watts.

Here's what happened. As the Reformation spread throughout Germany and all of Europe, the church started singing again; but there were differences of opinion about how this should be done. Whereas Luther and the Germans composed hymns ad infinitum, the Swiss Reformer Ulrich Zwingli and the French Reformer John Calvin believed that only biblical texts should be sung, particularly the Psalms. Calvin wanted nothing to do with organs, choirs, or hymns. He believed that metrical versions of the Psalms, sung in unison, were the proper songs for the assembled people of God. A great example is the "Old Hundredth," a metrical rendition of Psalm 100 in the 1551 *Geneva Psalter*, sung to the tune we associate with the "Doxology."

All people that on earth do dwell,
Sing to the Lord with cheerful voice.
Him serve with fear, His praise forth tell;
Come ye before Him and rejoice.

This became the attitude of the Reformers in England, and as a result, hymns were viewed with disfavor. In 1562, *The Whole Booke of Psalmes*

Alas! and Did My Savior Bleed

Isaac Watts   Hugh Wilson

1. A - las! and did my Sav - ior bleed And
2. Was it for crimes that I have done, He
3. Well might the sun in dark - ness hide And
4. Thus might I hide my blush - ing face While
5. But drops of grief can ne'er re - pay, The

did my Sov - ereign die? Would He de - vote that
suf - fered on the tree? A - maz - ing pi - ty,
shut His glo - ries in; When Christ the might - y
His dear cross ap - pears; Dis - solve my heart in
debt of love I owe; Here, Lord, I give my -

sa - cred head, For such a worm as I.
grace un - known, And love be - yond de - gree!
Ma - ker died For man, the crea - ture's sin.
thank - ful - ness And melt mine eyes to tears.
self a - way, 'Tis all that I can do.

was published by John Day, providing singable versions of all 150 of the psalms of the Bible. This became the primary hymnbook for English worship for the next one hundred years, until 1696 when Nahum Tate and Nicholas Brady published the *New Version of the Psalms of David, Fitted to the Tunes Used in Churches.* (This new version was widely criticized by those who preferred the "old version" of 1562; the sentiment was, the newer the translation the less its accuracy.)

In Scotland, skilled translators rendered the entire book of Psalms from the original Hebrew into metrical English for singing, and the Scottish Psalter became the national hymnal. Today one of those songs still stands as a beloved British hymn and one of my favorites—the Scottish Psalter's Twenty-third Psalm:

> *The Lord's My Shepherd, I'll not want,*
> *He makes me down to lie*
> *In pastures green; He leadeth me*
> *The quiet waters by.*

In the New World, the American Puritans introduced a volume known as the Bay Psalm Book (*The Whole Booke of Psalmes Truthfully Translated into English Meter*), which is considered the first substantial book published in English-speaking North America.

The problem, of course, is that the Psalms-only attitude of the English Reformers retarded the development and use of hymns in British congregations. A man named George Wither produced the earliest known English hymnbook in 1623, but it encountered withering criticism.

Poets like the saintly George Herbert wrote spiritual poetry, but it was seldom set to music. The first and oldest of the English hymns that would be widely recognized today was written by Thomas Ken, an educator who penned a devotional manual for students of Winchester College. Included was a morning hymn, "Awake, My Soul, and with the Sun," and an evening hymn, "All Praise to You This Night." Both hymns ended with a refrain that is today called "The Doxology":

Praise God from whom all blessings flow,
Praise Him all creatures here below.
Praise Him above ye heavenly host.
Praise Father, Son, and Holy Ghost.

One brave soul fought with every nerve to introduce hymn-singing to the Baptist churches of England. His name was Benjamin Keach, born in an English town on Leap Year's Day of 1640. He grew up under pious parents and become a Christian at age fifteen and a Baptist preacher at eighteen. When the Act of Uniformity was passed in 1662 requiring all English churches use the rites and ceremonies of the *Book of Common Prayer,* young Keach was seized by government troops and threatened with death by being trampled by horses. His crime was writing a book for children that presented some spiritual lessons at odds with the *Book of Common Prayer.*

Keach was imprisoned, fined, and forced to stand in the public pillory in the marketplace. He was bloody but unbowed, and shortly afterward he agreed to become the pastor of a small Baptist church that met in a private home in London. His congregation of Dissenters had to meet in secret.

When the laws changed in 1672, the church began worshipping openly, and soon the building was enlarged to seat nearly a thousand people. Keach had a streak of stubborn godliness that led him to introduce the highly controversial practice of the congregational singing of hymns. At that time, English Baptists were convinced that only the metrical psalms should be sung in church. But Keach led his church to sing a hymn at the Lord's Supper service. After some years, the practice was extended to Thanksgiving services.

Finally, about the year 1690, Keach's church voted (amid much debate and with some Dissenters) to sing hymns along with the metrical psalms every Sunday. It was agreed that the hymn would be sung at the close of service, after the sermon and prayer, so that those who opposed it could "go freely forth."

The next year, 1691, Mr. Keach published a book entitled *The Breach*

Repaired in God's Worship, or Singing of Psalms, Hymns and Spiritual Songs Proved to Be an Holy Ordinance of Jesus Christ. He also published a hymn-book that same year. It contained about three hundred hymns, and is known as the first Baptist hymnal published in England.

An undercurrent of discontent continued to disturb Keach's church, and on February 9, 1693, the church split, with those unwilling to sing hymns (six men and thirteen women) withdrawing from the church and organizing their own, Maze Pond Church, in the house of Luke Leader, on Tooley Street, Southwark. (Within a couple of generations, even the Maze Pond Church was singing hymns like everyone else, and in 1750, the pastor of the Maze Pond Church published a book of hymns!) Though Keach was heavily criticized by fellow Christians at the time, he stands as a pioneer who paved the way for the English hymn, which would be popularized by another young man a generation later—Isaac Watts.

Today we call Watts the "Father of the English Hymn," but he was a young "father." Many of his groundbreaking hymns were written when he was twenty years old, fresh home from college and living again with his parents in Southampton. The singing there was awful, and young Watts decided to write a simple hymn for the church. The congregation tried it out and asked for more. Watts later became a prominent London pastor, but he's best remembered for his hymns, including:

* Alas, And Did My Savior Bleed
* Am I a Soldier of the Cross?
* Come We That Love the Lord
* When I Survey the Wondrous Cross
* Jesus Shall Reign
* Joy to the World
* O God, Our Help in Ages Past

Then came the Wesley brothers, John and Charles, founders of the Methodist movement. Both Wesleys were preachers, theologians, church founders, and hymnists. But John is chiefly remembered for his sermons and Charles for his hymns. The mid-1700s was a time of revival—the Great Awakening in the American Colonies and the Wesleyan Revival on the British Isles. In America, the sensational preaching of George Whitefield paved the way for the popularization of Isaac Watts's hymns in the Colonies. And in England, Charles Wesley picked up where Watts had left it. He wrote thousands of hymns (some scholars put the total number at 8,989), including:

- And Can It Be?
- Come, Thou Long Expected Jesus
- Christ the Lord Is Risen Today
- Hark! The Herald Angels Sing
- O For a Thousand Tongues to Sing
- Rejoice, the Lord Is King
- Love Divine, All Loves Excelling

The sheer volume of Charles's lyrics unleashed a torrent of hymn composers, some of them writing in the old and more majestic styles; others wrote in a more popular folk medium.

In the preface of the 1761 volume of *Sacred Melody*, John Wesley listed seven rules for congregational singing:

1. Learn these tunes before you learn any others . . .
2. Sing them exactly as they are printed here . . .
3. Sing all. See that you join with the congregation as frequently as you can. Let not a slight degree of weakness or weariness hinder you . . .
4. Sing lustily and with a good courage. Beware of singing as if you were half dead, or half asleep, but let up your voice with strength . . .
5. Sing modestly. Do not bawl, so as to be heard above or distinct from the rest of the congregation, that you may not destroy the harmony . . .

6. Sing in time . . . . Do not run before nor stay behind . . .
7. Above all, sing spiritually. Have an eye to God in every word you sing. Aim at pleasing Him more than yourself . . .

In the wake of Watts and the Wesleys, whole generations of hymnists rose up, one after another, to produce some of the grandest music in the history of the church. William Williams (d. 1791), "the Watts of Wales," wrote "Guide Me, O Thou Great Jehovah." Edward Perronet (d. 1792) wrote "All Hail the Power of Jesus' Name," often considered the greatest hymn of the lordship of Christ ever penned. Robert Robinson (d. 1790) wrote the popular "Come, Thou Fount of Every Blessing."

And let's not forget John Newton (d. 1807), whose story is often repeated but never boring. He was a slave trader on the high seas, an evil and vile man who, following his conversion to Christ, became an Anglican minister, a powerful hymnist, a collaborator with the noted English poet William Cowper (d. 1800), and a fierce opponent of slave-trading in the British Empire. Newton's classic hymn of testimony "Amazing Grace" is arguably the most famous hymn in English history.

Newton and Cowper, the preacher and the poet, lived near each other in the little town of Olney, England, and they often met in a shed between their gardens. Their *Olney Hymns* (pronounced *All-knee*) was published in February 1779 and is one of the classics of hymnody.

Another prominent London pastor and hymnist of this period was Augustus Toplady (d. 1778), who also wrote a wonderful hymn on God's amazing grace, which says:

> *Grace first inscribed my name*
> *In God's eternal book;*
> *'Twas grace that gave me to the Lamb,*
> *Who all my sorrows took.*

> *Grace taught my soul to pray*
> *And made mine eyes o'erflow;*

And Can It Be That I Should Gain?

Charles Wesley   Thomas Campbell

1. And can it be that I should gain An in - t'rest
2. He left His Fa - ther's throne a - bove, So free, so
3. No con - dem - na - tion now I dread; Je - sus, and
4. Long my im - pris - oned spir - it lay Fast bound in

in the Sa - vior's blood? Died He for me, who caused His pain?
in - fi - nite His grace; Emp - tied Him - self of all but love,
all in Him, is mine! A - live in Him my liv - ing Head,
sin and na - ture's night; Thine eye dif - fused a quick-'ning ray,

For me, who Him to death pur - sued? A - maz - ing love! How
And bled for A - dam's help - less race. 'Tis mer - cy all, im -
And clothed in righ - teous - ness di - vine, Bold I ap - proach th'e -
I woke, the dun - geon flamed with light; My chains fell off, my

can it be That Thou, my God, shouldst die for me?
mense and free! For, O my God it found out me!
ter - nal throne, And claim the crown, through Christ my own.
heart was free; I rose, went forth and fol - lowed Thee.

'Twas grace which kept me to this day,
And will not let me go.

Toplady's greatest hymn was "Rock of Ages."

Other hymnists: John Fawcett ("Bless Be the Tie That Binds"), Reginald Heber ("Holy, Holy, Holy"), James Montgomery ("Angels from the Realms of Glory"), the blind Scottish pastor George Matheson ("O Love That Wilt Not Let Me Go"), and the invalid poet Anne Steele.

Another hymnist, Henry Lyte, lived on a beautiful estate (now a hotel) on the English coast and pastored a nearby church, but he contracted lung disease and left for a therapeutic holiday. He died shortly thereafter, leaving behind this beautiful hymn that says, "Abide with me, fast falls the eventide; the darkness deepens, Lord, with me abide."

Matthew Bridges and Godfrey Thring wrote alternating verses of "Crown Him with Many Crowns." Philip Doddridge wrote "O Happy Day."

One of the more interesting characters in English hymnology was Sabine Baring-Gould, an eccentric, brilliant, indefatigable pastor who wrote over one hundred books (including thirty novels) and a number of hymns. His popular "Onward, Christian Soldiers" was written for the children of his church to sing while marching to a Sunday school rally. He had stayed up the night before composing the words, having found nothing else suitable. The melody is by Arthur Sullivan, of Gilbert and Sullivan fame.

While Baring-Gould was writing simple songs like "Onward Christian Soldiers" and "Now the Day Is Over," his contemporary John Mason Neale, as we've already seen, was hard at work discovering ancient Latin hymns and translating them into English lyrics suitable for singing. Unimpressed with the hymns of Watts, Wesley, and Newton, he preferred the majestic sturdiness of the ancients. To him we owe our English renditions of "All Glory, Laud, and Honor," "Of the Father's Love Begotten," and the Christmas carols "O Come, O Come Emmanuel," "Good Christian Men, Rejoice," and "Good King

Wenceslas," which he wrote to teach children the legend of an ancient duke of Bohemia.

Charlotte Elliott, an invalid, was a bitter woman until she discovered she could come to Christ just as she was—and out of her experience came the great invitational hymn "Just as I Am."

And then there's Frances Ridley Havergal. But I feel like the writer of Hebrews 11 who said that time would not permit him to tell the stories of all the heroes he wanted to recount. "What more shall I say? For time would fail me to tell of" all the other source springs of English hymnody. This is my favorite genre of sacred song, the Golden Age of Church Hymnody. I never tire of it, never exhaust the diamond mines of its richness, never weary of the fascinating stories of its worthies.

Once you learn to love the English hymns, you'll find you just can't do without them; and like the promises of the Bible, you'll find there's always one available for every need you'll ever have and every circumstance you'll ever face.

From Gospel Songs to Contemporary Praise

T wo developments shaped the evolution of Christian music in the United States: the publication of the Bay Psalm Book, which has already been discussed, and the development of the "Singing School" and shaped notes. Harvard-educated ministers were distressed by the poor quality of congregational singing, and in 1721, Massachusetts pastor John Tufts published the first of what came to be hundreds of manuals for singing school and church use. Going into churches and schools, ministers and musicians used these manuals to teach Americans the rudiments of music and to introduce them to sacred melodies.

Out of this came the first hymn tunes written on American soil. One of the first was CORONATION, which is still used today with the words "All Hail the Power of Jesus' Name." It was written by a Massachusetts carpenter and real estate developer who led many Singing Schools and, on one occasion, composed a song for George Washington.

One of the most gifted American composers of Christian music was Lowell Mason (d. 1872), a banker in Georgia who pursued his love of music on the side. Mason eventually moved to Boston and became the director of music for churches there and a significant figure in early American music education. But he's best known as the "Father of American Church Music," and we're still singing his notes and sounding his praise. Among the melodies he composed or arranged are:

HAMBURG ("When I Survey the Wondrous Cross")
DENNIS ("Bless Be the Tie")
CLEANSING FOUNTAIN ("There Is a Fountain")
AZMON ("O For a Thousand Tongues")

All Hail the Power of Jesus' Name

Edward Perronet

Oliver Holden

1. All hail the power of Je - sus' name! Let an - gels pros - trate fall; Bring forth the roy - al di - a - dem, And crown Him Lord of all; Bring forth the roy - al di - a - dem, And crown Him Lord of all.

2. Ye cho - sen seed of Is - rael's race, Ye ran - somed from the fall, Hail Him who saves you by His grace, And crown Him Lord of all; Hail Him who saves you by His grace, And crown Him Lord of all.

3. Let ev - ery kin - dred, ev - ery tribe, On this ter - res - trial ball, To Him all maj - es - ty as - cribe, And crown Him Lord of all; To Him all maj - es - ty as - cribe, And crown Him Lord of all.

4. O that with yon - der sa - cred throng, We at His feet may fall! We'll join the ev - er - last - ing song, And crown Him Lord of all; We'll join the ev - er - last - ing song, And crown Him Lord of all.

BETHANY ("Nearer, My God, to Thee")
OLIVET ("My Faith Looks Up to Thee")
MISSIONARY HYMN ("From Greenland's Icy Mountains")
WORK SONG ("Work, for the Night Is Coming")
ANTIOCH ("Joy to the World")

Mason and his contemporaries wrote music in a warm devotional style, combining simplicity and dignity. But all that was about to change as America entered an era of popular ballads and folk music in the years prior to the Civil War. This had a strong stylistic influence on congregational singing.

Side by side with the nation's folk music was the rise of camp meetings, large assemblies where families would camp for extended periods to attend revival meetings. These began in Kentucky and rode a wave of revival that swept over America and changed the fabric of its culture. Singing was a large part of these meetings, but the songs had to be popular, rousing, and cheerful. One of the songs that resounded around a thousand campfires was a simple anonymous spiritual that said, "Give me the old time religion." Another said, "Just a closer walk with Thee, / Grant it, Jesus, is my plea."

It was D. L. Moody (d. 1899) and his era of urban revivalism that caused a seismic shift in Christian music around the world. Moody came to Christ as a teenager through the witness of his Sunday school teacher, Edward Kimball. After moving to Chicago, Moody was a walking turbine of energy who threw himself into Sunday school work and soon had the children of Chicago at his feet. When the nation ripped itself apart during the Civil War, Moody became a chaplain, leading many soldiers to faith in Christ. After the war, he teamed up with Gospel singer Ira Sankey and set the world afire in great campaigns in all the major cities of America and the United Kingdom. Evangelism moved from the country camps to urban auditoriums where the singing was simple, enthusiastic, emotional, personal, and heart-lifting, in the popular style of the era.

Ira Sankey wanted rousing, light, earnest music for the campaigns, songs that described the Christian's experience in emotional terms—and so was born the era of the Gospel song. Hymnist Philip P. Bliss coined that term as the title of a small collection of Sunday school hymns published in 1874, and the phrase stuck. Soon everyone was writing and singing Gospel songs, with music composed by gifted musicians like William Bradbury.[9]

It was Bradbury who, taking a poem from a popular novel by Anna and Susan Warner, wrote the music for the most enduring children's hymn of all time, "Jesus Loves Me." (The full story of the remarkable Warner sisters and their famous hymn is told in my book *Jesus Loves Me This I Know*, published by J. Countryman Books.)

By far, the most astonishing and prolific poet of the Gospel song era was Fanny Crosby, who had been blinded in infancy but grew up to become one of the best-known speakers and Christian personalities of her day. Her memory was astounding. Having memorized very much of the Bible, she drew from its inner resources to compose thousands of Gospel songs in her head and dictated them to waiting secretaries. William Bradbury, Robert Lowry (composer of the words and music to "Shall We Gather at the River?"), William Doane, and others put her poems to music, giving us timeless favorites like "To God Be the Glory."

Fanny Crosby's classic "Blessed Assurance" was written on the spot when her friend Phoebe Knapp played a melody she'd composed on the piano. Fanny clapped her hands and exclaimed, "Why, that says, 'Blessed Assurance!'" And she quickly composed the words for the verses and chorus for this song.

Fanny had a similar experience when composer William Doane gave her a melody he had written. To her the music said, "Jesus, Keep Me Near the Cross," and soon the world was singing it as an earnest devotional prayer.

After Moody's death in 1899, the era of Gospel hymns continued into the twentieth century under the direction of Charles M. Alexander (director of music for the evangelistic campaigns of R. A. Torrey and J. Wilber Chapman) and Homer Rodeheaver (who led the music for the

Billy Sunday campaigns). Rodeheaver was criticized for his popular-sounding melodies, but he wrote in his memoirs, "It was never intended for a Sunday morning service, not for devotional purposes—its purpose was to bridge the gap between the popular song of the day and the great hymns and gospel songs, and to give men a simple, easy lilting melody which they could learn the first time they heard it, and which they could whistle and sing wherever they might be."

But the songs found their way from evangelistic settings into the repertoire of churches for worship. Many of our greatest Gospel songs came out of the evangelistic ministries of faithful soul-winners of the late 1800s and early 1900s.

- The invitational hymn "Softly and Tenderly" was written by Will Thompson, an Ohio poet who made a fortune on his publishing house, but whose first love was loading his upright piano on an old wagon and traveling through the small towns of America's heartland, singing and sharing Jesus.
- George Bennard, a traveling evangelist, wrote "The Old Rugged Cross" as he trekked across the Midwest on preaching trips.
- Civilla Durfee Martin, an evangelist's wife, wrote "His Eye Is on the Sparrow" after she and her husband stayed with an infirmed couple in New York who told her that the secret of their optimism was remembering that "His eye is on the sparrow, and I know He watches me."
- "Bringing in the Sheaves" was composed by the "Singing Evangelist," Knowles Shaw, who was later to perish in a train wreck in Texas.
- Philip Bliss, an evangelistic song leader connected with D. L. Moody, gave us the old hymn "Let the Lower Lights Be Burning." (Bliss and his wife also died in a train wreck in Ashtabula, Ohio.)
- Elisha Hoffman was an earnest evangelist, but he's best remembered as a prominent music publisher and the author of "Are You Washed in the Blood?"

About this time, the African American Spiritual was finding an audience all over the world through the popularity of the Jubilee Singers of Fisk University of Nashville. The slave songs of the Old South, composed and sung amid suffering and oppression, were written down and taught to the world. The authors of these hymns are unknown, but their music strikes a cord in our hearts: "When the Saints Go Marching In," "Were You There," "Deep River," and the Christmas spiritual "Go Tell It on the Mountain."

Several African American musicians provided the church with deeply felt Gospel hymns. Charles A. Tindley (d. 1933), the son of slaves, found a job as janitor of Calvary Methodist Episcopal Church in Philadelphia, and eventually became its far-famed pastor. He's the author of "I'll Overcome Some Day," the basis for the Civil Rights anthem "We Shall Overcome." He also wrote "Stand by Me," "Nothing Between," and "We'll Understand It Better By and By."

Another black composer of unusual depth was Thomas A. Dorsey, who moved from Georgia to Chicago and wrote the classic "Precious Lord, Take My Hand," following the death of his wife and child. (One of the most moving moments I've ever observed was when I watched my friend Tom Tipton sing "Precious Lord, Take My Hand" to the feeble and ailing evangelist Billy Graham. While he was singing, Tom walked over to the wheelchair-bound Graham, who was ninety-two, took his hand, looked into his eyes, and sang as only he could: "Precious Lord, take my hand, lead me home, let me stand, I am tired, I am weak and I am worn. Through the storm, through the night, lead me on to the light; take my hand, precious Lord, lead me home.")

As the twentieth century was cranking up, the sounds of African American jazz were merging with the Pentecostal and Azusa Street movements to create a uniquely American form of Christian music—Black Gospel with its rhythm-and-blues sound—songs that are more popular today than ever, as evidenced in everything from Southern Gospel to the Brooklyn Tabernacle hymns that have thrilled Christians around the world.

Not unrelated was the development of Southern Gospel music with its singing schools, shaped notes, and specialized harmonies. James D. Vaughn helped launch the era of the traveling Southern Gospel quartet, and many of these songs like "I'll Fly Away" have become classics.

In the twentieth century, churches were still singing the hymns and Gospel songs of prior generations, freshened up with some great hymns born out of the Great Depression and the dark days of World War II. Many of them are hymns of assurance and comfort, and they focused on Jesus. Since I was born in 1952, these are the hymns I grew up on, and I never tire of hearing them. For example: "Since Jesus Came into My Heart," "All That Thrills My Soul Is Jesus," "Jesus Is All the World to Me," "No One Ever Cared for Me Like Jesus."

During this time, John W. Peterson and William and Gloria Gaither were writing Gospel songs and modern favorites. Cliff Barrows and the Billy Graham choirs were popularizing some of today's most beloved hymns and Gospel songs, including the classic "How Great Thou Art," which was introduced to North American audiences at the 1955 Billy Graham Crusade in Toronto. The next time was during the 1957 Billy Graham Crusade in New York City. It was sung by George Beverly Shea one hundred times, which included crusades in Madison Square Garden, Times Square, and Yankee Stadium—all in New York City—with the choir joining the chorus: *Then sings my soul, my Savior God to Thee, How great Thou art!*

Then came the 1960s, and the world changed. The Bay of Pigs, the Cuban Missile Crisis, the assassination of President John F. Kennedy, the Vietnam War, the Civil Rights Movement, the anti-war movement, the assassinations of Martin Luther King and Bobby Kennedy, Watergate. All this was happening while my generation lurched through a school system from which the United States Supreme Court had recently forcibly removed the Bible and the right to pray. It's no wonder thousands of young people were deceived by Timothy Leary's call to "turn on, tune in, and drop out." College campuses were burned and bombed across America, but the epicenter of the hippy movement was in California, especially at the corner of Haight and Ashbury Streets in San Francisco.

But the Lord was also at work, and in the midst of it all came the Jesus Movement of the late 1960s and early 1970s. I was a college student in the 1970s, as this mini-revival swept over the chaos of the counter-culture as the Lord began touching the lives of thousands of angry young people. And from the left coast of America, a new period of Christian music began emerging that is popularly called praise and worship, or sometimes contemporary Christian music. At the forefront of the revolution was Calvary Chapel in Costa Mesa, California, and its visionary pastor Chuck Smith. Hundreds of young barefoot, long-haired, newly converted believers flocked to the church, and they brought their guitars with them.

Soon praise and worship music was rolling into churches, campuses, and youth groups everywhere. Christians around the world were singing "Seek Ye First." Over the next several years, hymnals were replaced with projected lyrics, pianos and organs with guitars and drums, arm-waving worship leaders with praise teams, and stately hymns were supplemented with intimate songs of spiritual expression. All this resulted, as one would expect, in a series of worship wars that reminds us of the generational transitions that took place in Isaac Watts's day. But I'm indebted to arranger Don Marsh for helping me understand the evolution of praise and worship music. Over supper earlier this year, he offered this simple explanation of the progression of this era of Christian music.

First came the praise choruses, such as "Seek Ye First," "Pass It On," and "They'll Know We Are Christians by Our Love."

Then came the praise songs, still widely sung today, like: "As the Deer," "He Is Exalted," "Shout to the Lord," and "Lord, I Lift Your Name on High."

And now the church is discovering praise hymns, with Keith and Kristyn Getty and Stuart Townend leading the way. Today a new generation of writers and composers are leading us into a new era of both hymns and contemporary Gospel music. I'm a firm believer that we should sing the best of the newer Christian music without abandoning the heritage of our hymnody or the treasuries of our old hymnals.

Let's sing a new song to the Lord, as the Bible says—but let's not forget the old ones.

P.S. – Stay tuned. I'll have more to say about this later.

PART 2
DO YOU KNOW THESE HYMNS?

Glory Be to the Father

Traditional

Henry W. Greatorex
GLORIA PATRI

Glo - ry be to the Fa - ther, And to the Son, and to the
Ho - ly Ghost; As it was in the be - gin-ning, Is now and ev - er
shall be, World with-out end. A - men, A - men.

The Gloria Patri
("Glory Be to the Father")

About AD 100

*T*he word *doxology* comes from two Greek words: *Doxo*, meaning *praise*, and *-ology*, from *logos*, meaning *word*. A doxology then is a word or a burst of praise. The most famous doxology is the one written in 1674 by Thomas Ken, which begins: "Praise God from whom all blessings flow." It's one of our oldest English hymns, but as doxologies go it's the new kid on the block. The oldest doxology still commonly sung today is the "Gloria Patri," which dates almost to New Testament times and has been used in various forms by the ancient church, the Roman Catholic Church, Orthodox churches, Anglicans, and Protestants. Arguably Christianity's oldest universally sung hymn, the "Gloria Patri" is often called the Lesser Doxology to distinguish it from another prominent doxology in the early church, the "Gloria in excelsis."

In its most common English rendering, the "Gloria Patri" is a praise of the Triune God—Father, Son, and Holy Spirit—who was and is and is to be, forever, world without end. According to John Julian's *Dictionary of Hymnology*, the "Gloria Patri" is possibly (but not demonstrably) of apostolic antiquity. Its Trinitarian language is derived from our Lord's commission in Matthew 28. St. Basil the Great asserts that the first part of this doxology was being sung in both the Eastern and Western churches as early as the time of St. Clement of Rome, who died about AD 100, not long after John the apostle.[10]

When we sing the "Gloria Patri" today, we commonly use a joyful melody composed by Henry Wellington Greatorex, who was born in Burton upon Trent, England, in 1816. His father, the organist at Westminster Abbey, taught him music. In 1839, Henry immigrated to the United States, settled in New York, and himself became a church organist. Ten years later, he married an Irish immigrant, Eliza Pratt, who was a Wesleyan preacher's daughter.

Eliza went on to become one of the most famous artists of her day, as did their two daughters.

O Trinity of Blessed Light

Attr. to Ambrose of Milan
Trans. by John M. Neale

Jeremiah Clarke
BROMLEY

1. O Trin - i - ty of bless - ed light,
2. To Thee our morn - ing song of praise
3. All laud to God the Fa - ther be,

O U - ni - ty of prince - ly might,
To Thee our eve - ning prayer we raise;
All praise, e - ter - nal Son to Thee,

The fier - y sun now goes his way;
O grant us with Thy saints on high
All glo - ry, as is ev - er meet,

Shed Thou with - in our hearts a ray.
To praise Thee through e - ter - ni - ty.
To God the Ho - ly Par - a - clete.

O Trinity of Blessed Light

About AD 390

It hasn't been professional songwriters, but pastors and theologians who have composed many of the great hymns of the faith. Take for example Ambrose of Milan (340–397). Born into an upper-class Italian home, he was bright and bold enough at age twenty-nine to be appointed governor of the province around Milan.

He soon faced a challenge. When the bishop of Milan died, the city was torn apart trying to find a replacement. Difficult theological issues were involved. Ambrose sought to calm the storm; but in the midst of the commotion, a cry went up for Ambrose to be bishop. According to tradition, it was a child's voice that cried out the suggestion. The crowd took up the chant, and Ambrose was soon installed, rather against his will, as the city's pastor (though he himself was not baptized at the time).

Selling his estates, Ambrose gave his money to the poor, began fasting and studying the Scripture, and started preaching the gospel. He vehemently opposed false doctrines, and he pushed back against civil authorities who tried to meddle in church affairs. Often Ambrose was so absorbed by his studies and writing that he was totally inaccessible. It's said that visitors would be ushered into his presence to stand against the wall and watch him as he read silently and studied at his desk. From his intense study came a flood of sermons and songs. It's not known how many hymns Ambrose actually wrote. Nor can we verify that he wrote all the songs that are attributed to him. But he's the leader who took congregational singing to a new level. Many of the hymns of Ambrose focus on the Trinity—Father, Son, and Holy Spirit, as seen in this classic hymn: "O Trinity of Blessed Light."

On one occasion, Ambrose and his entire congregation were trapped in the Basilica at Milan by the armies of Justina, mother of the emperor Valentinian II. They fortified themselves by singing during the siege, as one hymn after another rose up from the church. The news of this unique worship service spread across the Roman Empire and elevated the use of hymns by congregations in times of both stress and celebration.

Come, Thou Redeemer of the Earth

Ambrose of Milan
Translated by John M. Neale

Trier manuscript
PUER NOBIS NASCITUR

1. Come, Thou Re - deem - er of the earth, And man - i -
2. Be - got - ten of no hu - man will, But of the
3. The vir - gin womb that bur - den gained With vir - gin
4. Forth from His cham - ber go - eth He, That roy - al
5. From God the Fa - ther He pro - ceeds, To God the
6. O e - qual to the Fa - ther, Thou! Gird on Thy
7. Thy cra - dle here shall glit - ter bright, And dark - ness
8. All laud to God the Fa - ther be, All praise, e -

fest Thy vir - gin birth: Let ev - ery age a -
Spir - it, Thou art still The Word of God in
hon - or all un - stained; The ban - ners there of
home of pur - i - ty, A giant in two - fold
Fa - ther back He speeds; His course He runs to
flesh - ly man - tle now; The weak - ness of our
breathe a new - er light, Where end - less faith shalll
ter - nal Son, to Thee; All glo - ry, as is

dor - ing fall; Such birth be - fits the God of all.
flesh ar - rayed, The prom - ised Fruit to man dis - played.
vir - ture glow; God in His tem - ple dwells be - low.
sub - stance one, Re - joic - ing now His course to run.
death and hell, Re - turn - ing on God's throne to dwell.
mor - tal state With death - less might in - vig - or - ate.
shine se - rene, And twi - light nev - er in - ter - vene.
ev - er meet To God the Ho - ly Par - a - clete.

Come, Thou Redeemer of the Earth

About AD 390

Ambrose of Milan made a powerful contribution to the history of church hymnology when he started writing hymns with meter and rhythm and even with occasional rhyme. Biblical hymns and those of the early church depended on poetic techniques such as parallelism to give them a singable quality. According to Augustine, Pastor Ambrose was the one who began setting hymns to the popular music styles of the day and to the metrical tunes of Roman soldiers. His lyrics were mathematical in meter and form.

Ambrose wanted to celebrate congregational singing and to use hymns as a method of spreading true theology to the masses. He was particularly keen to write hymns of solid theology to combat the Arian heresy, which tried to diminish the identity and authority of Christ. Under the pastoral ministry of Ambrose in Milan, the practice of congregational singing accelerated. Because of this, Ambrose is called the "Father of Latin Hymnody," and he's even been called the "Father of Christian Hymnody."

"Come, Thou Redeemer of the Earth" is a Christmas carol reportedly written by Ambrose and translated from Latin by John Mason Neale in 1862. Like many of the hymns of Ambrose, it was written partly to combat the Arian heresy that claimed Jesus was not God Himself, but the greatest of God's creation. This hymn takes pains to stress the divinity of Christ, referring to Him in various stanzas as "the God of All" and "the Word of God in flesh arrayed." One of the lines says plainly:

> *O equal to the Father, Thou!*
> *Gird on Thy fleshly mantle now . . .*

The final verses are a Trinitarian doxology (the word "Paraclete" is from the Greek term meaning *helper* or *comforter*, referring to the Holy Spirit).

Of the Father's Love Begotten

Aurelius C. Prudentius
Trans. by John M. Neale and Henry W. Baker

Plainsong
Arr. by C. Winfred Douglas
DIVINUM MYSTERIUM

1. Of the Fa-ther's love be-got-ten, Ere the worlds be-gan to be,
2. O ye heights of heaven, a-dore Him; An-gel hosts, His prais-es sing;
3. Christ, to Thee with God the Fa-ther, And, O Ho-ly Ghost, to Thee,

He is Al-pha and O-me-ga, He the Source, the End-ing He
powers, do-min-ions, bow be-fore Him And ex-tol our God-and King;
hymn and chant and high thanks-giv-ing, And un-wea-ried-prais-es be:

of the things that are that have been,
let no tongue on earth be si - lent;
hon-or glo-ry and do-min - ion

and that fu-ture years shall see, ev-er-more and ev-er-more.
ev-ery voice in con-cert ring, ev-er-more and ev-er-more.
and e-ter-nal vic-to-ry, ev-er-more and ev-er-more.

Of the Father's Love Begotten

About AD 400

ome time ago a college student sauntered into my office to tell me about a song he'd discovered, one with haunting melody and pensive words. I smiled when he played it for me, for it was one of our oldest hymns, "Of the Father's Love Begotten."

This ancient Latin hymn is by Aurelius Prudentius, who was born in northern Spain in AD 348, not long after Christianity was legalized in the Roman Empire following three centuries of persecution. Prudentius became a lawyer and provincial governor in Spain where his leadership skills attracted the attention of Emperor Theodosius I who appointed him to an imperial military post.

It may have been shortly afterward that Prudentius gave his life to Christ and began writing Christian poetry. At age fifty-seven, he retired from government and entered a monastery where he devoted himself to worship and writing. Today we have nearly four hundred poems from his hand.

Prudentius has been called "the prince of early Christian poets." Though he and Ambrose were both writing hymns about the same time, the ones by Prudentius are more reflective, displaying greater warmth and glow. Perhaps it was his warm Spanish blood.

"Of the Father's Love Begotten" is among the greatest Christmas carols in Western history, and thankfully its popularity is on the increase, partly owing to the tender beauty of its probing score, *Divinum Mysterium*, composed nearly a thousand years ago. My young collegian would say that if you've never heard "Of the Father's Love Begotten," throw down this book and run—don't walk—to your nearest music store and find a quality recording of it. I agree. It's worth learning.

Of the Father's love begotten, ere the worlds began to be,
He is Alpha and Omega, He the source, the ending He,
Of the things that are, that have been, and that future years shall see,
Evermore and evermore![1]

Now Praise We Christ, The Holy One

Caelius Sedulius
Trans. by Martin Luther

Eyn Enchiridion
CHRISTUM WIR SOLLEN LOBEN SCHON

1. Now praise we Christ, the Ho - ly One, The
2. He who Him - self all things did make A
3. The grace and power of God the Lord Up -
4. The no - ble moth - er bore a Son — For
5. Up - on a man - ger filled with hay In
6. The heaven - ly choirs re - joice and raise Their
7. All hon - or un - to Christ be paid, Pure

bless - ed vir - gin Ma - ry's Son, Far as the glo - rious sun doth
ser - vant's form vouch - safe to take That He as man man - kind might
on the moth - er was out-poured; A vir - gin pure and un - de -
so did Ga - briel's prom-ise run — Whom John con - fessed and leaped with
pov - er - ty con - tent He lay; With milk was fed the Lord of
voice to God in songs of praise. To hum - ble shep-herds is pro -
off - spring of the fav - ored maid, With Fa - ther and with Ho - ly

1-6 | **7**

shine, E'en to the world's re - mote con - fine.
win And save His crea - tures from their sin.
filed In won-drous wise con - ceived a Child.
joy Ere yet the moth - er knew her Boy.
all, Who feeds the ra - vens when they call.
claimed The Shep-herd who the world hath framed.
Ghost, Till time in end - less time be lost.

Now Praise We Christ, the Holy One

About AD 450

Beneath the merriment of Christmas, a melancholy stream flows like an underground river, casting a pensive—even a sad, mournful—vapor over the eve of Christ's birth. It isn't simply feelings of nostalgia or the holiday blues. It's the pathos of the imponderable, the unsearchable sorrow of God-in-flesh, coming to die for the sins of the world.

Hearing "Now Praise We Christ, the Holy One", one has the sense of attending Midnight Mass in an ancient torch-lit cathedral on Christmas Eve, or being present in the haunts of a medieval monastery as brown-robed monks shuffle through the cloisters, their haunting chants echoing through the shadowed corridors.

Caelius Sedulius was a Latin Christian who lived in the 400s, probably in Rome. We know little about him except that he seems to have been an expert in pagan literature who, following his conversion, devoted himself to writing Christian poetry and became one of the most influential hymnists in the early church.

"Now Praise We Christ," originally part of a longer Latin hymn entitled *A Solis Ortus Cardine*, was excerpted and translated into German by Martin Luther in the 1520s, and rendered into English in 1854 by Richard Massie, an Anglican rector in Eccleston, England.

We don't want to live in dark moods of imponderable mystery, but neither do we want to miss them altogether. They allow us to emerge from the tender sadness of the manger to sing with the angels in the skies above shepherds' field, even as Sedulius wrote in another ancient carol:

> *From east to west, from shore to shore,*
> *Let every heart awake and sing*
> *The holy child whom Mary bore,*
> *The Christ, the everlasting King.*[12]

Christ Is Made the Sure Foundation

Latin Hymn, 7th century
Translated by John M. Neale

Henry T. Smart
REGENT SQUARE

1. Christ is made the sure foun-da - tion. Christ the head and
2. To this tem - ple, where we call Thee, Come, O Lord of
3. Here vouch-safe to all Thy ser - vants What they ask of
4. Laud and hon - or to the Fa - ther; Laud and hon - or

cor - ner - stone, Cho - sen of the Lord and pre - cious,
hosts, to - day. With ac - cus - tomed lov - ing-kind - ness
Thee to gain, What they gain from Thee for - ev - er
to the Son. Laud and hon - or to the Spir - it;

Bind - ing all the Church in one, Ho - ly Zi - on's
Hear Thy peo - ple as they pray, And Thy full - est
With the bless - ed to re - tain, And here - af - ter
Ev - er Three and ev - er One. One in might and

help for - ev - er, And her con - fi - dence a - lone.
ben - e - dic - tion Shed with - in its walls al - way.
in Thy glo - ry Ev - er - more with Thee to reign.
One in glo - ry While un - end - ing a - ges run.

Christ Is Made the Sure Foundation

About AD 650

H ere's one of the best hymns you've likely never heard. It dates from the seventh century, authorship anonymous. But you can sing it to the well-known tune REGENT SQUARE ("Angels from the Realms of Glory"), which was composed by Henry Smart.

"Christ Is Made the Sure Foundation" was translated from Latin into English by the Anglican priest and hymnographer John Mason Neale, who also gave us English versions of many other ancient classics.

John Mason Neale was a high churchman who bore much criticism for tilting toward the catholic revival of the Established Church. He loved high church architecture. He disliked the modern hymns being written by Watts and company. Neale wanted to revive the ancient Latin hymns; and he was the one to do it, for he's said to have known twenty languages.

Neale relished compiling his hymnals of translated verse. "Some of the happiest and most instructive hours of my life," he recalled, "were spent in the sub-committee of the Ecclesiological Society appointed for the purpose of bringing out the (Hymnal). It was my business to lay before them the translations I had prepared, and theirs to correct. The study which this required drew out the beauties of the original in a way which nothing else could have done; and the friendly collisions of various minds elicited ideas which a single translator would in all probability have missed."[13]

One of the best quotations I've seen about the heritage of our hymnody was penned in the introduction to a 1914 edition of Neale's hymns: "Neale seems to me to have always needed some previous fire at which to kindle his torch. When that could be found, his success was very great."[14]

How many of us can say the same! In the great hymns—both ancient and modern—we find a glowing fire from a previous age with which to kindle our torch and give us success.

Commit Whatever Grieves Thee

Paul Gerhardt

Hans L. Hassler
Harm. by Johann Sebastian Bach
PASSION CHORALE

1. Com - mit what - ev - er grieves thee In - to the gra - cious hands
2. On Him place Thy re - li - ance If thou wouldst be se - cure;
3. Thy truth and grace, O Fa - ther, Most sure - ly see and know
4. Thy hand is nev - er short - ened, All things must serve Thy might;

Of Him who nev - er leaves thee, Who heaven and earth com - mands.
His work thou must con - sid - er If thine is to en - dure.
Both what is good and e - vil For mor - tal man be - low.
Thine ev - ery act is bless - ing, Thy path is pur - est light.

Who points the clouds their cours - es, Whom winds and waves o - bey,
By anx - ious sighs and griev - ing And self - tor - ment - ing care
Ac - cord - ing to Thy coun - sel Thou wilt Thy work pur - sue;
Thy work no man can hin - der, Thy pur - pose none can stay,

He will di - rect thy foot - steps And find for thee a way.
God is not moved to giv - ing; All must be gained by prayer.
And what Thy wis - dom choos - eth Thy might will al - ways do.
Since Thou to bless Thy chil - dren Wilt al - ways find a - way.

Commit Whatever Grieves Thee

1656

T he first stanza of this hymn is easy to memorize, and well worth the effort. In cadence and content, it flows as naturally as cascading water: "Commit whatever grieves thee into the gracious hands / of Him who never leaves thee, who heav'n and earth commands." I often quote it in sermons or counseling.

Paul Gerhardt knew what he was writing about. Considered Germany's greatest hymnist, he was a man whose whole life was encompassed by troubles. In 1618, while he was still a child, the Thirty Years' War broke out and he lived much of his life amid its horrors. The University of Wittenberg remained open, and there Gerhardt studied for the ministry, greatly influenced by two professors who were lovers of Lutheran hymns.

Upon graduation, Gerhardt accepted a position as tutor for a family in Berlin, and later he began pastoring in the nearby town of Mittenwalde. There he wrote many of the hymns for which he is remembered. He later moved to Berlin and became the pastor of St. Nicholas's Church. But this was a time of bickering between the Lutherans and the Reformed clergy, and the Elector Frederick William deposed Gerhardt from his position in 1666.

"This is only a small Berlin affliction," he said, "but I am also willing and ready to seal with my blood the evangelical truth, and like my name-sake, St. Paul, to offer my neck to the sword."

Gerhardt's wife, it seems, didn't immediately share his stalwartness. According to an old story (impossible to confirm), as they left Berlin for parts unknown, she was fearful and fretful. That evening at an inn, she poured out her problems and bemoaned her hard lot. Gerhardt tried to comfort her by quoting Psalm 37:5: "Commit your way to the LORD; trust in him and he will do this." But she had trouble resting in that assurance.

Going outside, Gerhardt sat on a garden seat and there composed the words to "Commit Whatever Grieves Thee." That evening as he quoted the hymn to her, her fear subsided and she was able to cast her cares into the gracious hands of Him who never leaves us, whom heav'n and earth commands.

All Praise to Thee, My God, This Night

Thomas Ken

Arr. from Thomas Tallis
TALLIS' CANON

1. All praise to Thee, my God this night For
2. For - give me, Lord, for Thy dear Son, The
3. Teach me to live that I may dread The
4. Oh, may my soul in Thee re - pose, And
5. When in the night I sleep - less lie, My
6. Praise God, from whom all bless - ings flow, Praise

all the bless - ings of the light, Keep me, oh, keep me,
ill that I this day have done, That with the world, my -
grave as lit - tle as my bed. Teach me to . die that
may sweet sleep mine eye - lids close, Sleep that shall me more
soul with heaven - ly thoughts sup - ply; Let no ill dreams dis -
Him, all crea - tures here be - low; Praise Him a - bove, ye

King of kings, Be - neath thine own al - might - y wings.
self, and Thee, I, ere I sleep, at peace may be.
so I may Rise glo - rious at the awe - some day.
vig - orous make To serve my God when I a - wake!
turb my rest, No powers of dark - ness me mo - lest.
heaven - ly host; Praise Fa - ther, Son, and Ho - ly Ghost.

All Praise to Thee, My God, This Night

1674

T homas Ken's mother died when he was four, and his father a few years later.[15] A godly older stepsister raised him, and he later became a clergyman and educator. At age thirty-seven, he published *A Manual of Prayers for the Use of the Scholars of Winchester College*. Churches in England didn't sing hymns at the time, only psalms. Ken was an advocate of hymns, but didn't try to force the issue. He wrote hymns for his students' use in private devotions, including this song for bedtime—"All Praise to Thee, My God, This Night."

He advised students: "Be sure to sing the Morning and Evening Hymn in your chamber devoutly, remembering that the Psalmist, upon happy experience, assures you that it is a good thing to tell of the loving kindness of the Lord early in the morning and of His truth in the night season."[16]

Thomas faced lifelong pressure due to the unstable politics of his day and finally spent his remaining years in retirement. His books of sermons were very popular, but it's his hymns that have endured—especially his classic doxology: *Praise God from whom all blessings flow*. He once commented that it would enhance his joy in heaven if when he reached that happy place he might be permitted to hear his songs being sung by worshippers still on earth.[17]

One wonders if Thomas's mother didn't cast a long doxology over his life. Despite her premature passing, he must have drank in her love and training. He later told parishioners to teach their children "with all the sweetness and gentleness" they could, "to instill good things into their minds as soon as ever they begin to speak; let the first words they utter, if it be possible, be these: 'Glory be to God.' Accustom them to repeat these words on their knees, as soon as they rise, and when they go to bed, and oft times in the day; and let them not eat or drink without saying 'Glory be to God.'"[18]

While Shepherds Watched Their Flocks

Nahum Tate

George F. Handel
CHRISTMAS

1. While shep - herds watched their flocks by night, All
2. "Fear not!" said he; for might - y dread Had
3. "To you, in Da - vid's town, this day Is
4. "All glo - ry be to God on high, And

seat - ed on the ground, The an - gel of the Lord came down,
seized their trou - bled mind, "Glad tid - ings of great joy I bring,
born, of Da - vid's line, The Sav - ior, who is Christ the Lord;
to the earth be peace: Good - will hence - forth from heaven to men,

And glo - ry shone a - round, And glo - ry shone a - round.
To you and all man - kind, To you and all man - kind.
And this shall be the sign: And this shall be the sign:
Be - gin and nev - er cease, Be - gin and nev - er cease!"

While Shepherds Watched Their Flocks

1700

Tis popular Christmas carol owes its endurance to two men with financial woes. The first, Nahum Tate, was born in Dublin in 1652 to a preacher who was literally named Faithful—Rev. Faithful Teate (original spelling). After attending Trinity College in Dublin, young Nahum migrated to London wanting to be a writer. His success was slow in coming, but he dabbled with plays, adapted the prose of others, and was eventually named poet laureate in 1692 and appointed royal historiographer ten years later. Unfortunately, Nahum was intemperate and careless in handling money, and he lived in perpetual financial distress. He died in an institution for debtors in 1715.

His chief claim to fame was his collaboration with Nicholas Brady in compiling a hymnbook entitled *The New Version of the Psalms of David*, published in 1696. It was reissued in 1700 with a supplement in which this carol first appeared. The words to "While Shepherds Watched Their Flocks" represent a literal paraphrase of Luke 2:8–14, making this one of our most biblically accurate Christmas carols.

The second man was George Frederick Handel, composer of the music to which this carol is sung. Handel was born in Germany with the inborn talent of a musical genius. His father, wanting to discourage his pursuit of music, pressured the young man to enter law school, but George would not be denied, writing his first composition by age twelve and amazing choirmasters with his artistry. He moved to London where he enjoyed great success for a season. Then his popularity waned, his income dwindled, and he went bankrupt. It was the remarkable success of *Messiah* that salvaged Handel's career—and bank account.

How ironic! Two men who never met, who struggled with poverty, who faced bankruptcy and worried about making ends meet—yet they enriched the world beyond measure, providing millions of people for scores of generations with the gift of song every Advent season.[19]

When I Can Read My Title Clear

Isaac Watts

Traditional American melody
PISGAH

1. When I can read my ti-tle clear To man-sions in the skies,
2. Should earth a-gainst my soul en-gage, And fi-ery darts be hurled,
3. Let cares like a wild del-uge come, And storms of sor-row fall!
4. There shall I bathe my wea-ry soul In seas of heaven-ly rest,

I'll bid fare-well to ev-ery fear, And wipe my weep-ing eyes;
Then I can smile at Sa-tan's rage, And face a frown-ing world;
May I but safe-ly reach my home, my God, my heaven, my all;
And not a wave of trou-ble roll A-cross my peace-ful breast,

And wipe my weep-ing eyes, And wipe my weep-ing eyes,
And face a frown-ing world, And face a frown-ing world,
My God, my heaven, my all, My God, my heaven, my all,
A-cross my peace-ful breast, A-cross my peace-ful breast,

I'll bid fare-well to ev-ery fear, And wipe my weep-ing eyes.
Then I can smile at Sa-tan's rage, And face a frown-ing world.
May I but safe-ly reach my home, My God, my heaven, my all.
And not a wave of trou-ble roll A-cross my peace-ful breast.

When I Can Read My Title Clear

1707

Isaac Watts popularized modern hymn-singing in the English church, but today even traditional churchgoers know only a handful of his hundreds of hymns: "We're Marching to Zion," "Alas, and Did My Savior Bleed," "I Sing the Mighty Power of God," "Jesus Shall Reign," "O God, Our Help," "When I Survey the Wondrous Cross," and "Joy to the World." Some *Then Sings My Soul* readers may know another Watts hymn, which begins: "When I can read my title clear to mansions in the skies, / I bid farewell to every fear, and wipe my weeping eyes."

In an old biography of Ulysses S. Grant, Headley and Austin relate the story of a dying captain in the Civil War, a man shot through both thighs at Shiloh. As he was carried off the field the next day mortally wounded, he said:

"While lying there, I suffered intense agony from thirst. . . . and the rain from heaven was falling around me . . . In a little while a pool of water formed under my elbow, and I thought, if I could only get to that puddle, I might quench the burning thirst . . . but was unable. . . .

"By and by, night fell, and the stars shone out clear and beautiful above the dark field, and I began to think of that great God who had given His Son to die a death of agony for me . . . and I felt that I was going home to meet Him and praise Him there. I could not help singing that beautiful hymn: 'When I can read my title clear to mansions in the skies, / I'll bid farewell to every fear, and wipe my weeping eyes.'

"There was a Christian brother in the brush near me. I could not see him, but I could hear him. He took up the strain, and beyond him another and another caught it up, all over the terrible battlefield of Shiloh. That night the echo was resounded, and we made the field of battle ring with hymns of praise to God."[20]

Lo, He Comes with Clouds Descending

Charles Wesley and Martin Madan
Based on John Cennick

Henry T. Smart
REGENT SQUARE

1. Lo, He comes with clouds de-scend - ing, Once for fa - vored sin - ners slain; Thou - sand thou - sand saints at - tend - ing Swell the tri - umph of His train. Al - le - lu - ia! Al - le - lu - ia! God ap - pears on earth to reign.

2. Ev - ery eye shall now be-hold Him, Robed in dread - ful maj - es - ty! Those who set at naught and sold Him, Pierced and nailed Him to the tree, Deep - ly wail - ing, deep - ly wail - ing, Shall the true Mes - si - ah see.

3. Now the Sav - ior long - ex-pect - ed, See in sol - emn pomp ap - pear. All His saints, by man re - ject - ed, Now shall meet Him in the air. Al - le - lu - ia! Al - le - lu - ia! See the day of God ap - pear.

4. Yes, a - men! let all a - dore Thee, High on Thine e - ter - na throne. Sav - ior, take the power and glo - ry; Claim the king - dom for Thine own. O come quick - ly! O come quick - ly! Ev - er - last - ing God come down!

Lo, He Comes with Clouds Descending

1752

*T*hough his grandparents were Quakers who bore persecution for their faith, John Cennick grew up in an Anglican household and gave scant thought to the things of Christ. By age sixteen his life revolved around playing cards, going to the theater, and music. One day, as he later said, while "walking hastily in Cheapside, London, the hand of the Lord touched me. I felt at once an uncommon fear and dejection, and though all my days had been bitter through the fear of going to hell, yet I knew not any weight before like this."

For two years John struggled with the burden of guilt. When he tried to pray, his words went nowhere. When he read his Bible, he felt nothing but pangs of conviction. He tried through austerity to find inner peace, subjecting himself to self-denial. He gave up rich food and existed on potatoes, acorns, crabs, and grass. Finally on September 6, 1737, a breakthrough came and he was born again. He began reading the journal of George Whitefield and longed to hear the great evangelist preach. Learning that Whitefield was going to be in a particular place, Cennick walked all night long to get there. Soon he was working alongside Whitefield as one of his closest friends and associates.

It wasn't long before John Cennick was traveling internationally, drawing great crowds and preaching multiple times a day with intense power. He was attacked by bullies who set their dogs on him. He was subjected to harsh treatment and exhausting conditions. He often addressed huge crowds in the pouring rain. He worked beyond the capacity of his frame to endure it, and he broke down while trying to get to a service at a Moravian meetinghouse on Fetter Lane in London. He passed away on July 4, 1755, at the age of thirty-six.

"Lo, He Comes with Clouds Descending" was printed in a collection of hymns two years before Cennick's death.

Awake, My Soul, Stretch Every Nerve

Philip Doddridge

Arr. from George F. Handel
CHRISTMAS

1. A - wake, my soul, stretch ev - ery nerve, And press with vig - or
2. A cloud of wit - ness - es a - round Hold thee in full sur -
3. 'Tis God's all - an - i - mat - ing voice That calls thee from on
4. Blest Sav - ior, in - tro - duced by Thee, Have I my race be -

on! A heaven - ly race de - mands thy zeal, And
vey; For - get the steps al - read - y trod, And
high; 'Tis His own hand pre - sents the prize To
gun; And, crowned with vic - tory, at Thy feet I'll

an im - mor - tal crown, And an im - mor - tal crown.
on - ward urge thy way, And on - ward urge thy way.
thine as - pir - ing eye, To thine as - pir - ing eye.
lay my hon - ors down, I'll lay my hon - ors down.

Awake, My Soul, Stretch Every Nerve

1755

Except for his upbeat hymn "O Happy Day," which has surprisingly showed up in several recent movies and an old book he wrote entitled *The Rise and Progress of Religion in the Soul*, Philip Doddridge isn't as well-known as he was in previous generations.[21] He is an esteemed British clergyman and hymnist, the last of twenty children born to a pickle-dealer and his wife in London. His mother, Monica, was the daughter of a Czech preacher who had fled Prague for his faith. Monica taught young Philip the Bible using fireplace tiles with scriptural scenes.

When both his parents died while he was a child, Philip was placed in the care of tutors and educators who further influenced him toward a life of Christian service. He preached his first sermon on July 22, 1722, from 1 Corinthians 16:22. Two people accepted Christ as Savior because of Philip's sermon that day.

Philip married Mercy Maris during the Christmas holidays of 1730, and the couple had five children, four of whom survived to adulthood. He was a Dissenter—a non-Anglican, who devoted his life to educating children in Dissenting Schools and pastoring churches. Like his close friend Isaac Watts, Philip became a prolific hymnist and writer. Most of his four hundred hymns were written to summarize and conclude his sermons.

Philip caught a cold in December 1750 while going to preach a funeral sermon, and his condition deteriorated quickly. He preached his final sermon in Northampton from the text Romans 14:8. Thinking a warmer climate would help, he departed for Lisbon. He wrote his friends, "If I survive my voyage, a line shall tell you have I bear it. If not, all will be well." He did survive the voyage, but not much longer. He passed away in Lisbon at age fifty.

The hymn "Awake, My Soul, Stretch Every Nerve" was published posthumously. You can sing it to the same tune as "While Shepherds Watched Their Flocks."[22]

Come, Thou Almighty King

Unknown

Felice de Giardini
ITALIAN HYMN

1. Come, Thou Al-might-y King, Help us Thy name to sing,
2. Come, Thou In-car-nate Word, Gird on Thy might-y sword,
3. Come, Ho-ly Com-for-ter, Thy sa-cred wit-ness bear
4. To Thee, great One in Three, E-ter-nal prais-es be

Help us to praise: Fa-ther all glo-ri-ous, O'er all vic-
Our prayer at-tend: Come, and Thy peo-ple bless, And give Thy
In this glad hour: Thou who al-might-y art, Now rule in
Hence, ev-er-more! Thy sov-ereign maj-es-ty May we in

to-ri-ous, Come, and reign o-ver us, An-cient of Days.
word suc-cess: Spir-it of ho-li-ness, On us de-scend.
ev-ery heart, And ne'er from us de-part, Spir-it of power.
glo-ry see, And to e-ter-ni-ty Love and a-dore!

Come, Thou Almighty King

1757

T his is one of our oldest English hymns, but its authorship is unknown. It was published in or before 1757, and one of the oldest imprints is in a four-page Methodist pamphlet. Some people have attributed it to Charles Wesley. But most hymnologists reject that attribution since it's written to a meter that Wesley never used and the great hymnist never claimed it as his own. A number of old sources speculate that the real author was Rev. Martin Madan (1726–1790), who was an English lawyer-turned-Methodist-preacher with a reputation as a stirring orator and a gifted musician.

At first, this hymn was sung to the same tune as "God Save the King." On the American side of the Atlantic, we use the same tune for "My Country 'Tis of Thee." Just as an experiment, try singing a verse of "Come, Thou Almighty King" to this slower, more somber melody. There's an interesting story connected with it. During the American Revolution, while British troops were occupying New York City and appeared to be winning the war, a group of English soldiers went to church one Sunday morning in Long Island. The setting was tense. The occupiers demanded the congregation sing "God Save the King" in honor of King George III. The organist was forced to begin playing the tune—but instead of singing "God Save the King," the congregation broke out in "Come, Thou *Almighty* King."[23]

Point made.

I don't remember *not* knowing this hymn. In the mountain church I attended in childhood, it was one of three songs that opened almost every Sunday morning service, the others being "Holy, Holy, Holy" and "O Worship the King." I love those hymns to this day. After all, what better prayer can a church offer than: "Come, and Thy people bless, and give Thy Word success"?

Since 1769, the majestic tune ITALIAN HYMN has been used as the musical setting for "Come, Thou Almighty King." It was composed by Felice de Giardini, the Italian composer and violinist.

Come, Ye Sinners, Poor and Needy

Joseph Hart
Refrain, unknown

Traditional American melody
Walker's *Southern Harmony*
ARISE

1. Come, ye sin-ners, poor and need-y, Weak and wound-ed, sick and sore;
2. Come, ye thirst-y, come, and wel-come, God's free boun-ty glo-ri-fy;
3. Let not con-science make you lin-ger, Nor of fit-ness fond-ly dream;
4. Come, ye wea-ry, heav-y lad-en, Lost and ru-ined by the fall;

Je-sus read-y stands to save you, Full of pit-y, love, and power.
True be-lief and true re-pen-tance, Ev-ery grace that brings you nigh.
All the fit-ness He re-quir-eth Is to feel your need of Him.
If you tar-ry till you're bet-ter, You will nev-er come at all.

I will a-rise and go to Je-sus, He will em-brace me in His arms;

In the arms of my dear Sav-ior, O, there are ten thou-sand charms.

Come, Ye Sinners, Poor and Needy

1759

nvitation hymns have been used powerfully in bringing sinners to faith in Christ: "Just as I Am," "Softly and Tenderly," "Have Thine Own Way," and "The Savior Is Waiting." One of the first in this genre was Joseph Hart's "Come, Ye Sinners, Poor and Needy." It originally appeared in a 1759 hymnal under the title "Come, and Welcome, to Jesus."

Joseph Hart was a Londoner, born in that city in 1712, to a Christian family. He was well educated and became a London schoolteacher specializing in classical languages, but he turned away from the Lord and became immoral. He even wrote a pamphlet attacking Christianity (and John Wesley in particular), entitled "The Unreasonableness of Religion."

Moving to the town of Sheerness, Kent, Hart became so dissolute and notorious that townspeople persuaded him to move back to London. He later testified, "I ran such dangerous lengths both of carnal and spiritual wickedness that I even outwent professed infidels and shocked the irreligious and profane with my horrid blasphemies and monstrous impieties."[24] But when he was forty-five, the Lord got hold of him. He was converted one afternoon in 1757 in a Moravian Chapel in London under the influence of a sermon from Revelation 3:10. Two years later he published this hymn.

Over a century later, the remarkable New York City pastor T. DeWitt Talmage referred to this hymn in a sermon, lamenting: "The word 'sinner' is almost dropped out of the Christian vocabulary; it is not thought polite to use that word now. It is methodistic or old-fashioned. If you want to tell me that they are sinners, you must say they are spiritually erratic or have moral deficits, or they have not had a proper spiritual development; and I have not heard in twenty years that old hymn, 'Come, Ye Sinners, Poor and Needy.'"[25]

Talmage said that in 1874.

What would he say now?

I Know That My Redeemer Lives!

Samuel Medley

John Hatton
DUKE STREET

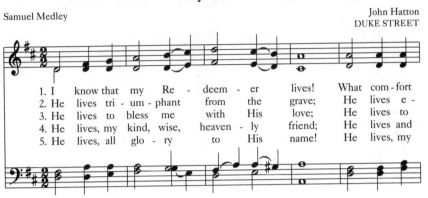

1. I   know that my Re - deem - er lives! What com - fort
2. He lives tri - um - phant from the grave; He lives e -
3. He lives to bless me with His love; He lives to
4. He lives, my kind, wise, heaven - ly friend; He lives and
5. He lives, all glo - ry to His name! He lives, my

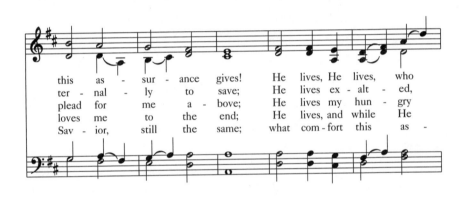

this as - sur - ance gives! He lives, He lives, who
ter - nal - ly to save; He lives ex - alt - ed,
plead for me a - bove; He lives my hun - gry
loves me to the end; He lives, and while He
Sav - ior, still the same; what com - fort this as -

once was dead; He lives my ev - er - liv - ing Head!
throned a - bove; He lives to rule His church in love.
soul to feed; He lives to help in time of need.
lives, I'll sing; He lives, my Proph - et, Priest, and King!
sur - ance gives: I know that my Re - deem - er lives!

I Know That My Redeemer Lives!

1775

Living up to his name, Samuel Medley gave us a handful of enriching hymns. He was born June 23, 1738, in an English village. His father and grandfather were sincere believers, who planted seeds of grace in Samuel's heart, though it took years for them to sprout. At age fourteen Samuel moved to London, and three years later joined the British navy.

His three years aboard a warship in the Mediterranean were spent in corruption and carelessness.[26] Though his remarkable personality made him everyone's friend, he wanted nothing to do with godliness or godly people. Then war broke out, and during a battle with the French his leg was badly injured and his wounds became gangrenous. One night the surgeon told him his leg would have to be amputated the next day unless there was improvement.

Samuel earnestly cried to God for mercy and, remembering that he had a Bible buried away in his chest, he sent for it. That night he read the Bible and prayed in anguish and great earnestness. The next morning the surgeon was amazed at the difference in the appearance of the wound. His leg was spared.

Samuel returned to his grandfather's house to convalesce, and afterward was baptized and called to preach. "He left the sea," it was said, "and became a faithful preacher of that Savior whose name in early life he often profaned."[27]

During his career Samuel wrote 230 hymns, including: "Awake, My Soul, to Joyful Lays," "O Could I Speak the Matchless Worth," and "Now, in a Song of Grateful Praise."

Medley was known as something of an eccentric and humorist. When asked, "In what town is your church?" he replied, "In one where sin makes many a fool, / known by the name of Liverpool." When asked, "Have you an assistant?" he answered, "O yes! I've One on whom I boast, / His name is called the Holy Ghost."[28]

He also had an emphatic death; but that's a story for the next entry.

Now, In a Song of Grateful Praise

Samuel Medley

Unknown
DEAR JESUS IS THE ONE I LOVE

1. Now, in a song of grate - ful praise, To
2. All worlds His glo - rious power con - fess, His
3. How sov - ereign, pow - er - ful, and free Has

(Refrain) Dear Je - sus is the One I love, Oh,

my dear Lord my voice I'll raise; With all His saints I'll join to
wis - dom all His works ex - press; But oh! His love what tongue can
been His love to sin - ful me! He plucked me from the jaws of

bless His name! He died for me; His blood now cleans - es me from

tell — My Je - sus has done all things well.
tell? My Je - sus has done all things well.
hell — My Je - sus has done all things well.

sin, Dear Je - sus now He sets me free.

Now, in a Song of
Grateful Praise

1776

I t seems a curious custom to us now, but deathbed scenes were fodder for Christian periodicals in an earlier era. One such article appeared about the final moments of pastor and hymnist Samuel Medley. His valuable friends came in, whom he cheerfully welcomed and to whom he said, "You see me now on my dying bed; and a sweet bed it is to me. What mercies am I now enjoying in it! Thanks be to God, I have now little or no pain. What blessings I have in my family! All my eight children a comfort to me. I am full of comfort and consolations, and able yet to recollect God's precious Word. The promises are like an army of soldiers; when I have finished with one another suitable portion presents itself. The doctrines I have preached, I am fully persuaded, are of the truth. They are now the support and consolation of my mind."

After a while his strength began failing and he slipped into unconsciousness. No one expected to hear from him again. But at two in the morning, he awoke smiling and said joyfully, "Look up, my soul and rejoice, for thy redemption drawth nigh!"

He fell back into a restless sleep, frequently rousing to recite passages of memorized Scripture.

"About half an hour before his departure, none of his family expecting to hear his voice more, he opened his eyes and with a smiling countenance said, 'Dying is sweet work! . . . Then with a dying voice he continued, 'Glory, glory! Home, home!' till his voice failed, and with a smiling countenance he yielded up his spirit into the hands of his heavenly father about half an hour before seven o' clock in the evening."[29]

Such was the home-going of the author who wrote this hymn with its happy lines: "With all the saints I'll join to tell—My Jesus has done all things well."

Come, My Soul, Thy Suit Prepare

John Newton

Henri A. César Malan
HENDON

1. Come, my soul, thy suit pre - pare, Je - sus loves to
2. Thou art com - ing to a King; Large pe - ti - tions
3. Lord, I come to Thee for rest; Take pos - ses - sion
4. While I am a pil - grim here, Let Thy love my
5. Show me what I have to do; Ev - ery hour my

an - swer prayer; He Him - self has bid thee pray,
with thee bring; For His grace and power are such,
of my breast; There Thy blood-bought right main - tain,
spir - it cheer: As my guide, my guard my friend,
strength re - new; Let me live a life of faith,

There-fore will not say thee nay, There-fore will not say thee nay.
None can ev - er ask too much, None can ev - er ask too much.
And with-out a ri - val reign, And with-out a ri - val reign.
Led me to my jour - ney's end, Lead me to my jour - ney's end.
Let me die Thy peo - ple's death, Let me die Thy peo - ple's death.

Come, My Soul, Thy Suit Prepare

1779

T he author of this hymn is John Newton, whose story I've told in the two previous volumes of *Then Sings My Soul*. He was the famous slave-trader who, following his conversion to Christ, became one of England's most celebrated preachers and the author of "Amazing Grace."

Newton's hymn "Come, My Soul, Thy Suit Prepare" deals with the subject of prayer, the word "suit" meaning *petition*. It holds a special place in my memory because when I was in college I had the privilege of spending time with Ruth (Mrs. Billy) Graham. In discussing prayer, she quoted the second verse of this hymn from memory and with a knowing smile: "Thou art coming to a King, / Large petitions with thee bring, / For His grace and power are such / None can ever ask too much."

Those words instantly engraved themselves on my mind in an unusual exercise of sudden memorization and I've often quoted them since.

"Come, My Soul, Thy Suit Prepare" originally appeared in *The Olney Hymns*, complied by Newton and his troubled friend William Cowper. Newton was vicar in the village of Olney, England. Wanting to encourage Cowper, Newton drew him into a partnership of writing hymns for their church. The two men lived on parallel streets with an orchard between them. They paid the orchard owner a guinea a year for the right to pass through his land to their respective gardens. Here they spent many hours discussing Newton's sermons and their corresponding hymns. Cowper called the garden his "verse manufactory."

When *The Olney Hymns* was published in 1779, Cowper's name was attached to over sixty of them; Newton's to over 280. The hymnal was so popular that by 1836 there were thirty-seven official editions and many unauthorized editions. *The Olney Hymns* presented the evangelical truths of the Christian faith in both theological and personal verse.

Holy Bible, Book Divine

John Burton

William B. Bradbury
ALETTA

1. Ho - ly Bi - ble, book di - vine, Pre - cious
2. Mine to chide me when I rove; Mine to
3. Mine to com - fort in dis - tress, Suf - fering
4. Mine to tell the joys to come, And the

trea - sure, thou art mine; Mine to tell me whence I
show a Sav - ior's love; Mine thou art to guide and
in this wil - der - ness; Mine to show, by liv - ing
reb - el sin - ner's doom; O thou ho - ly book di -

came; Mine to teach me what I am;
guard; Mine to pun - ish or re - ward;
faith, Man can tri - umph o - ver death;
vine, Pre - cious trea - sure, thou art mine.

Holy Bible, Book Divine

1805

G enerations of children (and adults) have learned to cherish their Bibles due to this simple song that tells us about God's Word: "Holy Bible, book divine, precious treasure, thou art mine." It was written in 1802 or 1803 and appeared in the *Evangelical Magazine* in 1805, attributed to J. B. Nottingham (Nottingham—J.B.). As the poem gained popularity, its readers were mystified. No one could find a J. B. Nottingham. Finally the truth came out. The author was a modest British layman named John Burton (sometimes spelled Barton), who had been born in Nottingham in 1773.

At that time, the Sunday school movement was picking up speed, having been launched by a British newspaper mogul named Robert Raikes, whose burden was to help illiterate and impoverished children gain the rudiments of an education and a knowledge of the Bible. As the movement spread to Nottingham, it captured Burton's passion and he poured himself into leading schools, teaching youngsters, and developing biblical resources for classroom and private use.

Shortly after writing "Holy Bible, Book Divine," Burton married, and the couple had a son, John Burton Jr., born in 1808, who later testified that he remembered being taught this song by his father before he was able to read. At age thirty, he published *The Youth's Monitor in Verse—In a Series of Little Tales, Emblems, Poems and Songs, Moral and Divine*, which became a standard study guide for the movement. Shortly afterward, Burton published songbooks for use in Sunday schools, and they included several of his hymns. More of his original hymns were discovered and published following his death at age forty-nine on June 24, 1822, though "Holy Bible, Book Divine" is the only hymn commonly sung today.

The most recognized tune for "Holy Bible, Book Divine" is ALETTA, written by William Bradbury, the composer who also gave us the melody to another beloved children's hymn, "Jesus Loves Me." He also composed the hymn tunes to "He Leadeth Me," "Just as I Am," "Sweet Hour of Prayer," "Savior, Like a Savior Lead Me," and "The Solid Rock."

Day by Day the Manna Fell

Josiah Conder

John B. Calkin
MUNUS

1. Day by day the man - na fell; O to learn this les - son well!
2. "Day by day," the prom - ise reads, Dai - ly strength for dai - ly needs;
3. Lord! my times are in Thy hand; All my san - guine hopes have planned,
4. Thou my dai - ly task shalt give; Day by day to Thee I live;
5. Fond am - bi - tion, whis - per not; Hap - py is my hum - ble lot.
6. Oh, to live ex - empt from care By the en - er - gy of prayer:

Still by con - stant mer - cy fed, Give me Lord, my dai - ly bread.
Cast fore - bod - ing fears a - way; Take the man - na of to - day.
To Thy wis - dom I re - sign, And would make Thy pur - pose mine.
So shall add - ed years ful - fill, Not my own, my Fa - ther's will.
Anx - ious, bus - y cares a - way; I'm pro - vid - ed for to - day.
Strong in faith, with mind sub-dued, Yet e - late with grat - i - tude!

Day by Day the Manna Fell

1836

No wonder Josiah Conder became a respected literary force in his day—he was born in a bookstore. His father, Thomas Conder, a devout Christian, ran a bookshop on Falcon Street in London. There Josiah was born in 1789. At age five, he endured a smallpox inoculation that destroyed the vision in his right eye. Hoping to save the sight in his other eye, he was treated with experimental electrical shocks. It seemed to work, and Josiah continued his schooling. At ten, his first essay was published, and his first book at age twenty. At twenty-one, he took over his dad's bookshop and gained a reputation for his literary knowledge and skill. He eventually disposed of his bookshop and devoted the rest of his life to writing and preaching.

Conder's Christian convictions guided everything he wrote and preached. He advanced evangelical causes such as the abolition of slavery and the repeal of laws against Jews. His books were widely read (including a thirty-volume geography of the world). And his hymns were more popular in England than those of any other author except Isaac Watts and Philip Doddridge. His son later described his father's hymns as "transcripts of personal experience and . . . proofs so often given that God tunes the heart by trial and sorrow, not only to patience but to praise."

Despite their popularity at the time, Conder's hymns have fallen into disuse, especially in America. Perhaps "Day by Day" will be a good introduction to a new generation of us. Though I've never heard this song in a congregational setting, it's become to me a cherished hymn of personal worship. On a recent trip, my granddaughter and I memorized it together, and I frequently quote it to friends—especially the line that says, "'Day by day' the promise reads, daily strength for daily needs." And the great final stanza about prayer: "Oh, to live exempt from care by the energy of prayer: / Strong in faith, with mind subdued, yet elate with gratitude!"

Based on the story of God's providing bread (manna) for the Israelites in the wilderness, this hymn is a reminder of our God's daily guidance and provision.

Once in Royal David's City

Cecil Frances Humphreys Alexander

Henry John Gauntlett
Harm. by Arthur Henry Mann
IRBY

1. Once in roy - al Da - vid's cit - y stood a low - ly cat - tle
2. He came down to earth from heav - en, Who is God and Lord of
3. And, through all His won - drous child - hood, He would hon - or and o -
4. For He is our child-hood's pat - tern, day by day like us He
5. And our eyes at last shall see Him, through His own re - deem-ing
6. Not in that poor low - ly sta - ble, with the ox - en stand-ing

shed, where a moth - er laid her Ba - by in a man - ger for His bed;
all, and His shel - ter was a sta - ble, and His cra - dle was a stall;
bey; love and watch the low - ly maid - en in whose gen - tle arms He lay;
grew; He was lit - tle, weak and help - less, tears and smiles like us He knew;
love; for that Child so dear and gen - tle, is our Lord in heaven a - bove,
by, we shall see Him; but in heav - en, set at God's right hand on high;

Ma - ry was that moth - er mild, Je - sus Christ her lit - tle Child.
with the poor, and mean, and low - ly lived on earth our Sav - ior ho - ly.
Chris-tian chil - dren all should be kind, o - be - dient, good as He.
and He feel - eth for our sad-ness, and He shar - eth in our glad-ness.
and He leads His chil - dren on to the place where He is gone.
when like stars His chil - dren crowned, all in white shall wait a - round.

Once in Royal David's City

1848

C ecil Frances Humphreys was born in 1818, in an Irish village called Redcross. Thirty-two years later, she married Rev. William Alexander, and the couple became a powerful duo in British Christianity. William was appointed the bishop for all of Ireland, but his wife's fame eclipsed his. Her poems and hymns became greatly beloved in the English-speaking world.

Mrs. Alexander, however, seemed less concerned about fame than she was about being faithful to Christ. She had a deep heart for children, devoting much time to teaching Sunday school and writing songs for youngsters. She helped establish a school for the deaf and founded a Girl's Friendly Society in Londonderry. She worked tirelessly to provide food for the hungry and comfort to the sick.

One day, Mrs. Alexander was working with one of her pupils in Sunday school—a little boy who happened to be her godson. He was struggling to understand the Apostles' Creed and portions of the Catechism. Mrs. Alexander began to mull the possibility of converting the Apostles' Creed into songs for children, using simple hymns to explain the phrases and truths of the Christian faith.

The Apostles' Creed begins: *I believe in God, the Father Almighty, Maker of heaven and earth, and in Jesus Christ, His only Son, our Lord.* For the phrase "Maker of heaven and earth . . ." she wrote the famous little song "All Things Bright and Beautiful."

The Creed goes on to say about Jesus Christ: ". . . who was conceived of the Holy Spirit, born of the Virgin Mary . . ." That spurred the writing of our great Christmas carol "Once in Royal David's City."

These hymns were published in 1848 in Mrs. Alexander's book *Hymns for Little Children*. It became one of the most successful hymn publishing projects in history, going through over one hundred editions and telling children the world over what happened "once in royal David's city."[30]

Jesus! Name of Wondrous Love

William How

Everett Titcomb
CARLSON

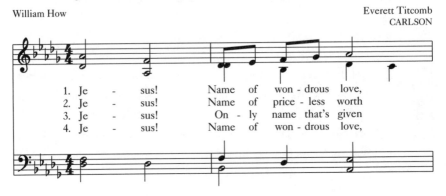

1. Je - sus! Name of won - drous love,
2. Je - sus! Name of price - less worth
3. Je - sus! On - ly name that's given
4. Je - sus! Name of won - drous love,

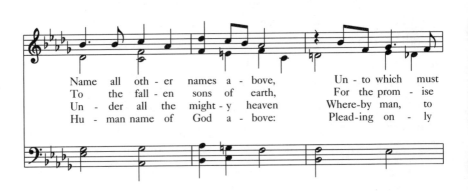

Name all oth - er names a - bove,   Un - to which must
To the fall - en sons of earth,   For the prom - ise
Un - der all the might - y heaven   Where-by man, to
Hu - man name of God a - bove: Plead-ing on - ly

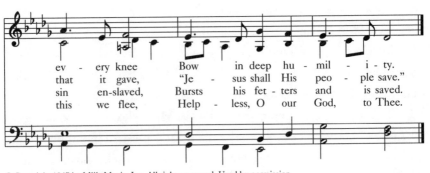

ev - ery knee   Bow   in deep hu - mil - i - ty.
that it gave,   "Je - sus shall His peo - ple save."
sin en-slaved,   Bursts his fet - ters and is saved.
this we flee,   Help - less, O our God, to Thee.

Jesus! Name of Wondrous Love

1854

William How was a renowned Anglican leader affectionately known as the People's Bishop. After laboring for years in rural areas, he accepted an appointment in East London where he worked among the poorer classes with simplicity and love. Masses who had never before seen a bishop were amazed at how frequently he was among them. At first, they said, "That's a bishop." Then it was: "That's *the* bishop." And finally it was: "That's *our* bishop."[31]

In 1888, rather against his will, he was appointed bishop of Wakefield at the age of sixty-four. His wife had died recently, and it was a difficult transition to make as he rendered his farewells, left his friends, and took up a new work. Wishing him Godspeed, the archbishop of Canterbury, William Temple, spoke for many when he said about Bishop How:

> *"We know him—know him by years of intimate knowledge . . . by his humility. We know him, for he has lived and worked amongst us; and we do not often come across such a man.*
>
> *"You will find men of great devotion. . . . You will find men sweet and gentle in society, whom you cannot help feeling in your inmost heart to be saints of God . . . You will find men so humble that they put themselves absolutely on one side, so simple in their humility that they walk through this world as if they were still children, carrying with them the charm of childhood even in the gravest matters. . . .*
>
> *"You will find such men; but you will not often find such men in whom all these things are combined at once.*
>
> *"Could we always get such men for Bishops assuredly the Church of Christ would so shine before the world that it would hardly be needful to preach sermons or to teach, for men would learn quickly from what they saw."*[32]

William How passed away after a few years at Wakefield, but he left behind about sixty hymns including "Jesus! Name of Wondrous Love."

Spirit of God, Descend upon My Heart

George Croly

Frederick C. Atkinson
MORECAMBE

1. Spir - it of God, de - scend up - on my heart;
2. I ask no dream, no proph - et ec - sta - sies,
3. Hast Thou not bid us love Thee, God and King?
4. Teach me to feel that Thou art al - ways right;
5. Teach me to love Thee as Thine an - gels love,

Wean it from earth, through all its puls - es move;
No sud - den rend - ing of the veil of clay,
All, all Thine own soul, heart and strength and mind.
Teach me the strug - gles of the soul to bear,
One ho - ly pas - sion fill - ing all my frame;

Stoop to my weak - ness, might - y as Thou art,
No an - gel vis - it - ant, no o - pening skies;
I see Thy cross — there teach my heart to cling:
To check the ris - ing doubt, the reb - el sigh;
The bap - tism of the heaven - de - scend - ed Dove,

And make me love Thee as I ought to love.
But take the dim - ness of my soul a - way.
O let me seek Thee, and O let me find.
Teach me the pa - tience of un - an - swered prayer.
My heart an al - tar, and Thy love the flame.

Spirit of God, Descend upon My Heart

1854

T his hymn, so often sung on Pentecost Sunday, is a deeply moving prayer for personal devotion or church use any time. Its author, George Croly, was born in Dublin in 1780. His father was a physician, but George decided to become a physician of souls and was ordained into the Anglican ministry when he graduated from Trinity College in Dublin in 1804. No church became available to him, so he moved to London, started writing, and developed a respected reputation as a gifted man of letters.

Eventually Croly was assigned to St. Stephen's, a church in the slums of London that had been closed for a hundred years. There Croly preached eloquent sermons without notes, and the crowds came. He spoke extemporaneously, sometimes changing his mind mid-service about his subject or text. His energy was boundless as he churned out seemingly endless compositions—hymns, dramas, biographies, historical and theological works, sermons, and novels.

In 1854, Croly published a volume of hymns entitled *Psalms and Hymns for Public Worship*. Just before the book was released, fire broke out and destroyed most of the copies. Extant copies are now extremely rare. But one hymn from the book has lived on—Croly's prayer to the Holy Spirit: "Spirit of God, Descend upon My Heart." He based it on Galatians 5:25—"If we live in the Spirit, let us also walk in the Spirit" (KJV).

Dr. Croly was described as tall, with a massive chest and head, short stubby iron-gray hair, a broad furrowed forehead, large gray eyes, a wide mouth, and an ample chin. He enjoyed good health until old age, but following the Christmas Day death of his son in a war in India and the subsequent passing of his wife, his strength declined. On November 24, 1860, leaving his home in Bloomsbury Square for a regular Saturday afternoon walk, he collapsed and was carried into a nearby shop where he was pronounced dead in his eightieth year.

As with Gladness, Men of Old

William C. Dix

Conrad Kocher
DIX

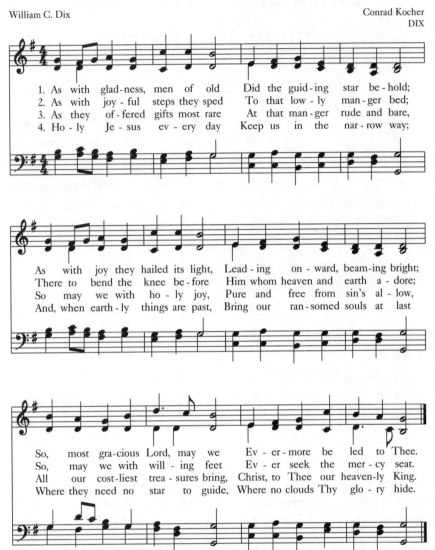

1. As with glad-ness, men of old   Did the guid-ing   star be-hold;
2. As with joy - ful steps they sped   To that low - ly   man-ger bed;
3. As they of - fered gifts most rare   At that man-ger   rude and bare,
4. Ho - ly Je - sus ev - ery day   Keep us in the   nar-row way;

As with joy they hailed its light,   Lead - ing   on - ward, beam-ing bright;
There to bend the knee be-fore   Him whom heaven and earth a - dore;
So may we with ho - ly joy,   Pure and   free from sin's al - low,
And, when earth-ly things are past,   Bring our   ran-somed souls at last

So, most gra-cious Lord, may we   Ev - er-more be led to Thee.
So, may we with will - ing feet   Ev - er seek the mer - cy seat.
All our cost-liest trea - sures bring,   Christ, to Thee our heaven-ly King.
Where they need no star to guide,   Where no clouds Thy glo - ry hide.

As with Gladness, Men of Old

1860

William Chatterton Dix was born into a home in which not all was well. His father, a surgeon and a biographer, appears to have abandoned his family. An 1872 periodical contained this cryptic report about William's father: "John Dix, author of the *Life of Chatterton*, died in America about seven years ago. For some time he practiced as a surgeon in Bristol, but owing to his unfortunate habits, with very limited success. With more circumspection he might have obtained emolument as a literary writer. . . . He proceeded to America some twenty years ago, leaving his young family to be brought up by the relations of his wife, traders in Bristol. The family (is) reluctant to refer to him or his writings. His son, William Chatterton Dix, is an accomplished verse-writer. He has composed one of our best hymns, beginning "As with Gladness, Men of Old."[33]

Well, no one can say that William himself suffered from "unfortunate habits." After attending grammar school in Bristol, he decided to follow "mercantile pursuits." About 1863, he moved to Glasgow, Scotland, and took a position with the Marine Insurance Office. It seems that when William was about twenty-nine or thirty, a serious illness left him nearly dead. He was confined to his bed for months, and many of his famous hymns can be dated from the period of his recovery.

Dix alluded to this in a letter to hymn-historian Francis Arthur Jones, who had inquired as to the circumstances behind "As with Gladness, Men of Old." He was unwell at the time, he said, recovering from a serious illness. One evening he felt his strength returning, and with newly felt energy began composing in his brain the idea for this hymn. Asking for writing materials, he jotted down the words. The following year it was published in a small hymnal that saw limited circulation, but it kept appearing in additional hymnals until it became a beloved carol.[34]

You can sing this song about the Magi using the tune to the thanksgiving hymn "For the Beauty of the Earth."

Joy Fills Our Inmost Hearts Today

William C. Dix

Samuel Smith
GAUDETE

1. Joy fills our in-most hearts to-day! The Roy-al Child is born:
2. Low at the cra-dle throne we bend, We won-der and a-dore;
3. For us the world must loose its charms Be-fore the man-ger shrine,
4. Thou Light of un-cre-a-ted Light, Shine on us Ho-ly Child:

And an-gel hosts in glad ar-ray His ad-vent keep this morn.
And fell no bliss can ours tran-scend, No joy was sweet be-fore.
When fold-ed in Thy moth-er's arms, We see Thee, Babe di-vine.
That we may keep Thy birth-day bright, With ser-vice un-de-filed.

Re-joice, re-joice! Th'In-car - nate Word Has come on earth to

Re-joice,   Th'In-car-nate

dwell; No sweet-er sound than this is heard Em-man-u-el!

Joy Fills Our Inmost
Hearts Today
1865

William Chatterton Dix reveled in celebrating the birth of Christ. He wrote two great carols, "What Child Is This?" and "As with Gladness, Men of Old." And he wrote several lesser-known carols including "Joy fills our inmost hearts today! The royal Child is born."

Though he was a businessman rather than a clergyman, Dix didn't shy away from writing hymns and Christian literature. In addition to his Christmas carols, he also explained the meaning of Christmas to children in his book *The Pattern Life.* He evidently believed children could understand good doctrine, for he didn't shy away from the great truths of the incarnation when he wrote:

"A birthday is a happy time in a house! There are presents given; and smiles and laughter and fun and good wishes and kind thoughts are the order of the day. All try to be sweet and good-tempered on a birthday, of all days of the year. But this day is the best birthday that the world has ever known; it is the Birthday of Jesus Christ."

Referring to the events in long-ago Bethlehem, Dix wrote: "The people were going and coming, and passing thoughtlessly by the poor shed wherein lay the Lord of Life and Glory, wrapped in baby's clothes. None knew that the little Baby lying in Mary's arms was God of God, Light of Light, very God of very God, by whom all things were made; and yet, perhaps, the creatures in the stable knew it, for Isaiah says, 'The ox knew his master, and the ass the manger of the Lord.'"

Dix went on to suggest that at Christmastide "every altar is a Bethlehem, for Bethlehem means 'House of Bread . . .' and He said, 'I am the Bread of Life . . . .' Oh, where shall we find such happiness on earth as at the altar of God? For there the Baby of Bethlehem waits to give us Himself, as more than eighteen hundred years ago He came to the manger-throne, true God and true Man, to give His Incarnate Life to all who would welcome and love Him as little children."[35]

Fill Thou My Life, O Lord My God

Horatius Bonar

Thomas Haweis
RICHMOND

1. Fill Thou my life, O Lord my God, In
2. Not for the lip of praise a - lone, Nor
3. Praise in the com - mon things of life, Its
4. Fill ev - ery part of me with praise: Let
5. So shalt Thou, Lord, from e - ven me Re -
6. So shall no part of day or night From

ev - ery part with praise, That my whole be - ing
for the prais - ing heart; I ask Thee for a
go - ings out and in; Praise in each du - ty
all my be - ing speak Of Thee and of Thy
ceive the glo - ry due; And so shall I be -
sa - cred - ness be free; But all my life, in

may pro - claim Thy be - ing and Thy ways.
life made up Of praise in ev - ery part.
and each deed, How - ev - er small and mean.
love, O Lord, Poor though I be, and weak.
gin on earth The song for - ev - er new.
ev - ery step, Be fel - low - ship with Thee.

Fill Thou My Life, O Lord My God

1866

This hymn comes from the pen of Horatius Bonar, a giant in the Scottish pulpit and the "Prince of Scottish Hymn Writers." Bonar was born just before Christmas 1808 in Edinburgh. He was from a long line of Scottish ministers (serving a total of 364 years). After completing theological studies in Edinburgh, Bonar was appointed assistant to the pastor of a church in Leith, where he oversaw the Sunday school program. It bothered him that the children had few lively songs to sing, so he found some popular tunes and wrote new words for them. He had leaflets printed with the new words, and he was delighted to find his Sunday school singing them heartily.

On November 30, 1837, Bonar was ordained the minister of the North Parish Church in Kelso. His attention turned to sermons and prose, but he kept a little notebook nearby in which he jotted down "stray poetical ideas."

His son later wrote about this habit, saying, "As I write now I have seven or eight (of these notebooks) lying before me. They contain most of the better-known hymns, hastily written down in pencil in his spare moments; they are full of contractions, with an occasional word or phrase in shorthand; sometimes a line is struck out and another substituted, yet in nearly every case the complete hymn, almost as it was afterward published, can be gleaned from this rough draft. Sometimes on the margin or in a blank corner of a page several possible rhymes are written down."

Even on vacation, Bonar kept a notebook in his pocket and was often seen jotting down outlines, thoughts, or snatches of possible sermons, poems, hymns, or articles. He was one of the most voluminous writers and pastors of the nineteenth century.

Today his best-known hymn is "I Heard the Voice of Jesus Say."

"Fill Thou My Life" was originally published under the title "Life's Praise"—and that's what it's about. It's a prayer for lifelong praise. In its original it's quite long, but several of the stanzas are well worth memorizing.

O Word of God Incarnate

William W. How

Neuvermehrtes Gesangbuch
Arr. by Felix Mendelssohn
MUNICH

1. O Word of God in - car - nate, O Wis - dom from on high,
2. The Church from her dear Mas - ter Re - ceived the gift di - vine,
3. It float - eth like a ban - ner Be - fore God's host un - furled;
4. O make Thy Church, dear Sav - ior, A lamp of pur - est gold,

O Truth un-changed, un - chang - ing, O Light of our dark sky;
And still that light she lift - eth O'er all the earth to shine.
It shin - eth like a bea - con A - bove the dark - ling world.
To bear be - fore the na - tions Thy true light as of old.

We praise Thee for the ra - diance That from the hal-lowed page,
It is the gold - en cas - ket Where gems of truth are stored;
It is the chart and com - pass That o'er life's surg - ing sea,
O teach Thy wan-dering pil - grims By this their path to trace,

A lan - tern to our foot - steps, Shines on from age to age.
It is the heaven-drawn pic - ture Of Christ, the liv - ing Word.
'Mid mists and rocks and quick-sands, Still guides, O Christ, to Thee.
Till, clouds and dark - ness end - ed, They see Thee face to face.

O Word of God Incarnate

1867

W illiam How, the beloved Anglican bishop of Queen Victoria's day, started composing hymns in childhood, and as a teen he wrote simple hymns for use on Sunday nights in the family circle. After attending Oxford University, How entered the ministry, and he was always eager to promote great singing in his churches. He helped compile a popular hymnal in 1854, with additions in 1864 and 1867. And he encouraged the printing of children's hymnals.

Bishop How was big-hearted, hardworking, and joyful. His sermons were tender, engaging, and well received. He was a High Churchman who wasn't inclined to jump on the Gospel song wagon of Moody and Sankey. Still, he wasn't all that critical. Writing to a friend, he said: "I went on Friday evening . . . to Moody and Sankey, and was agreeably surprised. It was a most marvelous sight to see twenty thousand people packed in Agricultural Hall; and the singing of the hymns by such a mass of voices was very grand, though the tunes were, of course, rather secular."[36]

No one ever called the bishop's hymns "secular." In some ways he was the last of the great British hymnists of the Golden Age of Watts, Wesley, and the others. In all, he published sixty hymns. This is one of his best. It appeared in the 1867 edition of his hymnal. The first verse is a prayer to Christ—Living Word and Living Wisdom—for the light of Scripture to shine from the hallowed page as a lantern for our footsteps. The second verse refers to the Bible as "the sacred Vessel where gems of truth are stored." In the third verse, the Scripture is a banner and a beacon, a chart and a compass. The fourth verse is a prayer that God's church might be a lamp of purest gold through which the message of Scripture shines to all the nations.

O teach Your wandering pilgrims by this their path to trace,
Till, clouds and darkness ended, they see You face to face.

The tune is MUNICH, named after a melody found in an old German hymnal and adapted by Felix Mendelssohn for his oratorio *Elijah.*

At the Name of Jesus

Caroline M. Noel

Ralph Vaughan Williams
KING'S WESTON

Unison

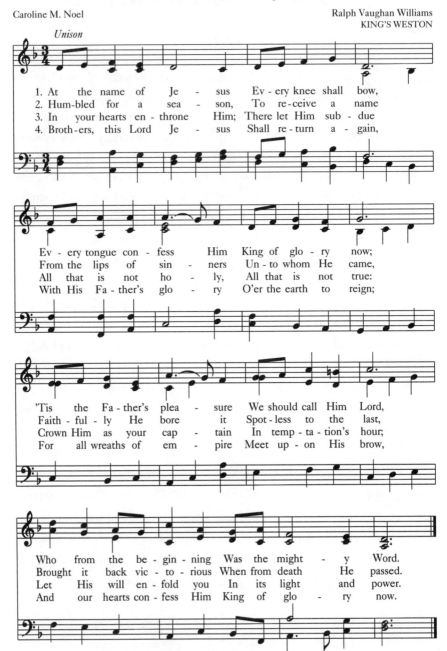

1. At the name of Je - sus Ev - ery knee shall bow,
2. Hum-bled for a sea - son, To re-ceive a name
3. In your hearts en - throne Him; There let Him sub - due
4. Broth-ers, this Lord Je - sus Shall re-turn a - gain,

Ev - ery tongue con - fess Him King of glo - ry now;
From the lips of sin - ners Un - to whom He came,
All that is not ho - ly, All that is not true:
With His Fa - ther's glo - ry O'er the earth to reign;

'Tis the Fa - ther's plea - sure We should call Him Lord,
Faith - ful - ly He bore it Spot - less to the last,
Crown Him as your cap - tain In temp - ta - tion's hour;
For all wreaths of em - pire Meet up - on His brow,

Who from the be - gin - ning Was the might - y Word.
Brought it back vic - to - rious When from death He passed.
Let His will en - fold you In its light and power.
And our hearts con - fess Him King of glo - ry now.

From *Enlarged Songs of Praise* by permission of Oxford University Press.

At the Name of Jesus

1870

I n earlier days not all hymnbooks were designed for the public at large. Some were published for specific audiences, and quite a few were designed for the sick, diseased, age-riddled, or bedfast. These hymnals usually resided on bedside tables rather than in pew racks, and were of incalculable encouragement to the ill.

The Name of Jesus and Other Verses for the Sick and Lonely was a book of poetry published originally in 1861 and expanded in subsequent editions. The author was London native Caroline Maria Noel, who wrote her first hymn, "Draw Nigh Unto My Soul," at age seventeen. She wrote a dozen more poems by age twenty, then her pen fell silent for twenty years. At age forty, she started writing again, spurred by an encroaching illness, and she wrote consistently for the next twenty years, passing away in 1877 at the age of sixty.

A memorial edition of her hymnal was printed after her death, and in the publisher's introduction we learn that Caroline's poems were borne of "a sickness prolonged for more than twenty years, with seasons of extreme suffering and weakness, so extreme at times that the end seemed imminent; a peculiar sensitiveness of nerve and brain, which could seldom bear the presence of earthly friends; long nights and days of throbbing sleeplessness."[37]

The publisher went on to say that the acceptance and popularity of her poems gave Caroline a "cheering and joyous brightness" to her sickroom, especially as she read notes from those whom she had helped.

Caroline's poems weren't all centered on illness. She also composed verses for the earthly history of Jesus Christ, with poems devoted to His birth, His infancy, His ministry, His visit to the home of Lazarus, His crucifixion, His resurrection, and His ascension. "At the Name of Jesus" was her ascension hymn, based on Philippians 2:10–11, and it's often sung to the same tune as "Like a River Glorious." Few of her other poems were set to music, but they should be.[38]

I Am Not Skilled to Understand

Dora Greenwell

William J. Kirkpatrick
GREENWELL

1. I am not skilled to understand What God has willed, what God has planned; I only know at His right hand Is One who is my Savior!
2. I take Him at His word indeed: "Christ died for sinners," this I read; For in my heart I find a need Of Him to be my Savior!
3. That He should leave His place on high And come for sinful man to die, You count it strange? so once did I, Before I knew my Savior!
4. And, oh, that He fulfilled may see The travail of His soul in me, And with His work contested be, As I with my dear Savior!
5. Yes, living, dying, let me bring My strength, my solace from this spring; That He who lives to be my King Once died to be my Savior!

I Am Not Skilled to Understand

1873

I t's funny how words change their meaning. In researching Dorothy (Dora) Greenwell's life, I found an 1885 biography and was shocked by the title of chapter 14: "Miss Greenwell's Interest in Imbeciles."

The writer said, "Among the great enthusiasms of her life, none deserve to be more especially mentioned than her concern for idiots and imbeciles."[39] I had to read further to understand the truth about it. Dora was concerned about children and adults with severe physical, emotional, and mental disabilities. The terms were used somewhat more charitably back then. Dora poured herself—passion and purse—into loving those who were misunderstood and mistreated by society. She visited the asylums, raised money for the unfortunate, and lifted the spirits of the lowest and lowliest.

Dora was born into a wealthy British family on a December day in 1821. As she grew up, she became known for her wise words and beautiful handwriting. Her personality was described as "rippling sunshine." When her father encountered financial troubles and the family lost their estate, Dora moved in with her brother, who was a vicar, and she occupied herself with delightful walks, good conversations, and the writing of poetry and prose. She also taught a youth class, worked with the "sick and sorrowful" in her brother's parish, and ministered earnestly to physically and mentally challenged children. One friend said, "Her life was hid with Christ in God, but it was also wonderfully transparent to all who knew her. . . . She had a wonderful knack of making one happy in her presence."

I had hoped to find something in her biography about the writing of her famous hymn "I Am Not Skilled to Understand," but there was nothing. Another old volume, however, said this: "In 1873, (Dora) wrote the eight *Songs of Salvation*, which describe the practical application of faith to the lives of the simple and the partially educated; and they have been loved by many who knew not the author's name."[40]

Among those eight songs was one entitled "Redemption," which we know today as "I Am Not Skilled to Understand."

More Holiness Give Me

Philip P. Bliss

Philip P. Bliss

1. More ho - li - ness give me, More striv - ing with - in;
2. More grat - i - tude give me, More trust in the Lord;
3. More pu - ri - ty give me, More strength to o'er-come;

More pa - tience in suf - fering, More sor - row for sin;
More pride in His glo - ry, More hope in His Word;
More free-dom from earth - stains, More long-ings for home;

More faith in my Sav - ior, More sense of His care;
More tears for His sor - rows, More pain at His grief;
More fit for the king - dom, More used would I be;

More joy in His ser - vice, More pur - pose in prayer.
More meek-ness in tri - al, More praise for re - lief.
More bless - ed and ho - ly, More, Sav - ior, like Thee.

More Holiness Give Me

1873

P hilip and Lucy Bliss died in a train wreck on December 29, 1876, while en route to sing at D. L. Moody's New Year's Eve service in Chicago. Their memorial service was held on Sunday morning, January 7, 1877, at the Presbyterian Church in Rome, Pennsylvania. Sleighs came from all directions, and the church was packed.

Rev. E. P. Goodwin spoke eloquently of Philip's life and work, saying, "I think I might safely call him the most joyous Christian I have ever known. It was a rare thing to see a shadow even transiently clouding his face. . . . His hymns and music are full of hope and exultation. There is hardly a melancholy verse or strain among them all. Almost invariably both songs and music swell and grow jubilant as they move on. Hallelujahs ring all thorough them."

Goodwin continued: "His buoyancy was contagious. I have known him, when a prayer meeting dragged, when very likely the minister was dispirited and others shared the feeling, to sweep his hand over the keys of the piano, and alike by touch and voice scatter the despondency. . . . On one of the last occasions when he was with us . . . he came in late and sat in the rear of the room. Espying him, I called him forward to sing the hymn entitled, 'My Prayer' ('More Holiness Give Me'). He struck the piano keys, stopped, and reading the words in the latter part of the first stanza, 'More joy in His service,' said, 'I don't think I can sing that as a prayer any more. It seems to me I have as much joy in serving the blessed Master as it is possible for me to bear.'"

Continuing, Goodwin said, "This is what the Master wants us all to be, what the world greatly needs to see—buoyant, cheerful singing believers. . . . Many grumble far more than they give thanks. They forget the daily manna, the sufficient grace, the fellowship of the Spirit, the better country. . . . This ought not so to be. Dear brethren, let this life so overflowing with gladness help us to better things."[41]

It seems Bliss lived up to his name!

Wonderful Words of Life

Philip P. Bliss

Philip P. Bliss
WORDS OF LIFE

1. Sing them o-ver a-gain to me, Won-der-ful words of Life;
2. Christ, the bless-ed One, gives to all Won-der-ful words of Life;
3. Sweet-ly ech-o the gos-pel call, Won-der-ful words of Life;

Let me more of their beau-ty see, Won-der-ful words of Life.
Sin-ner list to the lov-ing call, Won-der-ful words of Life.
Of-fer par-don and peace to all, Won-der-ful words of Life.

Words of life and beau-ty, Teach me faith and du-ty:
All so free-ly giv-en, Woo-ing us to heav-en:
Je-sus on-ly Sav-ior, Sanc-ti-fy for-ev-er:

Beau-ti-ful words, won-der-ful words, Won-der-ful words of Life.

Beau-ti-ful words, won-der-ful words, Won-der-ful words of Life.

Wonderful Words of Life

1874

P hilip Bliss was born in Pennsylvania on July 9, 1838, and fell in love with music in childhood when he heard a neighbor's piano. As a teen he nurtured his musical interests in the sawmills and lumber camps where he worked. At age twenty-two, Bliss, newly married, became an itinerant music teacher, traveling from town to town on horseback teaching music and writing songs. Four years later, Bliss moved his family to Chicago where he hoped to break into music publishing.

One night he and his wife, Lucy, attended a rally in which D. L. Moody spoke, and a friendship quickly formed. Moody urged Bliss to "give up his business, drop everything, and sing the Gospel." Philip and Lucy were hesitant. "I am willing that Mr. Bliss should do anything that we can be sure is the Lord's will," said Lucy, "and I can trust the Lord to provide for us, but I don't want him to take such a step simply on Mr. Moody's will."

Finally Moody, never one to mince words, wrote bluntly: "You have not faith. If you haven't faith of your own on this matter, start out on my faith. Launch out into the deep."

Horatio Spafford, whose four daughters perished in the sinking of the *Ville de Havre*, urged Philip to consider Moody's appeal. (Bliss would later write the music to Spafford's hymn "It Is Well.") Still Philip wavered.

Shortly afterward, Bliss led the singing at an evangelistic effort in Waukegan, Illinois, where Major Daniel Whittle was preaching. Bliss sang his hymn "Almost Persuaded," and every word seemed filled with power. The next afternoon, Bliss and Whittle gathered with the pastor at the church and spent several hours in prayer. There Bliss made a formal surrender of everything to the Lord. He gave up his business and his writing of secular music. As Whittle later recalled, ". . . gave up everything, and in a simple childlike trusting prayer placed himself with any talent, any power God had given him, at the disposal of the Lord for any use He could make of him in the spreading of His Gospel."

Philip Bliss spent the rest of his short life doing exactly what his song proclaims: "Sing them over again to me, wonderful words of life. . . ."

Breathe on Me, Breath of God

Edwin Hatch

Robert Jackson
TRENTHAM

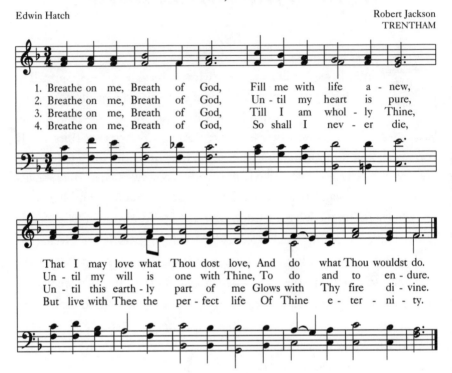

1. Breathe on me, Breath of God, Fill me with life a - new,
2. Breathe on me, Breath of God, Un - til my heart is pure,
3. Breathe on me, Breath of God, Till I am whol - ly Thine,
4. Breathe on me, Breath of God, So shall I nev - er die,

That I may love what Thou dost love, And do what Thou wouldst do.
Un - til my will is one with Thine, To do and to en - dure.
Un - til this earth - ly part of me Glows with Thy fire di - vine.
But live with Thee the per - fect life Of Thine e - ter - ni - ty.

Breathe on Me, Breath of God

1878

Solomon warned, "Much study is wearisome of the flesh" (Ecclesiastes 12:12 KJV), but that's a verse Edwin Hatch ignored. He's famous for his vigorous—almost severe—study habits. One obituary spoke of his "encyclopedic knowledge" and "unbounded mental activity." Many Oxford researchers and professors gave up various literary pursuits after it was learned Hatch himself was already pursuing the same topic for publication.

Hatch's love of knowledge started early. He was born in England in 1835, attended King Edwards School in Birmingham, and later studied at both Oxford and Cambridge. In his early twenties, he was ordained as an Anglican priest and took a professorship in Toronto and later in Quebec City. Returning to Oxford in 1867, he devoted the rest of his life to his studies, lectures, and scholarly works. His classes on church history were packed with stimulated students. It was a jolt to the university when Hatch died unexpectedly on November 10, 1889, at age fifty-four.

His books, many of them published posthumously, include volumes of poems and sermons as well as academic tomes such as *The Organization of the Early Christian Churches*, *The Growth of Christian Institutions*, *Influence of Greek Ideas and Usages upon the Christian Church*, *Essays in Biblical Greek*, and *A Concordance to the Septuagint*.

This hymn, originally titled "Spiritus Dei" ("Spirit of God") first appeared in a privately published, seventeen-page pamphlet in 1878. It was published as a hymn in 1886. In 1937, the popular Southern Baptist hymn-writer B. B. McKinney rewrote the stanzas, giving it new life under the title "Holy Spirit, Breathe on Me."

The hymn is based on the passage in John 20:21, when Jesus said to His disciples, "Peace to you! As the Father has sent Me, I also send you." The next verse adds, "And when He had said this, He breathed on them, and said to them, 'Receive the Holy Spirit'" (NKJV).

Redeemed, How I Love to Proclaim It

Fanny Jane Crosby

William James Kirkpatrick
REDEEMED

1. Re-deemed, how I love to pro-claim it! Re-deemed by the
2. Re-deemed, and so hap-py in Je - sus, No lan-guage my
3. I think of my bless-ed Re-deem - er, I think of Him
4. I know I shall see in His beau - ty The King in whose

blood of the Lamb; Re-deemed through His in - fi-nite mer - cy,
rap-ture can tell; I know that the light of His pres - ence
all the day long; I sing, for I can-not be - si - lent;
law I de - light; Who lov - ing - ly guard-ed my foot - steps

His child, and for - ev - er I am.
With me doth con - tin - ual - ly dwell. Re-deemed, re -
His love is the theme of my song. re-deemed,
and giv - eth me songs in the night.

deemed, re-deemed by the blood of the Lamb; re-deemed,
re-deemed, re-deemed,

re - deemed, His child, and for - ev - er I am.
re-deemed,

Redeemed, How I Love
to Proclaim It
1882

O ne June day long ago, the famous blind hymnist Fanny Crosby met with some children under an old apple tree. She thrilled them by reciting a few of her poems and telling them stories. Then she pulled out her "Wordless Book" and told them the significance of the colors—black, red, white, and gold. When she got to the "red" page, she said, "Red is for blood, and I want you ever to remember that you are redeemed by the precious blood of Christ. 'Unto Him who hath loved us and hath washed us from our sins in His own blood, unto Him be honor and praise forever.'"[42]

That was Aunt Fanny's unending message. Many of her eight thousand or so Gospel songs mentioned her favorite words: redeemed, blood, love, proclaim, lamb, mercy, forever. She was seldom at a loss for words, but she worked best when she had a good tune to go with them. One of her favorite composers was William James Kirkpatrick, a young Philadelphia music editor and publisher with whom she maintained a lively correspondence as long as she lived.

"I have visited Mr. Kirkpatrick at his home in Philadelphia several times," she once wrote, "and I look back upon these occasions with peculiar pleasure. To some of the melodies that he has sent I have written words that have been largely used for many years in gospel services everywhere. A few of the titles that come to mind now are 'He Hideth My Soul,' 'He Came to Save Me,' 'Redeemed . . .' and my readers will instantly recall many others."[43]

There's a forgotten verse to "Redeemed, How I Love to Proclaim It." When originally published as #7 in *Songs of Redeeming Love*, the hymn had five verses. In the years since, most hymnals have omitted the final stanza since it sounds a good deal like the previous one and few congregations will sing five verses to the same hymn.

God, Our Father, We Adore Thee

George W. Frazer
Alfred S. Loizeaux, st. 3

John Zundel
BEECHER

1. God, our Fa - ther, we a - dore Thee! We, Thy chil - dren, bless Thy name!
2. Son E - ter - nal, we a - dore Thee! Lamb up - on the throne on high!
3. Ho - ly Spir - it, we a - dore Thee! Par - a - clete and heaven - ly guest!
4. Fa - ther, Son, and Ho - ly Spir - it — Three in One! we give Thee praise!

Cho - sen in the Christ be - fore Thee, We are "ho - ly, with - out blame."
Lamb of God, we bow be - fore Thee, Thou has brought Thy pe - ple nigh!
Sent from God and from the Sav - ior, Thou hast led us in - to rest.
For the rich - es we in - her - it, Heart and voice to Thee we raise!

We a - dore Thee! we a - dore Thee! Ab - ba's prais - es we pro - claim!
We a - dore Thee! we a - dore Thee! Son of God, who came to die!
We a - dore Thee! we a - dore Thee! By Thy grace for - ev - er blest;
We a - dore Thee! we a - dore Thee! Thee we bless through end - less days!

We a - dore Thee! we a - dore Thee! Ab - ba's prais - es we pro - claim!
We a - dore Thee! we a - dore Thee! Son of God, who came to die!
We a - dore Thee! we a - dore Thee! By Thy grace for - ev - er blest;
We a - dore Thee! we a - dore Thee! Thee we bless through end - less days!

God, Our Father, We Adore Thee

1884

George Frazer, the twenty-year-old son of an Irish police inspector, was working in a Dublin bank when his older brother invited him to an evangelistic rally. The evangelist, Dr. H. Grattan Guiness, was drawing huge crowds in Dublin's Rotunda. George went with his brother but they were unable to get in because of the crowds. Climbing a guttering pipe George viewed the service through an upper window. Dr. Guiness's sermon pierced his heart, and George struggled for two weeks before yielding his life to Christ. He continued working at the bank, but George was a new man. He reveled in sharing his faith with others. Soon he was engaged in personal and public evangelistic work. At length, he entered full-time ministry, moving to England and settling in the town of Cheltenham. There he published three volumes on hymns, "Midnight Praises," "Day-Dawn Praises," and "The Day Spring."

His widely loved hymn on the Trinity, "God, Our Father, We Adore Thee," first appeared in "Midnight Praises" in 1884 and was published in the United States in 1904. (In 1952, Alfred Loizeaux replaced Frazer's original third verse with a revised stanza about the Holy Spirit.)

George Frazer was fifty-six when he passed away. "I grieve to leave my work for the Master . . . and all whom I love," he said, "but it is infinitely more precious to me to be with Christ than all besides." His tombstone says:

> GEORGE WEST FRAZER
> Departed to be with Christ
> January 24, 1896, Aged 56
> "THOU REMAINEST" (Heb. 1.11)
> His spirit now has winged its way to those bright realms
>   of cloudless day;
> Then, mourner, cease to weep; for better is it thus to be
> From self, the world, and Satan free, by Jesus put to sleep.

The Birthday of a King

William Harold Neidlinger

William Harold Neidlinger
Arr. by Robert F. Douglas
NEIDLINGER

1. In the lit - tle vil - lage of Beth - le - hem, There lay a Child one
2. 'Twas a hum - ble birth-place, but O how much God gave to us that

day, And the sky was bright with a ho - ly light O'er the
day; From the man - ger bed what a path has led, What a

place where Je - sus lay. Al - le - lu - ia! O how the
per - fect, ho - ly way.

an - gels sang. Al - le - lu - ia! How it rang! And the sky was bright with a

ho - ly light, 'Twas the birth - day of a King.

The Birthday of a King

1890

 illiam Harold Neidlinger loved music, he loved children, and he excelled in introducing one to the other. He was born in Brooklyn on July 20, 1863, and as a young man he studied under some of the greatest composers of his day in New York and London. His own career as a composer and singing teacher took him to London, Paris, and New York. He taught in the music department of the Brooklyn Institute of Art and Sciences, and served as organist and choral conductor in various societies and choirs. He was organist at St. Michael's Church in New York City.

He wrote comic operas, cantatas, church music, and secular songs. But he found his best audience in children. Some critics complained that he had reduced himself to writing "children's ditties." But his book *Small Songs for Small Singers* became a standard musical textbook in kindergartens across America for decades. As it turned out, the success of his book changed his life. Neidlinger became passionate about children's musical education and developed a deep burden for disabled youngsters, especially those with speech and vocal disabilities. He virtually abandoned his music career, studied child psychology, and established a school for "subnormal children" in East Orange, New Jersey. Failing health forced him to turn his work over to others as he devoted his remaining strength to finishing a book entitled *New Analysis of Human Speech*.

After a long illness he passed away at age sixty-two at his home in East Orange on a Friday night in 1924, at the beginning of the Christmas season. His obituary in the *New York Times* mentions his books, his school, his health, his operas, and his musical achievements. Strangely, it doesn't mention the one great achievement for which he is remembered to this day—his great Christmas carol about the birthday of a King.

> *Alleluia! O how the angels sang.*
> *Alleluia! How it rang!*
> *And the sky was bright with a holy light*
> *'Twas the birthday of a King.*

What a Wonderful Savior

Elisha A. Hoffman

Elisha A. Hoffman

1. Christ has for sin a - tone-ment made, What a won-der-ful Sav-ior!
2. I praise Him for the cleans-ing blood, What a won-der-ful Sav-ior!
3. He cleansed my heart from all its sin, What a won-der-ful Sav-ior!
4. He walks be - side me in the way, What a won-der-ful Sav-ior!

We are re-deemed! the price is paid! What a won - der-ful Sav - ior!
That rec - on - ciled my soul to God; What a won - der-ful Sav - ior!
And now He reigns and rules there-in; What a won - der-ful Sav - ior!
And keeps me faith - ful day by day, What a won - der-ful Sav - ior!

What a won - der - ful Sav - ior is Je - sus, my Je - sus!

What a won - der - ful Sav - ior is Je - sus, my Lord!

What a Wonderful Savior

1891

T he chorus of this hymn causes our spirits to smile with contentment: "What a wonderful Savior is Jesus, my Jesus! What a wonderful Savior is Jesus, my Lord!" Elisha Hoffman, one of the most popular heroes of the Gospel song era, wrote both words and music. I've enjoyed tracking down little newspaper accounts here and there of the old hymnists like Hoffman. In an old newspaper published in 1919, I found this notice in the section on church news under the headline: "Community Honors Hymn Writer."

"Cabery, Illinois, and the surrounding country honored with a community banquet May 7, the eightieth birthday of the Rev. Elisha A. Hoffman, pastor of Cabery Presbyterian Church and one of the oldest ministers in active service in the middle western states. Dr. Hoffman, who has given sixty years to preaching the gospel, looks little more than half his age. He was pastor of Cabery church from 1911 to 1916 and was again called in 1918 when seventy-nine years of age. His name has been well known for two generations as a writer of gospel hymns. . . . The community banquet as an appropriate manner of celebrating the pastor's four score years . . . and was executed by the ladies' aid society." [44]

Ten years later, on November 26, 1929, the *New York Times* ran this obituary datelined Chicago:

The Rev. Dr. Elisha A. Hoffman, world-renowned writer of hymns, died at his home here today after an illness of two weeks. He was ninety years old. Among his best-known hymns were 'What a Wonderful Savior,' 'Are You Washed in the Blood?' and 'I Must Tell Jesus.' These and hundreds of other hymns written by Dr. Hoffman have been translated into German, Spanish, Italian, Russian, Chinese, Japanese, Korean, and several African and Indian dialects. Dr. Hoffman was born in Orwigsburg, Pa., on May 7, 1839. For sixty years he served in the Presbyterian ministry until his retirement in 1922. [45]

Small records of a life devoted to the service of a wonderful Savior!

Boundless Salvation

William Booth

J. Ellis
MY JESUS I LOVE THEE

1. O bound - less sal - va - tion! deep o - cean of
2. My sins they are man - y, their stains are so
3. My tem - pers are fit - ful, my pas - sions are
4. Now tossed with temp - ta - tion, then haunt - ed with
5. O o - cean of mer - cy, oft long - ing I've
6. The tide is now flow - ing, I'm touch - ing the
7. And now, hal - le - lu - jah! the rest of my

love, O full - ness of mer - cy, Christ
deep, And bit - ter the tears of re -
strong, They bind my poor soul and they
fears, My life has been joy - less and
stood On the brink of thy won - der - ful,
wave, I hear the loud call of the
days Shall glad - ly be spent in pro -

brought from a - bove, The whole world re - deem - ing, so
morse that I weep; But use - less is weep - ing; thou
force me to wrong; Be - neath thy blest bil - lows de -
use - less for years; I feel some thing - bet - ter most
life - giv - ing flood! Once more I have reach - ed this
Might - y to save; My faith's grow - ing bold - er, de -
mot - ing His praise Who o - pened His bos - om to

Boundless Salvation

1893

General William Booth knew how to rev up his audiences. Just listen to these "fighting words" from one of his sermons—and he meant every syllable: "While little children go hungry, as they do now, I'll fight. While men go to prison, in and out, in and out, I'll fight. While there is a drunkard left, while there is a poor lost girl upon the streets, while there remains one dark soul without the light of God, I'll fight. I'll fight to the very end."

It was this indomitable passion that launched the Salvation Army. And Booth wasn't just content to meet the physical needs of a hurting world; he longed to bring people to Christ.

In 1893, Booth wrote this hymn as a prayer for those wishing to be saved. His colleague Theodore Kitching later said that he arrived at the general's house at 6 a.m. on a November morning in 1893 and found Booth finishing this song, having apparently worked on it through the night. It was for the Boundless Salvation Evangelistic Campaign at Exeter Hall in London. There it was sung on November 14, 1893. The words appeared later in the Salvation Army magazine, *The War Cry*. It became a theme song of the Salvation Army. Years later, "Boundless Salvation" was sung at Booth's final public appearance, on May 9, 1912, at an event at Royal Albert Hall celebrating his eighty-third birthday.

"Boundless" is a good word to describe William Booth. In Harold Begbie's 1920 biography of the general, he used that word fourteen times (though never referring to Booth's hymn). He spoke of the general's boundless faith, his boundless enthusiasm, his boundless charity, his boundless depths of pity and mercy, and his boundless compassion. "He helped create the Social Conscience," wrote Begbie, "not by a political formula or by any merely philanthropic invention, but by the force and energy of his boundless love."[46]

Of course, Booth was not boundless. We all have boundaries, limitations, and drawbacks. We are finite. But our God *is* boundless, and so is His salvation.

We've a Story to Tell to the Nations

H. Ernest Nichol

H. Ernest Nichol
MESSAGE

1. We've a sto - ry to tell to the na - tions That shall
2. We've a song to be sung to the na - tions That shall
3. We've a mes - sage to give to the na - tions That the
4. We've a Sav - ior to show to the na - tions Who the

turn their hearts to the right, A sto - ry of truth and mer - cy,
lift their hearts to the Lord, A song that shall con - quer e - vil
Lord who reign-eth a - bove Hath sent us His Son to save us,
path of sor - row hath trod, That all of the world's great peo - ples

A sto - ry of peace and light, A sto - ry of peace and light.
And shat-ter the spear and sword, And shat-ter the spear and sword.
And show us that God is love, And show us that God is love.
Might come to the truth of God, Might come to the truth of God.

For the dark-ness shall turn to dawn-ing, And the dawn-ing to noon-day bright,

And Christ's great king-dom shall come to earth, The king-dom of love and light.

We've a Story to Tell to the Nations

1896

Where have all the great missionary hymns gone? If Christ's last commandment is our greatest commission—if the gospel is global and the mission universal—shouldn't we be singing about it? The history of hymnody is filled with mission hymns, such as "Anywhere with Jesus," "Bring Them In," "Christ for the World We Sing," "From Greenland's Icy Mountains," and "So Send I You." Hymns like "O Zion Haste" encompass the entire mission effort, and Gospel songs like "Rescue the Perishing" and "Send the Light" provide personal motivation.

"We've a Story to Tell to the Nations" has been one of the most popular of this genre. It was written by an eclectic musician, poet, artist, and writer named Henry Ernest Nichol, who was born in 1862 in Hull, a port city north of London. He had planned to be a civil engineer, but Nichol's love of music led him to change careers when he was twenty-three and earn his degree at Oxford in music. He excelled in music, art, poetry, and writing. He taught music, wrote musical textbooks, composed popular poetry, wrote on diverse themes, and established a wide-ranging reputation in his day for literary dexterity and excellence.

Nichol found personal fulfillment writing Sunday school songs, and for a time he served as the music editor for the *London Sunday School Times*. He wrote about 130 hymn tunes and on occasion supplied the words. Whenever he wrote both the words and music, he would list the lyricist as Colin Sterne, which was an anagram or rearranging of the letters of his name. He listed his real name for the composer of the music.

Nichol passed away in 1926, and most of his secular and sacred works have been forgotten, but this one hymn lingers in missionary circles. It's a rousing anthem with an enthusiastic refrain that practically shoves us out the door and across the seas.

We Praise Thee, O God, Our Redeemer

Julia Cady Cory

Netherlands Folk song
Arr. by Edward Kremser
KREMSER

1. We praise Thee, O God, our Re - deem - er, Cre - a - tor;
2. We wor - ship Thee, God of our fa - thers, we bless Thee;
3. With voic - es u - nit - ed our prais - es we of - fer,

In grate - ful de - vo - tion our trib - ute we bring.
Through life's storm and tem - pest our guide Thou hast been.
And glad - ly our songs of true wor - ship we raise.

We lay it be - fore Thee; we kneel and a - dore Thee;
When per - ils o'er - take us, Thou wilt not for - sake us,
Thy strong arm will guide us; our God is be - side us.

We bless Thy ho - ly name, glad prais - es we sing.
And with Thy help, O Lord, life's bat - tles we win.
To Thee, our great Re - deem - er, for - ev - er be praise.

We Praise Thee, O God, Our Redeemer

1902

Hymn tunes have names all their own, which are usually listed in small capital letters. For example, the tune KREMSER is a Dutch melody from the seventeenth century, which was arranged by composer Eduard Kremser in 1877. In America, it is associated with Thanksgiving and serves as the melody of the traditional hymn "We Gather Together." That hymn, which begins "We gather together to ask the Lord's blessing," isn't an American hymn at all. It was written in Holland to celebrate the Dutch victory over Spain and first appeared in the sixteenth century. It was brought to America by early Dutch settlers and became a Thanksgiving prayer among the founders of New Amsterdam, which today is called New York.

In the early 1900s, J. Archer Gibson was organist at New York's Brick Presbyterian Church. He wanted to use the tune KREMSER for a Thanksgiving hymn, but with a different set of words—some that would be distinctively worshipful. He asked Julia Cady Cory, twenty, to try her hand at some new verses.

Julia was the daughter of a prominent New York architect named J. Cleveland Cady, the designer of the American Museum of National History. He also designed New York's Metropolitan Opera House. Mr. Cady was a devout Presbyterian, a leader in his local Sunday school, and a faithful member of the Presbyterian Church of the Covenant on East 42nd Street. He was a lay hymnist, and his example had prompted his daughter Julia to attempt some hymns. Hence Gibson's request.

Julia struggled to compose new words for KREMSER before coming up with the lyrics. It was sung for the first time at the Church of the Covenant on Thanksgiving in 1902.

Julia married businessman Robert C. Cory in 1911, and they established their home in Englewood, New Jersey, where they raised three sons and faithfully attended a nearby Presbyterian church. She enjoyed her role as mother, grandmother, poet, and hymnist. She passed away in 1963.

All I Need

Charles P. Jones

Charles P. Jones
ALL I NEED

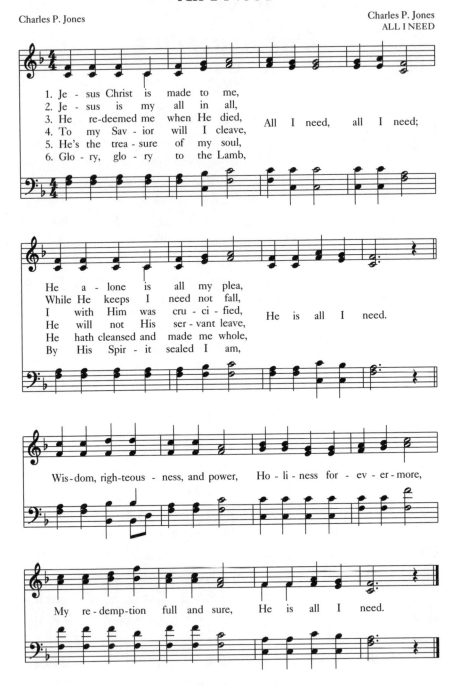

1. Je - sus Christ is made to me,
2. Je - sus is my all in all,
3. He re-deemed me when He died,
4. To my Sav - ior will I cleave,
5. He's the trea - sure of my soul,
6. Glo - ry, glo - ry to the Lamb,

All I need, all I need;

He a - lone is all my plea,
While He keeps I need not fall,
I with Him was cru - ci - fied,
He will not His ser - vant leave,
He hath cleansed and made me whole,
By His Spir - it sealed I am,

He is all I need.

Wis-dom, righ-teous - ness, and power, Ho - li - ness for - ev - er-more,

My re - demp-tion full and sure, He is all I need.

All I Need

1906

I first heard this simple song at Columbia Bible College (now Columbia International University) in South Carolina. I took to it at once, because its words summed up the victorious nature of the Christian life: Jesus Christ does not simply *give* me everything I need; He *is* everything I need—*wisdom, righteousness, and power, holiness for evermore, my redemption full and sure. He is all I need.*

The author was leader Charles Price Jones, who penned both the words and music in 1906. In an old volume on the history of African American trailblazers, I found this background:

> *"Dr. Jones was born December 9, 1865, in North Georgia and reared principally about Kingston. He was the son of Mary Jones-Latimer. She was a slave of William Jones of Floyd County, Georgia, and was a God-fearing woman who prayed fervently for the salvation of the soul of her son and Divine guidance through life. . . .*
>
> *"Later he went to night school. Shortly afterwards his mother died. This caused the lad to shift for himself, which he did with success. He went to Chattanooga, Tennessee, where he found employment, and later to Arkansas, and thence to Cat Island, Arkansas, where he picked cotton. In this he was above the average; he believed in excellency in whatever he attempted to do.*
>
> *"While young Jones was on Cat Island he was converted, in October 1884. . . . In the fall of the (next) year he went to preach the Gospel of Christ."*

During his career, Dr. Jones pastored some of the largest Baptist churches in the South. He was also involved in Christian publishing and oversaw a popular magazine. And he wrote popular hymns like "Jesus Only," "Deeper, Deeper," and "All I Need."

According to the book I found, Charles Jones moved to California in 1917 "to escape overwork."[47] But, of course, he kept right on working—and writing hymns, over one thousand of them, until his death in 1949.

Thy Word Have I Hid in My Heart

From Psalm 119
Adapt. by Ernest O. Sellers

Ernest O. Sellers

1. Thy Word is a lamp to my feet, A light to my path al -
2. For - ev - er, O Lord, is Thy Word Es - tab-lished and fixed on
3. At morn - ing, at noon, and at night I ev - er willl give Thee
4. Through Him whom Thy Word hath fore-told, The Sav - ior and Morn - ing

way, To guide and to save me from sin, And show me the
high; Thy faith - ful-ness un - to all men A - bid - eth for -
praise; For Thou art my por - tion, O Lord, And shall be through
Star, Sal - va - tion and peace have been brought To those who have

heaven - ly way.
ev - er nigh.
all my days!   Thy Word have I hid in my heart (in my heart), That
strayed a - far.

I might not sin a - gainst Thee (a - gainst Thee); That I might not sin, That

I might not sin, Thy Word have I hid in my heart.

Thy Word Have I Hid
in My Heart

1908

A Michigander named Ernest Orlando Sellers wrote this popular hymn and chorus. He was a civil engineer who became the superintendent of public works in Lansing, but his career was cut short when God saved him during a YMCA rally in Lansing and later called him into full-time ministry. In 1895, he enrolled at the Moody Bible Institute of Chicago and later had a rich and varied career in the Lord's work. He served as the song leader for evangelists like R. A. Torrey, Gipsy Smith, and J. Wilber Chapman.

During World War I, Sellers worked with the YMCA in Europe, traveling through France and England doing evangelistic work and sending his reports back to the *Christian Workers Magazine*. After the war, he directed the music department of the Bible Baptist Institute in New Orleans (New Orleans Baptist Theological Seminary) until his retirement in 1945. During his retirement, oil was found on the property of his home in Eola, Louisiana, providing abundantly for his remaining years.

One interesting footnote to Sellers' story is his influence on artist Warner Sallman. In January 1914, Sallman signed up for a Saturday night Bible study at Moody Bible Institute. E. O. Sellers, who was serving as dean, asked to see him. Sellers encouraged Sallman to paint a picture of Christ showing him as forceful and masculine rather than weak and effeminate as was often the case. Sellers suggested that Jesus had been physically strong during His earthly ministry, walking great distances, tanned under the sun. Later Sallman painted the head of Christ in oil in what became the most popular artistic rendering of Christ in the twentieth century. You've seen it in Sunday school magazines and hanging on the walls of churches everywhere.[48]

This hymn, "Thy Word Have I Hid in My Heart," is composed from various verses in Psalm 119. The refrain is taken directly from Psalm 119:11, and the stanzas are adapted from verses 41, 44, 62, 89, 90, 105, and 164.

Grace Greater than Our Sin

Julia H. Johnston

Daniel B. Towner
MOODY

1. Mar - vel-ous grace of our lov - ing Lord, Grace that ex - ceeds our
2. Sin and de - spair like the sea waves cold, Threat-en the soul with
3. Dark is the stain that we can - not hide, What can a - vail to
4. Mar - vel-ous, in - fi - nite, match - less grace, Free - ly be - stowed on

sin and our guilt, Yon - der on Cal - va - ry's mount out - poured,
in - fi - nite loss; Grace that is great - er, yes, grace un - told,
wash it a - way? Look! there is flow - ing a crim - son tide;
all who be - lieve; All who are long - ing to see His face,

There where the blood of the Lamb was spilt.
Points to the ref - uge, the might - y cross.
Whit - er than snow you may be to - day.
Will you this mo - ment His grace re - ceive?

Grace, grace,
Mar - vel-ous grace,

God's grace, Grace that will par - don and cleanse with - in; Grace,
in - fi-nite grace, Mar - vel-ous

grace, God's grace, Grace that is great-er than all our sin.
grace, in - fi-nite grace,

Grace Greater than Our Sin

1911

O n the bookshelves in my office is an old volume I picked up many years ago in an antiquarian bookstore—*Fifty Mission Heroes Every Boy and Girl Should Know*. It's as informative for adults as for youngsters, and I've gleaned a lot of personal inspiration (and sermon illustrations) from these fifty profiles of men and women like John Eliot, Bartholomew Ziegenbald, David Brainerd, William Carey, Alexander Duff, Adoniram Judson, David Livingstone, Agnes Agnew, and all the rest.

Only today did I realize the author of that book is also the author of this hymn—Julia Harriette Johnston. She wrote about the messengers, and sang about their message.

Julia was born in Salineville, Ohio, of good stock. Thirteen of her immediate relatives had been clergymen, and both her mother and grandmother were poets. When she was six, her family moved to Peoria, Illinois, where her father became pastor of the First Presbyterian Church. Julia lived in Peoria the rest of her life, and spent over four decades as superintendent of the younger children's Sunday school department and as a worker and teacher in the nursery.

For twenty years she served as president of the Presbyterian Missionary Society of Peoria, which had been founded by her mother. Julia also served as vice president for the Presbyterian Board of Missions for the Northwest. She wrote children's Sunday school lessons for a major publisher, authored several books for children, and churned out about five hundred hymns, many of them Sunday school songs for children. Only "Grace Greater than Our Sin" is widely sung today. But consider the chorus of Julia's hymn "Saving Grace." In it, Julia wrote that when her pilgrim song is over and she stands "on yonder shore" her theme will still be—grace!

I wish we knew the exact circumstances under which Julia Johnston wrote her hymns. But a glance of her biography tells us her passions—children, missions, music, and most of all grace—saving grace, marvelous grace of our loving Lord, grace that is greater than all our sin.

The Blood Will Never Lose Its Power

Andraé Crouch

Andraé Crouch
THE BLOOD

1. The blood that Je - sus shed for me,
2. It soothes my doubts and calms my fears,

'Way back on Cal - va - ry; The blood that gives me strength from
And it dries all my tears; The blood that gives me strength from

day to day, It will nev - er lose its power.
day to day, It will nev - er lose its power.

It reach-es to the high - est moun - tain. It flows to the

low - est val - ley. The blood that gives me strength from

day to day, It will nev - er lose its power.

The Blood Will Never Lose Its Power

1912

Perhaps you know the song "The Blood Will Never Lose Its Power" by Andraé Crouch. He's the Grammy Award–winning songwriter and Gospel singer who also gave us "Bless the Lord, O My Soul," "My Tribute," "Soon and Very Soon," and "Through It All." Andraé was a pioneer of the Jesus Movement of the 1960s and '70s, and God used him to help usher in the era of contemporary Christian music. Remarkably, Andraé wrote "The Blood Will Never Lose Its Power" when he was only fourteen years old.

Years before Andraé wrote "The Blood Will Never Lose Its Power," a husband and wife team, Walter and Civilla Martin, published this hymn with the same title, opening with similar words, and rejoicing in the identical theme. The Martins were quite a team. Walter was born in Massachusetts and attended Harvard before entering the ministry (first as a Baptist then as a member of the Disciples of Christ). Civilla hailed from Nova Scotia and was a schoolteacher before marrying Walter. Much of their ministry was spent traveling, singing, preaching, and soul-winning. But they were also hymnists. Civilla wrote the words and Walter the music for "The Blood Will Never Lose Its Power" and "God Will Take Care of You." Civilla also wrote the lyrics to the classic "His Eye Is on the Sparrow."

It's not surprising to have two similar hymns from different eras about the great reality behind our redemption. The Bible says we were not redeemed from our empty way of life with perishable things like silver or gold, "but with the precious blood of Christ, a lamb without blemish or defect" (1 Peter 1:19). There's a scarlet stream coursing through the Bible from Genesis to Revelation. Think of it as the circulatory system of the Bible. The beating heart of the love of God creates for us a fountain filled with blood drawn from Emmanuel's veins. We must never lose our message of the Blood, for the Blood will never lose its power.

He Giveth More Grace

Annie Johnson Flint

Hubert Mitchell
HE GIVETH MORE GRACE

1. He giv - eth more grace when the bur - dens grow great - er; He
2. Whe we have ex - haust - ed our store of en - dur - ance, When

send - eth more strength when the la - bors in - crease. To
our strength has failed ere the day is half done, When

add - ed af - flic - tion He add - eth His mer - cy; To
we reach the end of our hoard - ed re - sourc - es, Our

mul - ti - plied tri - als, His mul - ti - plied peace.
Fa - ther's full giv - ing is on - ly be - gun.

He Giveth More Grace

1922

A nnie Johnson Flint wrote this hymn sometime prior to 1922, because the earliest reference I've found to it is in a magazine of daily devotions for October of that year.[49] Miss Flint was a schoolteacher who became disabled by severe arthritis and began writing poems and hymns. Her most famous poem begins, "God hath not promised skies always blue . . ." Her best-known hymn is "He Giveth More Grace."

This hymn played a role in the survival of a missionary, Darlene Deibler Rose, who was caught in the horrors of the Japanese invasion of the Pacific during World War II. Forcibly separated from her husband, who subsequently perished, Darlene was interred in a horrific Japanese POW camp. In her account, *Evidence Not Seen*, she wrote:

> "I never shed a tear before [my inquisitors] during the hearings. But when the guard had returned me to my cell, and the sound of his footsteps had vanished—when I was certain that no one could hear me—I wept buckets of tears. In desperation I poured out my heart to the Lord. . . . When there were no more tears to cry, I would hear Him whisper, 'But my child, my grace is sufficient for thee. Not was or will be but is sufficient.' Oh, the eternal, ever-present, undiminished supply of God's glorious grace!
>
> "Just two weeks before I was brought to this prison, the Lord had laid it on my heart to memorize a poem by Annie Johnson Flint. Now I knew why. After drying the tears from my face and mopping the tears from the floor with my skirt, I would sit up and sing, 'He giveth more grace when the burdens grow greater. / He sendeth more strength when the labors increase. / To added affliction, He addeth His mercy, / To multiplied trials, His multiplied peace.'"[50]

None of us knows what we'll face from day to day, but our burdens will never outstrip God's all-sufficient grace. For out of His infinite riches in Jesus, He giveth and giveth and giveth again.

Now I Belong to Jesus

Norman J. Clayton

Norman J. Clayton
ELLSWORTH

1. Je - sus my Lord will love me for - ev - er, From Him no power of
2. Once I was lost in sin's deg - ra - da - tion, Je - sus came down to
3. Joy floods my soul for Je - sus has saved me, Freed me from sin that

e - vil can sev - er, He gave His life to ran - som my soul,
bring me sal - va - tion, Lift - ed me up from sor - row and shame,
long had en-slaved me, His pre-cious blood He gave to re - deem,

Now I be-long to Him;
Now I be-long to Him; Now I be-long to Je - sus, Je-sus be-longs to
Now I be-long to Him;

me, Not for the years of time a-lone, But for e-ter-ni-ty.

Now I Belong to Jesus

1938

A huge photograph appeared in the *New York Times* on October 1, 1944, showing Madison Square Garden the previous evening packed with twenty thousand young people, including soldiers and sailors just back from World War II. It was a Youth for Christ Victory Rally. The meeting was scheduled to begin at 6 p.m., but by midafternoon the lobby was already packed with hymn-singing crowds. Following an exuberant song service that night, Jack Wyrtzen, director of Word of Life, gave an evangelistic message. When he asked those who wanted to receive Christ to stand, hundreds of people rose to their feet, including many men and women in uniform. Right in the middle of it all, working alongside Jack Wyrtzen, was Norman J. Clayton, author of "Now I Belong to Jesus."

Clayton was a Brooklyn boy, born January 1903, the ninth of ten children. His mother, a devout member of the Church of England, had helped establish South Brooklyn Gospel Church, and there she attended regularly with her children. Norman was saved at the church at the age of six, and by age twelve he was playing the pump organ (and later the trumpet) for his church—a role he occupied for fifty years.

Though initially a builder by profession, Norman's real passion was Scripture memory, evangelism, and the ministry of music. In 1942, he joined the staff of Jack Wyrtzen's ministries and helped coordinate the New York City rallies for Word of Life, such as the one profiled in the *New York Times*. For fifteen years, he played the organ and vibraharp at these meetings and directed the work of the inquiry room and the follow-up teams. He also worked with Word of Life's radio broadcasts, as well as the "Sunday Morning Radio Bible Class" of the Bellerose Baptist Church.

Throughout the 1940s and '50s, Clayton published some thirty Gospel songbooks, and he became a writer and editor for the Rodeheaver Company. He remained active in the Lord's work until his death in 1992. He's also the author of the hymn "My Hope Is in the Lord."

"Now I Belong to Jesus" is one of those hymns that provides endless comfort for today . . . "not for the years of time alone, but for eternity."

Victory in Jesus

Eugene M. Bartlett

Eugene M. Bartlett
HARTFORD

1. I heard an old, old sto - ry, how a Sav - ior came from glo - ry,
2. I heard a-bout His heal - ing, of His cleans-ing power re - veal-ing,
3. I heard a-bout a man-sion He has built for me in glo - ry,

How He gave His life on Cal - va - ry to save a wretch like me;
How He made the lame to walk a - gain and caused the blind to see;
And I heard a - bout the streets of gold be - yond the crys - tal sea;

I heard a-bout His groan-ing, of His pre-cious blood's a - ton-ing,
And then I cried, "Dear Je - sus, come and heal my bro - ken spir - it,"
A - bout the an - gels sing - ing, and the old re - demp - tion sto - ry,

Then I re - pent-ed of my sins and won the vic - to - ry.
And some - how Je - sus came and brought to me the vic - to - ry.
And some sweet day I'll sing up there the song of vic - to - ry.

O vic-to-ry in Je-sus, my Sav-ior, for-ev-er,

He sought me and bought me with His re-deem-ing blood;

He love me ere I knew Him, and all my love is due Him,

He plunged me to vic-to-ry be-neath the cleans-ing flood.

Victory in Jesus

1939

E ugene Bartlett was in the strength of mid-life when he suffered a serious stroke. He was born on Christmas Eve 1885 in Waynesville, Missouri, and had grown up in Arkansas. He gave his life to Christ early in life, and in childhood demonstrated a strong voice and a love for music. After attending schools in Tennessee and Missouri, Bartlett took to the road, teaching Singing Schools and writing songs. His words and tunes ("Everybody Will Be Happy over There" and "Just a Little While") were fodder in the Singing Conventions of the early 1900s. His "Take an Old Tater and Wait" became a country music hit for Grand Old Opry star Little Jimmy Dickens.

Bartlett was also a businessman. He established his career working for the Central Music Company, an Arkansas concern that published shaped-note songbooks. In 1918 he helped establish the Hartford Music Company in the coal-mining town of Hartford, Arkansas. This company became a driving force in the development of Southern Gospel Music.

Bartlett also established the Hartford Music Institute, which trained hundreds of teachers and musicians each year. One day in 1926 a penniless young man showed up at the Hartford Music Institute, and finding Bartlett in his office, said, "Mr. Bartlett, I hear that you'll teach a fella how to sing and how to write music. I've come to learn and I understand I don't have to have any money." Bartlett asked the young man if he had money for room and board. He didn't. "Well, in that case," said Bartlett, "you better go over to my house and board." The young man, Albert E. Brumley, later became the dean of Southern Gospel Publishing and the author of "I'll Fly Away."

E. M. Bartlett suffered his stoke in 1939, and it left him partially paralyzed. His days of traveling and performing were over, and he was to live only two more years. But during his illness he devoted his time to studying the Bible and counting his blessings. The last of his eight hundred hymns and songs was the most difficult to write due to his impaired condition. It came painfully, phrase by phrase and note by note. It was the culmination of his life's work—"Victory in Jesus."

In Times Like These

Ruth Caye Jones

Ruth Caye Jones
TIMES LIKE THESE

1. In times like these you need a Sav - ior, In times like
2. In times like these you need the Bi - ble, In times like
3. In times like these I have a Sav - ior, In times like

these you need an an - chor; Be ver - y sure, be ver - y
these O be not i - dle; Be ver - y sure, be ver - y
these I have an an - chor; I'm ver - y sure, I'm ver - y

sure Your an - chor holds and grips the Sol-id Rock!
sure Your an - chor holds and grips the Sol-id Rock!
sure My an - chor holds and grips the Sol-id Rock!

This Rock is Je - sus, Yes, He's the One; This Rock is

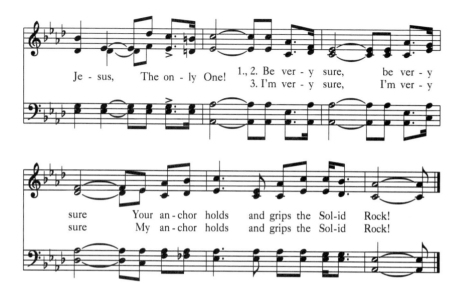

Je - sus, The on - ly One!
1., 2. Be ver - y sure, be ver - y
3. I'm ver - y sure, I'm ver - y

sure Your an - chor holds and grips the Sol-id Rock!
sure My an - chor holds and grips the Sol-id Rock!

In Times Like These

1943

In Times Like These" has encouraged my heart since childhood and I've never grown tired of hearing it or singing it. Ruth Caye Jones, who was born in Wilmerding, Pennsylvania, in 1902, crafted both words and music. Early in life she taught herself to play the piano and organ, then married a pastor and raised five children. In 1948, she established an unusual radio ministry, a program that was broadcast each week from the Jones's home in Erie, Pennsylvania. By then she was well-known as the author of "In Times Like These."

William J. Reynolds in his *Companion to Baptist Hymnal*, quoted from a letter from Ruth's son, Bert L. Jones, regarding the writing of the words and music to this hymn:

> *"Mother wrote this song during the dark days of World War II, with the words of 2 Timothy 3:1 in mind: 'This know also, that in the last days perilous times shall come' (kjv). The song was written in our family home in the Dormont area of Pittsburgh, Pennsylvania.*
>
> *"Inspiration for the words and music came very spontaneously as she was in the middle of her housework—actually while she was ironing. She took a pad of paper from her apron pocket, jotted down the words and melody and harmony. When I came home from high school that day, Mother said, 'Bert, you must try a new song that the Lord gave me today.' As I played the song for the first time, and our family group sang it several times, we never dreamed how far the song would go to bless so many people.*
>
> *"It has been frequently used in the Billy Graham Crusades. A very special high point for Mother came on the closing day of the Crusade at Columbus, Ohio, when George Beverly Shea asked her to sit on the platform, and he introduced her to the crowd before singing the song."*[51]

Ruth Caye Jones passed away in Erie on August 18, 1972, but her works have followed her. Now more than ever we need to be very sure our anchor holds and grips the Solid Rock.

It Took a Miracle

John W. Peterson

John W. Peterson

1. My Fa - ther is om - nip - o - tent, And that you can't de - ny;
2. Though here His glo - ry has been shown, We still can't ful - ly see
3. The Bi - ble tells us of His power And wis - dom all way through;

A God of might and mir - a - cles — 'Tis writ - ten in the sky.
The won-ders of His might, His throne, 'Twill take e - ter - ni - ty.
And ev - ery lit - tle bird and flower Are tes - ti - mo-nies, too.

It took a mir - a - cle to put the stars in place, It took a

mir - a - cle to hang the world in space; But when He saved my soul,

Cleansed and made me whole, It took a mir - a-cle of love and grace!

It Took a Miracle

1948

John W. Peterson was a remarkable man whose autobiography, *The Miracle Goes On*, is a delight to read. He wrote of how his grandparents emigrated from Sweden, settled in Kansas, and always maintained a strong Christian testimony. "Three times a day . . ." wrote Peterson, "grandfather would go to his desk, pull out his Bible and hymnbook, sing a song and read from the Scriptures, and finally pray—always aloud; always in Swedish."

One by one, John's brothers, having gone through some wild years, were converted; and through their influence John gave his life to Christ at the end of a service at Salina Bible Hall. Soon John and his brothers were singing at churches and on local radio stations. By the time he graduated from high school, John was writing Gospel music.

When World War II erupted, John found himself in the U.S. Air Corps. He earned his wings and flew endless supply routes in B-47s through all kinds of weather over the Hump—the Himalayas. Though the missions were dangerous and John had close calls, he never forgot the dazzling beauty he saw from the cockpit.

After the war, Peterson enrolled in Moody Bible Institute. One day sitting in class, he began thinking about the grace of God and the work of Calvary. Soon he had lost contact with the lecture and was thinking of the remarkable changes in his brothers and in his own life. The words of a song emerged, and John composed the chorus in his mind. Hurrying to the music building, he found a vacant studio and wrote "It Took a Miracle." Shortly after, John sold his song, along with eleven others, for thirty-six dollars. Soon it was the most popular new hymn in the nation.

At the time John didn't earn a single penny in royalties, having sold away the rights. His friends told him he'd been swindled, but he rejoiced that God was using his song. Eventually the copyright did come back to him, which was as it should be. "It Took a Miracle" was John W. Peterson's signature song, for it was his testimony: "When He saved my soul, cleansed and made me whole, it took a miracle of love and grace."[52]

Burdens Are Lifted at Calvary

John M. Moore

John M. Moore

1. Days are filled with sor-row and care, Hearts are lone - ly and drear;
2. Cast your care on Je - sus to - day, Leave your wor - ry and fear;
3. Trou - bled soul, the Sav-ior can see Ev - ery heart-ache and tear;

Bur-dens are lift - ed at Cal - va - ry, Je - sus is ver - y near.
Bur-dens are lift - ed at Cal - va - ry, Je - sus is ver - y near.
Bur-dens are lift - ed at Cal - va - ry, Je - sus is ver - y near.

Bur-dens are lift - ed at Cal - va - ry, Cal - va - ry, Cal - va - ry;

Bur-dens are lift - ed at Cal - va - ry, Je - sus is ver - y near.

Burdens Are Lifted at Calvary

1952

J ohn M. Moore was a Scottish lad, born in the tongue-twisting town of Kirkintilloch, Dunbartonshire, in 1925. He grew up under the tutelage of a godly mother and came to Christ at age sixteen. Soon he was volunteering for Sunday school work, open air meetings, tract distribution, and whatever he could do for the Lord. As a young man, he attended the Evangelical Baptist Bible College in Glasgow, then took a position as assistant superintendent of the Seaman's chapel in Glasgow, Scotland.

That's where he found the inspiration for this song. One day in 1952 he was asked to visit a young merchant seaman in critical shape at Glasgow Hospital. Walking into the man's room, Moore was well received, and after chatting a few moments reached his hand into his case to draw out a gospel tract. It was a brochure based on John Bunyan's classic *Pilgrim's Progress*. The tract described how Pilgrim had trudged his way up Mount Calvary with a heavy burden on his back. When he knelt sincerely at the cross, the burden suddenly fell from his shoulders, rolled down the hill, and disappeared into the empty tomb.

Moore told the sick man, "Pilgrim's experience had been my experience too." The sailor, listening carefully, grew anxious and started weeping. He was deeply burdened for his sins. "We prayed together," said Moore, "and never shall I forget the smile of peace and assurance that lit up his face as he said that his burden was lifted!"

Later that evening while by the fireside with pen and paper, John M. Moore scribbled down both the words and music to "Burdens Are Lifted at Calvary."

Moore went on to serve in other churches and evangelistic centers in Scotland before accepting a call to pastor Willowdale Baptist Church in Willowdale, Ontario, Canada. During his career, he wrote over 150 hymns and choruses. But his most enduring song has been the simplest: "Burdens Are Lifted at Calvary."[53]

Over the Sunset Mountains

John W. Peterson

John W. Peterson

1. O - ver the sun - set moun - tains Some-day I'll soft - ly
2. Toil-ing will all be end - ed, Shad-ows will flee a -

go, In - to the arms of Je - sus — He who has
way; Sor-row will be for - got - ten — O what a

loved me so. O - ver the sun - set moun -
won - der - ful day!

tains, Heav-en a - waits for me; O - ver the sun - set

moun - tains, Je - sus my Sav - ior I'll see.

Over the Sunset Mountains

1953

W hile a student at Moody Bible Institute, songwriter John W. Peterson worked for the school's radio station, WBMI, both behind the scenes and as a broadcaster. He also began publishing songbooks with Moody Press. Things were tight financially as Peterson tried to juggle his work with the demands of his growing family. He longed for a big commercial success for one of his songs.

In 1953, he introduced his song "Over the Sunset Mountains" to his WMBI audience and it provoked a strong and positive response. With Bill Pearce and Dick Anthony, he made a demonstration record and started sending it to various companies. An important secular publisher became interested and offered a tempting contract. He painted a grand picture of the commercial success and piles of royalty income. But there was a problem. The publisher wanted him to change the lyrics "to avoid possible offense." Could John water down the mention of Jesus in the song and simply elaborate on heaven?

John anguished over the decision, but he knew that as a Christian and as a songwriter he could not shun the name of the Lord Jesus. He walked away from the contract, his dreams of a major hit song shattered. But on the way home he knew he had made the right decision, and soon another song began to form in his mind. "When it was completed," he wrote later, "it became my public answer to the request that I water down the message of the Gospel. I called it simply 'My Song.'"

> *I have no song to sing*
> *But that of Christ my King;*
> *To Him my praise I'll bring forevermore.*
> *His love beyond degree,*
> *His death that ransomed me,*
> *Now and eternally, I'll sing it o'er.*[54]

The Savior Is Waiting

Ralph Carmichael

Ralph Carmichael
CARMICHAEL

1. The Sav - ior is wait - ing to en - ter your heart, Why don't you
2. If you'll take one step toward the Sav - ior, my friend, You'll find His

let Him come in? There's noth - ing in this world to keep you a - part,
arms o - pen wide; Re - ceive Him, and all of your dark - ness will end,

What is your an - swer to Him? Time af - ter time He has wait - ed be -
With - in your heart He'll a - bide.

fore, And now He is wait - ing a - gain To see if you're

will - ing to o - pen the door, Oh, how He wants to come in.

The Savior Is Waiting

1958

R alph Carmichael, who crafted the words and music of "The Savior Is Waiting," was born in Quincy, Illinois, in 1927. His mother was a gifted Bible teacher and his father a pastor. His dad also played the fiddle, but some in the church called fiddles the devil's instruments. Because of criticism, Rev. Carmichael retired his fiddle from church services. He gave it to four-year-old Ralph and arranged music lessons for him. Over time, Ralph also mastered the piano and trumpet, and excelled in voice lessons.

After committing his life to Christ at age seventeen, Ralph enrolled in a Bible college in Southern California. He struggled with Hebrew and Greek, but he reveled in music and in organizing choirs and orchestras. While still in school, Ralph produced a local weekly television show called *The Campus Christian Hour.*

For five years, Ralph served as minister of music at a Los Angeles Baptist church, and while there he wrote his classic invitation hymn "The Savior Is Waiting." He also began writing the music for many of the films being produced by the Billy Graham ministries.

Sitting here on my desk is a small paperback hymnal I purchased for fifty cents while a student at Columbia Bible College. The cover says: "He's Everything to Me Plus 53, Complied by Ralph Carmichael." It's a compilation of fifty-four of the songs we were singing day and night on campus. My favorite is Carmichael's little song about having a daily quiet time, and if pages had sound I'd be glad to sing it for you as you read its words:

There is a Quiet Place, far from the rapid pace,
Where God can sooth my troubled mind.
Sheltered by tree and flow'r, there in my quiet hour
With Him, my cares are left behind.
Whether a garden small or on a mountain tall
New strength and courage there I find;
Then from this quiet place I go prepared to face
A new day with love for all mankind.

He Touched Me

William J. Gaither

William J. Gaither
HE TOUCHED ME

1. Shack - led by a heav - y bur - den, 'Neath a load of guilt and shame; Then the hand of Je - sus touched me, And now I am no long-er the same.
2. Since I met this bless - ed Sav - ior, Since He cleansed and made me whole; I will nev-er cease to praise Him, I'll shout it while e - ter - ni - ty rolls.

He touched me oh, He touched me, And oh, the joy that floods my soul; Some-thing hap-pened, and now I know, He touched me and made me whole.

He Touched Me

1964

Bill Gaither longed to serve the Lord in full-time music ministry, but when he graduated from college the doors didn't open. Instead he found a job teaching English. In 1962 he married Gloria Sickal, a fellow teacher (Bill taught English, and Gloria taught both English and French). Their evenings and weekends were spent collaborating on songs. One of them would make a comment like "There ought to be a song that says . . . ," and they would write a song on that topic, crank it out on an old mimeograph machine, and hand the copies out at Wednesday night choir rehearsal.

During those days Dr. Dale Oldham was a beloved preacher in the area. His son, Doug Oldham, a gifted musician, helped his father in his meetings. When Doug's life fell apart, he started attending the same church the Gaithers attended. Doug had lost his family and fallen into a depression so deep he had contemplated killing himself. Realizing that he had brought all his troubles upon himself, he began reaching out to the Lord for help. Little by little, he traded his bad habits for holiness and healing. He was able to put his life—and his family—back together.

Eventually Doug began helping his father again, providing music when Dr. Dale preached. One Saturday night in 1963, as Bill, Doug, and Dale returned home from an evangelistic service they talked about how wonderfully the Lord can touch and heal a person's life. Dr. Dale looked over at Bill and said, "Bill there's something special about that word *touch*. You ought to write a song about how God touches lives."

By the next morning, Bill had scrawled out the lyrics to two verses and the chorus and had composed a simple melody. The following Tuesday before another of Dr. Dale's revival services, Bill handed Doug a copy of the handwritten song and said, "Let's see if we can sing this one tonight."

Doug became the first to record the song in 1964, and soon it was being recorded by the greatest names in the music industry (including Elvis Presley), and congregations around the world are still testifying through song: ". . . the hand of Jesus touched me, and now I am no longer the same."[55]

The Longer I Serve Him

William J. Gaither

William J. Gaither
THE SWEETER HE GROWS

1. Since I start-ed for the King-dom, Since my life He con-trols,
2. Ev - ery need He is sup - ply - ing, Plen-teous grace He be-stows;

Since I gave my heart to Je - sus, The long-er I serve Him, the
Ev - ery day my way gets bright-er, The long-er I serve Him, the

sweet-er He grows.
sweet-er He grows. The long-er I serve Him the sweet-er He grows, The

more that I love Him, more love He be-stows; Each day is like heav-en my

heart o-ver-flows, The long-er I serve Him the sweet-er He grows.

The Longer I Serve Him

1964

Bill Gaither was born in Alexandria, Indiana, in 1936, and formed his first musical group while a student at nearby Anderson College. After graduating in 1959, he got a job teaching English and, in 1962, married his sweetheart, Gloria Sickal. One day Bill took Gloria to meet his grandmother, a warm and well-liked woman affectionately known as "Mom" Hartwell.

Gloria later wrote, "I loved her from the start. She was Irish like my own grandmother. . . . When Bill first took me to Mom Hartwell's house, I felt as if I had come home to someone I'd lost at age fourteen, when my own dear grandmother had died." Gloria was amazed at the number of children, strangers, guests, even stray dogs and cats who showed up at Mom Hartwell's house.

When Bill and Gloria brought their first baby to show Mom Hartwell, she held the child in an old maple rocker and sang her the old hymns, like "Leaning on the Everlasting Arms." She also reveled in Bill's newest song, "He Touched Me."

One day, Mom suffered a stroke and her health quickly declined.

"As we sat by her bedside she would sing in her delirium the old songs about her precious Jesus," wrote Gloria. "One day toward the end, Mom was lucid and able to talk to us. We sat by her bed, Bill and I, with our baby girl, Suzanne. She was recalling moments both rewarding and difficult. After a while Bill said, 'Mom, you've lived a long time. We're just starting out with our baby and our lives. Tell me, has it been worth it, serving Jesus all these years?'

"She looked at him with that Irish twinkle in her still snappy brown eyes. 'Billy,' she said, 'the longer I serve Him, the sweeter He grows.'

"Not long after that, still forming the name of Jesus with her lips, she slipped out of our arms and into His. By then, the words she'd lift us had shaped themselves into a song. It was published with the title, 'The Longer I Serve Him,' but for Bill and me it will always be 'The Last Will and Testament of Mom Hartwell.'"[56]

Let's Just Praise the Lord

Gloria Gaither and William J. Gaither

William J. Gaither

Let's just praise the Lord! Praise the Lord! Let's just

lift our *hearts to heav-en and praise the Lord; Let's just

praise the Lord, Praise the Lord, Let's just

Fine

lift our *hearts to heav-en and praise the Lord.

Alternate words "voice," "hands."

1. Oh, we thank You for Your kind - ness, we thank You for Your love,
2. Just the pre - cious name of Je - sus is wor - thy of our praise.

We have been in heaven-ly plac - es, felt bless-ings from a - bove;
Let us bow our knees be - fore Him, our hands to heav-en raise:

We've been shar - ing all the good things, the fam - ily can af - ford.
When He comes in clouds of glo - ry, with Him to ev - er reign,

D.C.

Let's just turn our praise toward heav - en and praise the Lord.
Let's just lift our hap - py voic - es, and praise His name.

Let's Just Praise the Lord

1972

*I*n a concert on the East Coast some years ago, Bill and Gloria Gaither sang their popular hymns: "Because He Lives," "There's Something about that Name," and "The King Is Coming." They were overwhelmed at the end of the concert when the large crowd leapt to its feet and kept applauding. As the ovation continued, Bill and Gloria grew uncomfortable. The Bible says, "Not to us, O LORD, not to us but to your name be the glory" (Psalm 115:1). Bill sat down at the piano and began singing "Oh, How I Love Jesus." And soon the audience stopped applauding and joined in the song. Gloria relaxed, because she felt the praise was going where it should—to the Lord Jesus.

Later that evening Bill and Gloria talked about that incident. "We need a song," said Bill, "that would thank people for being so kind and loving to us but would help us all turn the praise heavenward."

"Why don't we just say exactly that," Gloria said.

Bill turned to an electric keyboard and Gloria grabbed a yellow tablet and "Let's Just Praise the Lord" emerged.

It's a secret of Christian graciousness to turn compliments heavenward. The Bible doesn't forbid our showing appreciation and honor to others. It tells us to render honor to whom honor is due. Yet how easy we worship honor and begin to think more highly of ourselves than we ought. I learned a great lesson from a preacher who was known for his powerful sermons. When people would compliment him afterward, he would simply say, "Thank you. I hope it was helpful." He knew that he was powerless within himself to do anything of significance for the Lord. But the sufficiency was in the Word and in the Spirit.

In times of adulation or tribulation, on good days and bad ones, when the crowds applaud or the way seems lonely . . . let's just praise the Lord.[57]

Shout to the Lord

Darlene Zschech

Darlene Zschech
Arr. by Eric Wyse
SHOUT TO THE LORD

My Je - sus, my Sav - ior, Lord, there is none like You.

All of my days I want to praise the won-ders of Your

might - y love. My com - fort, my shel - ter,

tow-er of ref - uge and strength. Let ev-ery breath, all that I am,

nev-er cease to wor - ship You. Shout to the Lord, all the earth,

Shout to the Lord

1993

*T*he Bible contains promises for every problem and a word of assurance for every need. When faced with anger or anxiety, we can always find a word from God to nudge us onward and upward—if only we'll open His Book. That's what Darlene Zschech did one dark day in 1993.

Darlene was born in 1965, in Brisbane, Australia, and she grew up singing. When she was about fifteen, her father, who had recently given his life to Christ, enrolled her in a Christian scouting program; and through that program she received Jesus Christ as her Savior.

Years later, one day in 1993, Darlene faced a daunting and discouraging personal problem. In her heaviness, she entered the study of her home and sat at the old and out-of-tune piano her parents had given her when she was five. Opening her Bible, she started reading Psalm 96.

As Darlene meditated on that psalm, her fingers pressed the keys of the piano, and the music and words began to flow. In about twenty minutes the song was done. For several days she sang it to herself as the truths of the song ministered to her own heart. She had not previously called herself a songwriter, so Darlene was reluctant to share it with anyone. But mustering her courage, she finally asked the music pastor at her church to listen to it. She was so nervous she kept stopping and apologizing. She even asked him to stand over by the wall and turn away from her while she sang it.

He assured her the song was wonderful, and shortly afterward they sang "Shout to the Lord" during the offering at church. The congregation took to it quickly, standing and joining in the song, though the words hadn't been prepared for bulletin or screen. Darlene's pastor, Brian Houston, predicted it would be sung around the world.

And so it has.

How Deep the Father's Love for Us

Stuart Townend

Stuart Townend
Arr. by Eric Wyse
FATHER'S LOVE

1. How deep the Fa - ther's love for us, How vast be - yond all mea - sure, That He should give His on - ly Son To make a wretch His trea - sure. How great the pain of sear - ing
2. Be - hold the Man up - on a cross, My sin up - on His shoul - ders; A - shamed, I hear my mock-ing voice Call out a - mong the scoff - ers. It was my sin that held Him
3. I will not boast in an - y - thing, No gifts, no power, no wis - dom; But I will boast in Je - sus Christ, His death and res - ur - rec - tion. Why should I gain from His re -

loss; The Fa - ther turns His face a -
there Un - til it was ac - com -
ward? I can - not give an an -

way, As wounds which mar the Cho - sen
plished; His dy - ing breath has brought me
swer, But this I know with all my

One Bring man - y sons to glo - ry.
life: I know that it is fin - ished.
heart: His wounds have paid my ran - som.

How Deep the Father's Love for Us

1995

Some people hearing "How Deep the Father's Love for Us" think they're listening to an old hymn, one that seems surprisingly fresh. That's because it's a Stuart Townend hymn. Stuart, who grew up in the home of an English vicar, offers this story behind writing it.

I'd already written quite a few songs for worship, but all in a more contemporary worship. . . . But I distinctly remember getting this feeling one day that I was going to write a hymn! Now, like most people, I am familiar with hymns—they form part of my church background, and I love the truth contained in many of them. But I don't go home at the end of a busy day and put on a hymns album! So I don't think of hymns as where I'm at musically at all!

Nevertheless, I'd been meditating on the cross, and in particular what it cost the Father to give up His beloved Son to a torturous death on a cross. And what was my part in it? Not only was it my sin that put Him there, but if I'd lived at that time, it would probably have been me in that crowd, shouting with everyone else 'crucify Him'. It just makes His sacrifice all the more personal . . . all the more humbling.

As I was thinking through this, I just began to sing the melody, and it flowed in the sort of way that makes you think you've pinched it from somewhere! So the melody was pretty instant, but the words took quite a bit of time, reworking things, trying to make every line as strong as I could. . . .

I was worried it was perhaps too twee, too predictable. . . . It was only when I began to use it in worship, and all sorts of people of different ages and backgrounds responded to it so positively, that I thought that it might be a useful resource to the church at large. Now I'm finding it gets used all over the world, by all sorts of churches . . . and I'm excited by that. But it has perhaps branded me as an old man before my time. It was fed back to me that at a conference a couple who loved the song were surprised to hear I was still alive.[58]

In Christ Alone

Keith Getty and Stuart Townend

Keith Getty and Stuart Townend
Arr. by Eric Wyse
IN CHRIST ALONE

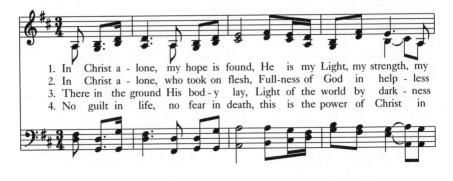

1. In   Christ a - lone,   my hope is found, He   is my Light, my strength, my
2. In   Christ a - lone,   who took on flesh, Full-ness of   God   in   help - less
3. There in the ground His bod - y   lay, Light of the world by   dark - ness
4. No   guilt in   life,   no fear in death, this   is the power of Christ   in

song;   This Cor - ner-stone,   this Sol - id Ground,   firm through the
Babe;   This gift   of love   and righ-teous - ness   scorned by   the
slain;   Then burst - ing forth   in   glo - rious   day,   up   from the
me;   From life's first cry   to   fi - nal   breath,   Je - sus   com-

fierc - est drought   and storm.   What heights of   love,   what depths of
ones   He came   to   save.   'Til   on that   cross   as   Je - sus
grave He rose   a - gain.   And   as He stands   in   vic - to -
mands my   des - ti - ny.   No   power of   hell,   no scheme of

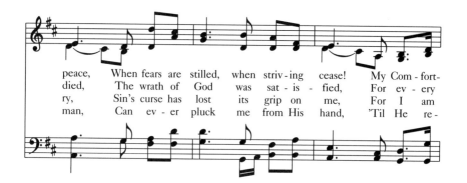

peace,   When fears are stilled, when striv-ing cease! My Com - fort-
died,   The wrath of God was sat - is - fied, For ev - ery
ry,   Sin's curse has lost its grip on me, For I am
man,   Can ev - er pluck me from His hand, 'Til He re -

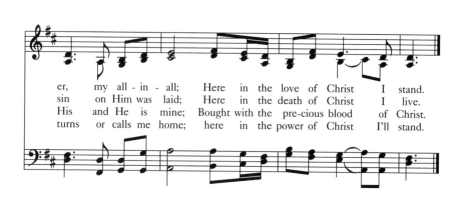

er,   my all - in - all; Here in the love of Christ I stand.
sin   on Him was laid; Here in the death of Christ I live.
His   and He is mine; Bought with the pre-cious blood of Christ.
turns   or calls me home; here in the power of Christ I'll stand.

In Christ Alone

2001

We've some new names to add to the roll call of classic hymnists—Keith and Kristyn Getty, the Irish couple who have richly expanded our hymnbooks. In 2001, they teamed up with Stuart Townend to give us "In Christ Alone."

"Of all the hymns we have written," Keith wrote, "this hymn is the most popular wherever we go. Ironically it is the first hymn we ever penned together.

"I had a strong very Irish melody that I could imagine a large crowd singing. I wanted it to become a hymn that would declare the whole life of Christ and what it meant. . . .

"Stuart penned an incredible lyric, which the two of us edited, developed and rewrote for a couple of weeks until it became 'In Christ Alone.'

"As well as being a creedal song, it fires people with hope that there is the God who even death cannot hold. 'No guilt in life, no fear in death, this is the power of Christ in me.'"

Keith tells of one particularly moving letter from a soldier at war, who said he listened to this hymn day and night. "As I drive down the highway," wrote the soldier, "with my M-16 pointed out the window and my 9MM pistol tucked in my flak jacket pocket, I can tell you that I feel more secure in claiming the promise, 'No power of hell, no scheme of man can ever pluck me from His hand till He returns or calls me home' than I do with that rifle and pistol."

A couple of years ago I had the opportunity of sharing a cup of coffee with Keith and Kristyn and found them as sincere, gentle, and devoted to Jesus as their hymns indicate. He explains there are two reasons he and Kristyn write modern hymns. "First, it's to help teach the faith. . . . The second reason is to try to create a more timeless musical style every generation can sing."[59]

For that we're thankful!

PART 3
SIX HYMN STORIES I LOVE TO TELL

It Is Well with My Soul

Horatio G. Spafford

Philip P. Bliss
VILLE DU HAVRE

1. When peace like a riv - er at - tend - eth my way, When
2. Though Sa - tan should buf - fet, Though tri - als should come, Let
3. My sin — oh, the bliss of this glo - ri - ous thought, My
4. And, Lord, haste the day when the faith shall be sight, The

sor - rows like sea - bil - lows roll; What - ev - er my lot, Thou hast
this blest as - sur - ance con - trol, That Christ has re - gard - ed my
sin — not in part but the whole, Is nailed to the cross and I
clouds be rolled back as a scroll, The trump shall re - sound and the

taught me to say, "It is well, it is well with my soul."
help - less es - tate, And hath shed His own blood for my soul.
bear it no more, Praise the Lord, praise the Lord, O my soul!
Lord shall de - scend, "E - ven so" — it is well with my soul.

It is

well with my soul, It is well, it is well with my soul.
It is well with my soul,

The Real Story Behind
"It Is Well with My Soul"

erhaps the most famous of our hymn stories involves the incredible tragedy that prompted Horatio Spafford to write the immortal hymn "It Is Well with My Soul." In the first volume of *Then Sings My Soul*, I related it like this:

When the great Chicago fire consumed the Windy City in 1871, Horatio G. Spafford, an attorney heavily invested in real estate, lost a fortune. About that time, his only son, age four, succumbed to scarlet fever. Horatio drowned his grief in work, pouring himself into rebuilding the city and assisting the one hundred thousand who had been left homeless.

In November of 1873, he decided to take his wife and daughters to Europe. Horatio was close to D. L. Moody and Ira Sankey, and he wanted to visit their evangelistic meetings in England, then enjoy a vacation.

When an urgent matter detained Horatio in New York, he decided to send his wife, Anna, and their four daughters, Maggie, Tanetta, Annie, and Bessie, on ahead. As he saw them settled into a cabin aboard the luxurious French liner Ville du Havre, an unease filled his mind, and he moved them to a room closer to the bow of the ship. Then he said goodbye, promising to join them soon.

During the small hours of November 22, 1873, as the Ville du Havre glided over smooth seas, the passengers were jolted from their bunks. The ship had collided with an iron sailing vessel, and water poured in like Niagara. The Ville du Havre tilted dangerously. Screams, prayers, and oaths merged into a nightmare of unmeasured terror. Passengers clung to posts, tumbled through darkness, and were swept away by powerful currents of icy ocean. Loved ones fell from each other's grasp and disappeared into foaming blackness. Within

two hours, the mighty ship vanished beneath the waters. The 226 fatali-
ties included Maggie, Tanetta, Annie, and Bessie. Mrs. Spafford was found
nearly unconscious, clinging to a piece of the wreckage. When the forty-seven
survivors landed in Cardiff, Wales, she cabled her husband: "Saved Alone."

Horatio immediately booked passage to join his wife. En route, on a cold
December night, the captain called him aside and said, "I believe we are now
passing over the place where the Ville du Havre went down." Spafford went
to his cabin but found it hard to sleep. He said to himself, "It is well; the will
of God be done."

He later wrote his famous hymn based on those words.

♭ ♭ ♭

The melody for "It Is Well," titled Ville du Havre, was written by Philip
Bliss who was himself soon to perish, along with his wife, in a terrible train
wreck in Ohio.*

* See the story of "I Will Sing of My Redeemer."

All that is true, as far as it goes. But there's more to the story. For
the last year, I've had internal debates in my head about telling the fuller
version in this final installment of *Then Sings My Soul*; but I've decided
to do it because it is fascinating, understandable, and a display of both
the ravages of grief and the grace of God. The Spaffords' story has more
twists and turns than the mountain roads snaking through my native East
Tennessee and Western North Carolina. I find it strangely comforting. It
reminds me that I can't figure everything out, that no one is perfect, and
that if we sometimes get a little off track under the strains of life, the Lord
knows how to bless us anyway.

Horatio was born in Troy, New York, and his childhood was marked by
scholastic excellence. After completing law school, he was attracted to the
adventure of the West and traveled to Chicago where, in the days before
the Civil War, he championed the abolition of slavery and the election
of Abraham Lincoln. He inserted himself into community causes, began

teaching law at Lind University, and gained a reputation for being one of the most eligible bachelors on the shores of Lake Michigan. As his income grew, he ventured into real estate and purchased extensive holdings along the lakefront. Unfortunately he often overextended himself and his credit.

A devout Presbyterian, Horatio taught Sunday school in a local church, and that's where he met Anna, who had immigrated to America at age four with her parents from Norway. She visited his class at the invitation of a friend. Despite their age difference (he was fourteen years older), they were married in 1861, a few months after the outbreak of the Civil War. Union forces were not doing well, and the mood in Chicago was glum. No one was interested in large weddings at the time, and the Spaffords were married in a small, private service at the Second Presbyterian Church. Anna wore a simple blue dress.

One day during a lunch break, Horatio heard shouts coming from the steps of the Chicago courthouse at the corner of Randolph and Clark Streets. He turned aside and listened to evangelist D. L. Moody, who was preaching an open-air sermon on the subject of repentance. Horatio caught Moody's enthusiasm and soon was pouring himself into evangelistic work, visiting jails and hospitals, and helping fund Moody's projects. Horatio and Anna often entertained Christian leaders and workers at Lake View, their fashionable Victorian home on twelve beautiful acres on Chicago's north shore.

Land speculation in Chicago was at fever pitch; and as Horatio took the train to his downtown office each morning, he began thinking more of real estate than of law. Along with two other partners, Spafford purchased a large tract of land near Lincoln Park, borrowing heavily to finance the transaction. He expected to divide the land into lots, sell them quickly, repay the loan, and pocket a sizable return. Thinking he had a buyer in Indiana, he reluctantly packed his bags and left to seal the deal, though he fretted about Anna who was still very weak from the difficult delivery of their fourth daughter.

While Horatio was away that evening, October 8, 1871, Mrs. O'Leary's cow kicked over a lantern in a barn on the south side of town.

Fanned by wind, flames spread quickly to Chicago's downtown blocks and consumed one landmark after another in rapid succession. The streets were mobbed with crowds of people and animals, fleeing amid falling embers and billowing smoke. A feeling of apprehension swept over Anna as she stood on her porch at Lake View and gazed at the distant glow. Neighbors and refugees soon poured onto the Spafford property, which was thought far enough to the north to escape the flames. Then news came that the flames were spreading through the trees, heading their way. Buggies were quickly harnessed and the house evacuated.

After spending the night in the open air, Anna and the girls returned to find the fire had stopped short of Lake View. But Chicago was a smoldering wasteland—three hundred people dead, one hundred thousand homeless, seventeen thousand buildings destroyed. Horatio was ruined financially. His holdings and properties were worthless. His debts staggering. His law offices gone.

Furthermore, Horatio had apparently "borrowed" money not only from legitimate lenders but also from funds he was managing for others, and he suddenly found himself in ethical and financial crisis. Because of Anna's fragile health, he shared little of this news with her; he bore it alone. Anna was losing weight and appeared increasingly frail. At the urging of friends and despite his disastrous finances, Horatio booked a family trip to Europe on one of the most luxurious passenger ships on the Atlantic—the French liner S.S. *Ville du Huvre*. They planned to travel with their friends, the Goodwins.

Just before leaving, another disaster struck—the 1873 financial collapse. The New York Stock Exchange closed for nearly two weeks, thousands of banks collapsed, eighteen thousand businesses failed, and nearly a hundred railroads went bankrupt. Horatio sustained further losses from risky bonds. Nevertheless, hearing a rumor that a particular man might be interested in purchasing one of his real estate holdings, Horatio told Anna to take the girls to Europe without him while he tried to negotiate a deal. He'd catch up soon.

Anna and the girls left on the *Ville du Havre*. And the potential buyer promptly died of a heart attack. Wondering what to do now, Horatio was near the breaking point when the telegram came.

Atlantic Cable Message

The Western Union Telegraph Company

To Spafford, 153 LaSalle Street, Chicago, Dec. 2d.,

5:40 AM, 1873

Saved alone. What shall I do. Mrs. Goodwin Children Willie Culver lost. Go with Lorriaux until answer reply . . .

Paris . . . Spafford.

The Gospel songwriter Major Daniel Whittle, a close friend, rushed to Horatio's side and stayed with him that evening as the bereaved father paced the floor in anguish. Dr. Hedges, the Spaffords' family physician, also stayed near.

Meanwhile, D. L. Moody, who was on the British Isles for an evangelistic campaign, tracked down Anna Spafford in her hotel room in London. Walking in and seeing her, he broke into uncontrollable tears. Anna told him softly, "Christ permitted me to take them only that they be wafted up to Him. Christ saved my life so that I might come back and work a little longer for him."

She told Moody how the youngest had been swept from her arms. She told of clinging to a plank in the icy ocean and feeling she was being spared for further work. "God gave me four little daughters," she said. "Now they have been taken from me. Someday I will understand why."

Horatio sailed to Europe to join Anna, passing over the site of the shipwreck and penning the ideas for the hymn "It Is Well." There's no record of what happened when the two were reunited, but as they returned to Chicago they seemed strangely cheerful. They were likely still in shock. Probably in denial. Certainly the Lord was giving them His peace that passes understanding. But how do you interact with old friends who now identify you only as victims of horrific tragedy? Friends who wanted to comfort them found them detached. No one knew quite how to relate with them, and the Spaffords didn't know how to receive the proffered sympathy. Tongues began to wag. Critical comments floated around like driftwood, and some wondered privately what the Spaffords had done to incur such loss.

A new minister, Dr. William Young, arrived at the Spaffords' Fullerton Avenue Presbyterian Church, and Horatio welcomed him with enthusiasm. But that relationship soon soured too. Spafford began questioning the pastor's theology, which was conservative and Calvinistic. Using his position as head of the finance committee, Horatio mounted a campaign to unseat the man, resulting in a contentious church business meeting. By a vote of 126 to 20, the congregation supported Pastor Young. Horatio angrily left the church and began building a chapel on his own land.

Anna was too preoccupied to be fully engaged in the conflict. She was about to give birth to a baby boy, Horatio Junior, who arrived on November 16, 1876. Two years later, Bertha was born. But in February 1880, both children contracted scarlet fever while traveling with their mother. Anna tried to return home with the feverish youngsters, but the harsh winter was too much for them—cold waiting rooms, chilly trains, open buggies, falling snow. By the time Anna got the children back to Lake View, four-year-old Horatio was unconscious. The home was quarantined. Two-year-old Bertha recovered, but the little boy died in his parents' arms.

Meanwhile, unknown to Anna, Horatio was still borrowing heavily, mortgaging and re-mortgaging properties in a futile effort to stay afloat. Former friends shied away, and it was generally believed the Spaffords in their intense grief were losing touch with reality. Whispers bounced around Chicago that Horatio was in debt for one hundred thousand dollars, a staggering sum in those days. To make matters worse, Horatio didn't even receive royalties for "It Is Well with My Soul," which had been published in Moody's hymnal amid great fanfare and astounding success. The proceeds went to help finance Moody's ministries.

By now Horatio had stopped practicing law altogether. He burrowed himself in his study working on materials having to do with the second coming of Christ. He became convinced Jesus was preparing to return to Jerusalem, and he decided he wanted to be there for the glorious event. He really meant it when he had written: "And Lord, haste the day when the faith shall be sight, / The clouds be rolled back as a scroll, / The trump shall resound and the Lord shall descend, / Even so, it is well with my soul."

In August 1881, the Spaffords and a small group of followers bid a bitter farewell to the Windy City and made the long and difficult trek to Palestine where they rented a home from a Joffa hotelier named Ustinov (the grandfather of British actor Peter Ustinov). As they settled down in Jerusalem, the group undeniably assumed some of the characteristics of a sect, giving themselves different names, looking for signs, insisting on celibacy, discouraging the use of doctors and medicine, and sporting a handful of strange beliefs. The American consul in Jerusalem didn't know what to make of them. He wrote:

"There has recently been an arrival at Jerusalem of eighteen persons for permanent residence from Chicago and vicinity, under the influence of some strong religious impulse, sustained by their interpretation of unfilled prophecies. They are praying, watching, waiting for, the grand events soon to transpire in this land as they suppose. They appear to be people of culture and wealth: they have taken a very large house in the Mohammedan quarter of the city, and are living as one religious household."[60]

It was here in Jerusalem, weighed down by the strains of his life, that Horatio grew weaker and sicker, eventually passing away on October 16, 1888. Anna assumed leadership of the group with, some would say, an iron hand. One of the best glimpses into this movement—they were variously called the Spaffordites, the Overcomers, and the American Colony—was a report written in a Methodist publication in 1891 by a sympathetic visitor named R. C. Morgan.

The coming of the Lord had evidently taken hold of the sufferers as an expectation to be speedily fulfilled, and about ten years ago with a few relatives and friends they left Chicago for Jerusalem, where they formed a community living as one family. They were not only subjected to severe criticism, but also to not a little misrepresentation. I think that they were undoubtedly under some hallucination. . . . I cannot but think they are under some hallucination still. They regard themselves as having received special illumination. . . . They live in harmony and peace. . . . They are a well-ordered and exemplary family in every respect; though I must add my conviction that all such communities are out of God's order and are therefore perilous. . . . There were at the beginning some married couples; but the rule was that they should live separately as brothers and sisters.

They have morning worship with their guests, at which they do not kneel but stand. They make no confession of sin and very little prayer. It is for the most part praise of the beautiful God and for the grace which He has given to them and the ministry to which He has called them. Subsequently they have a more private meeting, to which guests are not invited unless they manifest a receptive spirit. Here they read the Scriptures together, the prophecies relating to Israel being a subject of special interest."

The foundation on which the harmony of the community is based is evidently the implicit confidence with which they receive the teachings of Sister Anna (Mrs. Spafford). . . .

Mrs. Spafford wrote me a few weeks since: "It is truly wonderful to see how quickly God is working here. The Jews have been coming to us so changed from their former times. Hope is entering into them that God is really beginning to restore the land to them."[61]

Despite Morgan's allusion to harmony, the group's intrigues and infightings reads like the plot of a long-running soap opera. But Anna Spafford was a determined and earnest woman with a better head for business than her husband. Under her leadership, the Overcomers started a school, a farming enterprise, a bakery, a carpentry shop, a photography division, and an array of humanitarian works in Jerusalem. Since they didn't seek to proselytize others, both Jews and Muslims readily accepted their help. Their photographs of the Holy Land became the widespread iconic images sent to Christians around the world and inserted into books about the Land of the Bible. When World War I broke out, the American

Colony set up soup kitchens, orphanages, and other outlets for helping those in desperate straits. When the Turks fled the city, the Overcomers took over the hospitals and tended to the sick and wounded.

The group set up an insurance agency, imported the first steamroller into the Holy Land, and introduced the first telephone to Jerusalem.

Anna lived to be eighty, but in her final years she struggled with diabetes and the effects of a stroke. She passed away on April 17, 1923, and was buried on Jerusalem's Mount Scopus.

The surviving Spafford daughter, Bertha Spafford Vester, became one of the most colorful characters in the history of the new nation of Israel. She's the only Christian woman to have ever received the Jordanian Star, awarded to her in 1963 by Jordan's King Hussein in recognition of her humanitarian work. Israelis dubbed her "Mother of Mercy." The Bedouins called her "Murtha," the closest they could come to pronouncing her name. One magazine said she was "the uncrowned queen of Jerusalem."[62]

Bertha passed away in Jerusalem in 1968, leaving behind a legacy of her own. On Christmas Eve 1925, while preparing to go to Bethlehem to oversee carol singing at Shepherds' Field, she met a young Arab mother carrying a tiny infant. The mother had been walking six hours, but was terribly sick. She later said, "Here before me stood a rustic Madonna and babe, and, similar to Mary's plight, there was no place for them to stay."[63] Jerusalem's general hospital was closed to outpatients for the holiday. Bertha arranged for the woman to be admitted, but she died during the night. Bertha took in the baby. It was the beginning of an orphan and childcare ministry that continues to this day. It was originally named the Spafford Baby Home, and then the Anna Spafford Memorial Children's Hospital. Today it operates as the Spafford Children's Center.

Looking back, we can also say the Spaffords were at the forefront of the Zionist movement, encouraging the return of the Jews to Palestine. Their emphasis on the end times (though a bit extreme in Spafford's original calculations) contributed to the longing of Christians around the world to study the prophetic portions of Scripture and to anticipate the soon appearing of the Lord Jesus. They advanced the cause of biblical archaeology, and were instrumental in the discovery of Hezekiah's Tunnel and its famous inscription.

It was also from the American Colony that a bed sheet was used as the white flag (now in the Imperial War Museum in London) that was draped at the end of the first World War to initiate the truce that freed Jerusalem from three hundred years of Turkish rule.

Here's another surprising twist: When the legendary British general Charles Gordon visited the Spaffords in Jerusalem, he made an interesting discovery. Sitting on the roof of their communal home, he scanned the horizon and saw on the nearby hillside a rocky formation that looked like a giant skull. A keen student of the Bible, Gordon investigated the site and found an adjacent empty tomb and garden. To this day when I take a group of travelers to Israel, one of our most meaningful stops is at "Gordon's Tomb" with its haunting overview of Golgotha. It's largely thought to be the authentic site of the death, burial, and resurrection of Christ.

And the old American Colony headquarters?

Today it's a luxury hotel that's out of my price range but referred to as the best hotel in the Middle East. Near Jerusalem's fabled Damascus Gate, its archived registers hold the signatures of guests like Winston Churchill, Lawrence of Arabia, Lauren Bacall, Peter O'Toole, Tony Blair, and novelist John le Carré, who wrote one of his famous books there.

It is still owned by thirty-five descendants of the Spafford family.[64]

Isaac Watts:
The Father of English Hymnody

I f I were an artist, I'd love to paint scenes from Isaac Watts's life: A baby being nursed on the prison steps. A boy giggling during family worship. A teen pouring over college work. A youth penning the world's greatest hymns. A suitor whose marriage proposal is spurned. A semi-recluse, living in borrowed rooms of a lovely estate near London. A weak-voiced pastor who packed the pews. A brilliant educator who never got away from the "plain promises" of Scripture. A sickly old man whose last days were filled with "cheerful piety."

Meet Isaac Watts. He was a little man and none too handsome; but he was proud of his heritage, and rightly so. His grandfather, Thomas Watts, had commanded a warship for the British navy, and, on one occasion, had fought off an attacking tiger with his bare hands. Thomas survived the tiger only to die a hero's death when his ship exploded during a battle against Holland.

Isaac's father, Isaac Watts Sr., was an educator, a tailor, and a devout Christian who separated himself from the Church of England and was classified among the Dissenters—those in England who chose to attend Independent Christian congregations. For this, he was jailed off and on during the 1670s. One of those imprisonments occurred about a year after his marriage, and his wife brought newborn Isaac to the prison where she sat on the prison steps so her husband could be comforted by the sound of the baby's crying.

The Wattses lived in the English port city of Southampton, which had been the departure port for the *Mayflower* several decades earlier and, later, of the *Titanic*. There they established a Christian home for Isaac and his seven subsequent siblings. Isaac showed early signs of brilliance and

Behold the Glories of the Lamb

Isaac Watts

Hugh Wilson
Arr. by Ralph E. Hudson
MARTYRDOM

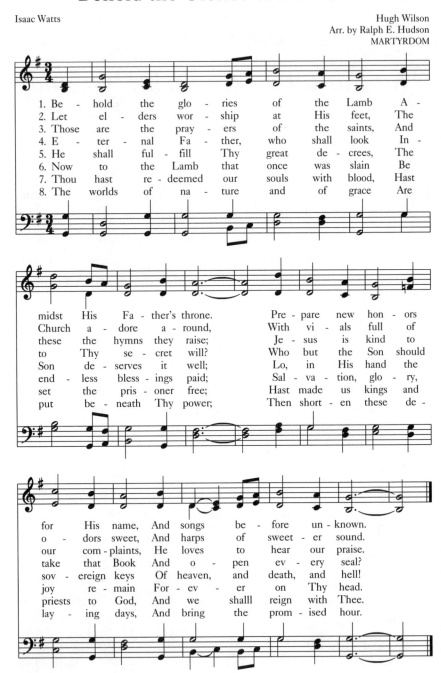

1. Be - hold the glo - ries of the Lamb A -
2. Let el - ders wor - ship at His feet, The
3. Those are the pray - ers of the saints, And
4. E - ter - nal Fa - ther, who shall look In -
5. He shall ful - fill Thy great de - crees, The
6. Now to the Lamb that once was slain Be
7. Thou hast re - deemed our souls with blood, Hast
8. The worlds of na - ture and of grace Are

midst His Fa - ther's throne. Pre - pare new hon - ors
Church a - dore a - round, With vi - als full of
these the hymns they raise; Je - sus is kind to
to Thy se - cret will? Who but the Son should
Son de - serves it well; Lo, in His hand the
end - less bless - ings paid; Sal - va - tion, glo - ry,
set the pris - oner free; Hast made us kings and
put be - neath Thy power; Then short - en these de -

for His name, And songs be - fore un - known.
o - dors sweet, And harps of sweet - er sound.
our com - plaints, He loves to hear our praise.
take that Book And o - pen ev - ery seal?
sov - ereign keys Of heaven, and death, and hell!
joy re - main For - ev - er on Thy head.
priests to God, And we shalll reign with Thee.
lay - ing days, And bring the prom - ised hour.

displayed a natural talent for rhyme. Once during family devotions, he started snickering. His father looked up sharply, but Isaac explained that he'd just seen a mouse run up the bell-rope by the fireplace. He diverted his father's irritation by composing a little poem on the spot: "There was a mouse, for want of stairs, / Ran up a rope to say his prayers."

Seeing his son's genius, Isaac's father began teaching him Latin, beginning at age four. When Isaac was six, wanting to prove to his mother that he could compose poetry cleverly and swiftly, he crafted this acrostic using his name:

I I am a vile polluted lump of earth.
S So I've continue'd ever since my birth;
A Although Jehovah grace does daily give me,
A As sure this monster Satan will deceive me,
C Come, therefore, Lord, from Satan's claws relieve me.
W Wash me in Thy blood, O Christ,
A And grace divine impart,
T Then search and try the corners of my heart,
T That I in all things may be fit to do
S Service to Thee, and sing Thy praises, too.

Realizing their son needed the best possible education, the Wattses placed him in a private Christian school operated by Rev. John Pinhorne, who became one of Isaac's most valuable mentors and his primary teacher for the next ten years. At one point during these years, Isaac was stricken by a "great and dangerous sickness." It was evidently during this time that he confirmed his personal faith in Christ. His journal says: "Feel under considerable convictions of sin, 1688. And was taught to trust in Christ, I hope, 1689."

A local physician in Southampton, seeing Isaac's brilliance and knowing of his desire to go into the ministry, offered to finance his education at an English university. At that time, however, Dissenting students weren't allowed to enroll at Cambridge or Oxford. Isaac wasn't willing to convert

I Sing the Mighty Power of God

Isaac Watts

from *Gesangbuch der Herzogl*, Württemberg

1. I   sing the might - y power of God, That made the mountains rise;
2. I   sing the good-ness of the Lord, That filled the earth with food;
3. There's not a plant or flow'r be - low But makes Thy glo - ries known,

That spread the flow-ing seas a - broad, And built the loft - y skies.
He formed the crea-tures with His word, And then pro-nounced them good.
and clouds a - rise and tem-pests blow, By or - der from Thy throne.

I sing the wis-dom that or - dained The sun to rule the day;
Lord, how Thy won-ders are dis - played, Wher - e'er I turn my eye;
While all that bor-rows life from Thee Is ev-er in Thy care;

The moon shines full at His com-mand, And all the stars o - bey.
If I sur - vey the ground I tread, Or gaze up - on the sky.
And ev - ery - where that man can be, Thou, God, art pres-ent there.

to the Church of England for the sake of college, so he enrolled himself in the Nonconformist Academy at Stoke Newington Green, outside of London. He was sixteen years old, and hesitant to leave the family he so loved. But his college years were happy ones under the wise tutelage of Rev. Thomas Rowe, and the friendships he made with fellow students stayed with him all his life.

Upon graduation, Isaac returned home to spend an additional two and a half years with his parents in Southampton. Here he devoted his time to reading, meditating, walking, praying, and seeking God's will for his next steps. He went faithfully with his family to Above Bar Congregational Church.

It was during this period—from age twenty to twenty-two—that Isaac became the "Father of the English Hymn." It stemmed from a conversation with his dad as they walked from church one Sunday. At that time congregational singing in English churches was limited to metrical versions of the Psalms, which were "lined out." The leader sang the line, then the congregation repeated it. Most British Christians thought only the psalms of David should be sung, and these had been hammered into wooden verses for congregational singing. These were ponderous and difficult to sing. Being from the Old Testament, these psalms were also devoid of much of the truth and imagery contained in the New Testament. When Isaac complained about all this, his father reportedly replied, "Try then whether you can yourself produce something better."

Isaac seized on the idea, and within a week had composed a hymn for the congregation to try. His first attempt is still sung to this day: "Behold the Glories of the Lamb," the first verse of which appropriately says:

Behold the glories of the Lamb
Amidst His Father's Throne.
Prepare new honors for His name,
And songs before unknown.

This wasn't the first English hymn, but previous attempts had been

We're Marching to Zion

Isaac Watts

Robert Lowry

1. Come, we that love the Lord, And let our joys be known.
2. Let those re - fuse to sing Who nev - er knew our God;
3. Then let our songs a - bound, And ev - 'ry tear be dry.

Join in a song with sweet ac - cord, Join in a song with sweet ac - cord,
But chil - dren of the heav'n - ly King, But chil - dren of the heav'n - ly King,
We're march - ing thro' Im - man - uel's ground, We're march - ing thro' Im - man - uel's ground.

And thus sur - round the throne, And thus sur - round the throne.
May speak their joys a - broad, May speak their joys a - broad.
To fair - er worlds on high, To fair - er worlds on high.

We're march - ing to Zi - on, Beau - ti - ful, beau - ti - ful Zi - on. We're

march - ing up - ward to Zi - on, The beau - ti - ful cit - y of God.

widely criticized and few English churches had adopted the habit of hymn-singing; so it must have taken a lot of mettle for the Above Bar Congregational Church to launch into this "contemporary" Christian song. But they tried it and liked it. Thereafter, Isaac began preparing a new hymn for them every week.

In the fall of 1696, Isaac realized he had to go to work, so he accepted a position as tutor to a wealthy family back in Newington, outside London. Sir John Hartopp and his wife had one son and six daughters; and since they traveled between their various homes and estates, they wanted a private teacher for their children. Isaac fit the bill perfectly and settled into his job with relish. He also began attending church with them at Mark Lane Independent Chapel in London. The church sat on a fashionable street not far from the famous Tower of London, but Isaac again found himself chaffing under the dullness of the worship.

All that began to change on July 17, 1698, when Isaac celebrated his twenty-fourth birthday by preaching his first sermon. Before long he was serving as the church's assistant pastor and preaching every Sunday morning. His sermons were fresh and lively, and the congregation at Mark Lane began to revive. He preached extemporaneously from an outline rather than reading a manuscript. The church also began singing his hymns.

They did not, however, see as much of their young assistant pastor as they'd have liked. Isaac was a bit reclusive, given to study, and not as apt to visit in their homes. Despite some grumbling, the church came to accept the fact that what they lost in pastoral visits they gained in pastoral sermons. In early 1702, the church asked Isaac to become senior pastor.

Isaac moved from Sir John Hartopp's home and took lodgings near Mark Lane. He had a secret room included in his quarters where he daily retired for Bible study, prayer, and meditation. "Abandon the secret chamber," he once warned, "and the spiritual life will decay."

Isaac's spiritual life thrived, but his body broke down early in his work. We aren't sure as to the nature of this illness—one of many that incapacitated Isaac at various times in his life—but he was so ill that he offered to resign from his pastorate. Instead the church hired an assistant

When I Survey the Wondrous Cross

Isaac Watts

Gregorian Chant
Arr. by Lowell Mason

1. When I sur - vey the won - drous cross
2. For - bid it, Lord, that I should boast,
3. See, from His head, His hands, His feet,
4. Were the whole realm of na - ture mine,

On which the Prince of glo - ry died,
Save in the death of Christ, my God;
Sor - row and love flow min - gled down;
That were a pres - ent far too small;

My rich - est gain I count but loss,
All the vain things that charm me most,
Did e'er such love and sor - row meet,
Love so a - maz - ing, so di - vine,

And pour con - tempt on all my pride.
I sac - ri - fice them to His blood.
Or thorns com - pose so rich a crown?
De - mands my soul, my life, my all.

for him and gave him as much time off as needed. Meanwhile, a wealthy family in the Mark Lane congregation invited Isaac to recover at their stately mansion on the outskirts of London. Sir Thomas Abney (the Lord Mayor of London) and his wife, Mary, offered a suite in their home so Isaac could get some "country air." He came for a week; and he stayed nearly four decades!

Meanwhile, Isaac fell in love. The object of his affections was one of his readers, Miss Elizabeth Singer, who had come from a Non-Conformist family. She loved his writings, and, after an exchange of correspondence, came to visit him. He mustered his courage and proposed to her. But though she loved his mind and his material, she couldn't get over his odd appearance, large head, and diminutive frame (Watts was a mere five feet tall). She politely declined, telling him as kindly as she knew how that she loved the jewel but not the box that contained it; and Watts accepted that as from the Lord and buried himself in his work, preparing sermons, writing poems, and composing hymns. He never married.

As hymns were still controversial novelties (critics called them "whims"), Watts had shied away from offering them to a publisher. But his brother Enoch did us all a favor by sending Isaac a letter, encouraging him to "oblige the world by showing it your hymns in print." He made a sound case for publishing them, telling Isaac that his hymns presented the old truths in new clothing and made singing at church seem "younger by ages."

Watts did start publishing his hymns. His *Hymns and Spiritual Songs* appeared in 1707–1709. A children's hymnal, *The Divine and Moral Songs for the Use of Children*, was published in 1715, and his landmark *The Psalms of David Imitated in the Language of the New Testament*, appeared in book-shops in 1719. We're still singing Watts's "whims" today, including:

- Alas! and Did My Savior Bleed?
- Am I a Soldier of the Cross?
- I Sing the Mighty Power of God
- I'll Praise My Maker
- Jesus Shall Reign

- Join All the Glorious Names
- Joy to the World
- We're Marching to Zion
- O God Our Help in Ages Past
- When I Survey the Wondrous Cross

Incredibly, Watts wrote many of these hymns while between the ages of twenty and forty-four. Afterward, Watts essentially stopped writing hymns and moved on to published sermons, textbooks, and works of prose.

Watts was a prolific educator and writer of faith-based academic literature. While still maintaining his pastorate in the city (though preaching a sermon so exhausted him that he had to go immediately to bed), he recused himself in the Abney's estate, took long morning walks, and churned out biblically based textbooks that were used in schools across England. His first was published in 1721: *The Art of Reading and Writing English*. He also published a widely used textbook on logic, *The Right Use of Reason in the Inquiry After Truth*, in 1724. It was used at Oxford, Cambridge, Harvard, and Yale for over one hundred years. He also wrote texts on astronomy and geography.

His *Prayers Composed for Children* came out in 1728, a set of catechisms in 1730, and *A Brief Scheme of Ontology* in 1733. Books of his sermons also sold well, and so did his book about heaven, *The World to Come*, published three years before his death.

He also conceived the idea for a book on *The Rise and Progress of Religion in the Soul*, but his growing illnesses prevented him from writing it. After sketching out its outline and emphases, he turned the project over to one of his best friends and fellow hymnist, Philip Doddridge, and the book became one of our greatest English Christian classics. This is the book that was responsible for the conversion of the great British statesman William Wilberforce, who later championed the cause of the abolition of slavery in the British Empire.

Watts was a popular preacher and became the best-known pastor in London, but his church was never huge. Christianity was plagued in those days by "empty pews," and maintaining a spiritual ministry was an uphill battle. In his latter years, however, Watts detected the stirrings of revival. He carefully followed news of the Great Awakening in America under the preaching of Jonathan Edwards. He received visits at Abney Park by Count Zinzendorf, the Wesleys, and George Whitefield (though it took him a while to warm up to the young Whitefield's unorthodox methods).

All the while, however, Isaac's health was declining. He finally stopped his prodigious output of writing and retired from his literary pursuits. His last months were devoted to getting his papers in order, praying and meditating, catching up on correspondence, and visiting with his close friends. He told one guest about an older minister who once told him the most learned and knowing Christians, when they come to die, have only the same plain promises of the gospel for their support as the common and unlearned believer. "And so I find it," Isaac said. "They are the plain promises of the Gospel which are my support, and I bless God they are plain promises, which do not require much labour or pains to understand them; for I can do nothing now but look into my Bible for some promise to support me, and live upon that."

Watts passed away during the afternoon of Friday, November 25, 1748, at the age of seventy-five, and was buried in the Dissenter's Cemetery at Bunhill Fields in London, across the street from Wesley's City Road Chapel. Today a statue of him stands in his native Southampton, where four times a day the central bell tower tolls out the notes of "O God Our Help in Ages Past." A bust of Watts is displayed in Westminster Abbey, and his hymns—among the first in the English language—are still sung around the world. It's also safe to say that Watts opened the floodgates of English hymnody, paving the way for Charles Wesley and a host of hymnists who gave the world the greatest collection of Christian songs in history.

I'm drawn to Isaac Watts for so many reasons; I identify with him—not in his brilliance, giftedness, or renown—but in his struggles to balance the demands of pastoring with writing, in his love of meaningful worship, and in his attempt to modify a secluded personality with what he called "cheerful piety."

In his lifetime, Watts composed about 750 hymns. I've already listed his most famous ones, but you might be interested in this lesser-known stanza from an Easter hymn based on Psalm 118:24, the verse that tells us this is the day the Lord has made so we should rejoice in it. Watts put it like this, and in so doing expressed his great theme in life:

> *This is the day the Lord hath made;*
> *He calls the hours His own;*
> *Let Heav'n rejoice, let earth be glad,*
> *And praise surround the throne.*

The Old Rugged Cross: A Hymn "First Sung" in Three Different Places

L ake Michigan cuts deeply into the northern United States, piercing like an index finger as far south as Chicago, Illinois, and Gary, Indiana. If you drive north from the Windy City past Milwaukee, you come to Green Bay. Halfway on up the Wisconsin coast, the water cuts around a knife-shaped little peninsula, and there you'll find the fishing town of Sturgeon Bay, population about ten thousand.

About a hundred years ago, a midwestern evangelist named George Bennard came to Sturgeon Bay to hold a revival meeting at the Sawyer Friends Church, a small but stately stone building that still stands at 204 West Maple Street. The local newspaper, in announcing the revival meetings, said, "The rush and excitement of the Christmas season will be over and the members of the Friends Church are looking forward to these meetings with much interest."

George Bennard was, after all, well-known in the area for his Gospel singing and preaching. He'd been born February 4, 1873, in Youngstown, Ohio, the son of a coal miner. George himself had worked in the Ohio coal mines as a teenager to help support his mother and sisters after the death of his father. In his early twenties, he was drawn into Salvation Army gospel meetings and was soon traveling through the Midwest conducting revivals. He carried his Bible and a guitar, and he frequently worked on Gospel songs he was composing.

In 1894, Bennard married a fellow Salvation Army worker, Arminta Beeler, who was still recovering from her mother's death and her father's

The Old Rugged Cross

George Bennard

George Bennard
OLD RUGGED CROSS

1. On a hill far a-way stood an old rug-ged cross, The
2. Oh, that old rug-ged cross, so de-spised by the world, Has a
3. In the old rug-ged cross, stained with blood so di-vine, A
4. To the old rug-ged cross I will ev-er be true, Its

em-blem of suf-fering and shame; And I love that old cross where the
won-drous at-trac-tion for me; For the dear Lamb of God left His
won-drous beau-ty I see; For 'twas on that old cross Je-sus
shame and re-proach glad-ly bear; Then He'll call me some day to my

dear-est and best For a world of lost sin-ners was slain.
glo-ry a-bove To bear it to dark Cal-va-ry.
suf-fered and died To par-don and sanc-ti-fy me.
home far a-way, Where His glo-ry for-ev-er I'll share.

So I'll cher-ish the old rug-ged cross,
cross the old rug-ged cross,

Till my

tro - phies at last I lay down; I will cling to the old rug-ged cross, the

cross, And ex-change it some day for a crown.
old rug - ged cross,

suicide. The couple made their home near the Methodist College in Albion, Michigan, renting an apartment from Professor Delos Fall on 1101 East Michigan Avenue. From here, Bennard journeyed out on evangelistic forays and wrote Gospel songs. His friendly smile and sparkling blue eyes added to the passion of his message as he preached and sang from church to church and from town to town.

It was apparently in the kitchen of his rented home, now demolished, that Bennard started working on a hymn about the meaning of the cross of Christ. It's likely that he began composing "The Old Rugged Cross" during the Christmas season of 1912. As soon as the holiday was over, he packed his bag again, picked up his guitar, kissed his pregnant wife good-bye, and headed for the train station.

He was due to preach a revival at the Friends Church of Sturgeon Bay, starting on December 29, 1912.

Bennard's friend Ernest Mieras joined him in Sturgeon to lead the music. The meetings attracted great interest in the little town, and every night the church was packed. The local newspaper followed the story. On Thursday, January 2, 1913, it reported: "The revival now in progress at the Friends Church conducted by Revs. Bennard and Mieras is creating much interest with a good attendance, and souls are finding Christ."

A week later, the newspaper reported: "The revival . . . conducted by Bennard and Mieras continues with unabated interest. We say, 'Let the good work go on.' All who can should attend these meetings and hear these evangelists preach the word and sing the sweet songs of salvation. Their duets and music from the guitar are an inspiration to all."

On Friday, January 17, the paper said: "The revival conducted by the evangelists, Bennard and Mieras, closed Sabbath evening about the midnight hour in a blaze of glory. One hundred and forty came to the altar . . . and found Christ as the lifegiver."

During this revival in Sturgeon Bay, Bennard kept working on his song about the cross. Several church members later recalled seeing him preoccupied with his song, even as he came to their homes for meals. One woman, Alice Torstensen, remembered, "At the time Bennard was here at our place for dinner, I observed him working on the song, 'The Old Rugged Cross.' He was sitting in the living room waiting until dinner was ready."

Late in the afternoon of the last day of the meetings, January 12, 1913, Bennard sat around the table in the parsonage with several others. He suddenly rose and said, "I've got something that I have been working on. Let's try it out and see how it is." One of the ladies sat down at the organ and was given the alto part to sing. Henry Maples took the bass part. Mieras took the tenor, and Bennard himself sang the lead. Later that evening, the church was packed for the final meeting of the revival. Before the full house, Bennard and Mieras sang "The Old Rugged Cross" as a duet, with Pearl Torstensen playing the organ.

From Sturgeon Bay, Bennard traveled to Pokagon, Michigan, to begin another revival meeting at the First Methodist Episcopal Church. He was coming at the invitation of his friend, Rev. Leroy O. Bostwick, and he had his new hymn with him, of course. One night he sang it in its entirety for the church. Later four members of the First Methodist Episcopal Church choir sang "The Old Rugged Cross," accompanied by a pianist and a violinist.

For about a hundred years, three different places have claimed to be the home of "The Old Rugged Cross."

At Albion, Michigan, there's a historical marker near the site of the house where the Bennards lived. It says: "The Old Rugged Cross, one of the world's best-loved hymns, was composed here in 1912 . . ."

In Sturgeon Bay, Wisconsin, the Friends Community Church maintains a beautiful garden with a cross commemorating the first singing of the hymn in their church.

In Pokagon, Michigan, another garden and historical marker claims to be the birthplace of "The Old Rugged Cross," and a group of earnest hymn-lovers is working hard to restore the old building where the completed version of "The Old Rugged Cross" was first sung by the four-person choir.

It seems only right that a traveling singing evangelist would leave memories and traces of the old rugged cross wherever he went.

Lord, Give Us Souls

George Bennard

George Bennard

1. Gath - ered are we in the name of our God, Lord, give us souls,
2. Loved ones are lost, and our friends are a - stray, Lord, give us souls,
3. Come, Ho - ly Ghost, on Thy peo - ple de-scend, Lord, give us souls,
4. Har - vest is pass - ing, yes, soon 'twill be gone, Lord, give us souls,

Lord, give us souls; Trust-ing His grace and His won - der - ful Word,
Lord, give us souls; Help us to win them while yet it is day,
Lord, give us souls; Make our hearts ho - ly, Thy king-dom ex - tend,
Lord, give us souls; Bring us at last to our heav - en - ly home,

Lord, give us souls, we pray. Seals to our la-bor, and souls for our hire,

This bless-ed Lord, is our one great de-sire; Souls for whom Je - sus His

pre - cious life gave, Lord, give us souls, we pray.

Eventually, Araminta's health problems caused them to move to Redondo Beach, California, where Bennard continued writing Gospel songs—over three hundred in all, some of which are on the left-hand pages of this chapter. In early 1958, his health began failing and he was admitted to Hollywood Presbyterian Hospital. A reporter for the *Los Angeles Times* visited him to talk about the hymn he'd written a half century ago. "I was going through a great travail," Bennard explained in a faltering voice. "I needed help. Then I remembered an old wooden cross I had once seen. The first ten words came to me: 'On a hill far away stood an old rugged cross.' It must have been two weeks later before I went back and finished it."

But writing one of the world's most famous hymns wasn't his greatest fulfillment. "Saving souls was my greatest thrill," he said. "That hymn's just runner up."[65]

So I'll cherish the old rugged cross,
Till my trophies at last I lay down;
I will cling to the old rugged cross,
And exchange it some day for a crown.

From a Bucket of Blood
to a Beloved Hymn

his story came to me compliments of my friend Dennis
Donnelly, an insurance executive in Kansas and the international president of the Gideons International. You know that
organization. They've placed or distributed more than 1.6 bil-
lion Bibles in over 190 countries of the world. They've been distributing
Bibles since 1908.

Ironically, as it turns out, that was the year a man named Vernon
Spencer was born into a large family in the frontier town of Webb City,
Missouri, north of Joplin. Times were hard, and Vernon's family moved to
New Mexico and later to Picher, Oklahoma. At age thirteen, Vernon purchased a banjo ukulele and ran into problems. His father, needing every
nickel to pay the bills and provide for the necessities, was furious at the
boy's purchase. Vernon ran off to Texas, but his father tracked him down
and persuaded him to return home.

Picher was a rough-and-tumble frontier town in those days, with all
the vices typical of the time. The Spencer men worked in the lead and
zinc mines there. One day Vernon had a terrible accident at the mine and
broke his back. Though he recovered, he was unable to return to mining.
Searching for something to do, he began playing music at the Bucket of
Blood, a local bar and dance club in eastern Oklahoma. In his mind, playing music in a bar was far better than mining lead under the earth. He
liked his first exposure to the entertainment business, such as it was. And
in 1931, Vernon took a train to Hollywood, hoping to make it big. He
found a day job in a local grocery store. Nights and weekends were devoted
to making the rounds of country shows, clubs, dances, and looking for
contacts to help him get established as an entertainer.

How Great Thou Art

Carl Boberg

Swedish Folk Melody

1. O Lord, my God, When I in awe - some won - der, Con - sid - er
2. When thru the woods and for - est glades I wan - der, And hear the
3. And when I think that God, His Son not spar - ing, Sent Him to
4. When Christ shall come With shout of ac - cla - ma - tion And take me

all the worlds Thy hands have made; I see the stars, I hear the roll - ing
birds sing sweet - ly in the trees; When I look down from loft - y moun-tain
die, I scarce can take it in; That on the cross my bur - den glad - ly
home, What joy shall fill my heart! Then I shall bow In hum - ble ad - o -

thun - der, Thy pow'r through - out The u - ni - verse dis - played.
gran - deur And hear the brook and feel the gent - le breeze.
bear - ing, He bled and died To take a - way my sin.
ra - tion, And there pro - claim, "My God, how great Thou art!"

Then sings my soul, My Sav - ior God, to Thee, How great Thou art! How great Thou art!

Then sings my soul, My Sav - ior God, to Thee, How great Thou art! How great Thou art!

Vernon took up with a couple of other would-be-stars—Leonard Slye and Bob Nolan, and soon they were calling themselves The Pioneer Trio. Vernon was dubbed "Tim" and from then on was known by his stage name—Tim Spencer.

Leonard Slye changed his name too. He called himself Roy Rogers— yes, *the* Roy Rogers. The trio added a fourth musician and changed their group's name to the Sons of the Pioneers. And they *did* make it big, becoming one of the most popular country-and-western singing groups in the nation. Bookings were no problem. Money rolled in. Publicity was great. Movie roles appeared. And Tim Spencer was on top of the world writing music and performing. He married a woman named Velma, had two children, and settled his family into a nice house in Hollywood.

In 1949, Tim's song "Room Full of Roses" flew to the top of the charts and became the number one pop hit in the nation. It was followed by another hit titled "Cigarettes, Whiskey, and Wild, Wild Women."

Unfortunately, those were subjects in which Tim had become an expert. But while he was living it up on the road, Velma was faithfully taking the children to the Hollywood Presbyterian Church and praying for her husband. She was burdened for her husband and sometimes discussed him with her minister. "Pastor, what do I do?" she asked. "My husband needs to know Jesus and he needs to be in church. But when he comes in off the road he doesn't want me complaining to him all the time. He wants to come home and rest."

Her pastor suggested she start writing letters to him when he was touring. This was before the days of instant communication; it was often hard to make long-distance calls. So Velma started writing Tim each day, and she included a verse of Scripture in every letter. Knowing his itinerary, she would send her letters to the next hotel, and when he checked in it would be waiting for him.

One day in 1949, Tim checked into a hotel in Hazelton, Pennsylvania, and there was a letter from Velma. He went to his room, opened the note, and began to read it. He saw the verse of Scripture she had quoted, and he also spied a Bible on the bedside table, one that had been placed there by a faithful Gideon. Picking up the Bible, Tim looked up the verse and read it in the context of his wife's letter. Intrigued, he kept reading from that Gideon Bible until the Lord gripped his heart and he was led to trust Jesus Christ as his personal Lord and Savior.

That year Tim retired from singing with the Sons of the Pioneers, and shortly afterward organized a Gospel music publishing company called Manna Music.

A few years later, Tim's son, Hal, a teenager at the time, attended a youth conference and a missionary was there from India. During the conference, the young people were taught a new song, one that contained stirring words. The tune was an old Swedish melody. Deeply moved by the song, Hal introduced himself to the evangelist and told him, "My dad is in the music business. Can you get me a copy of that? I think maybe my dad can do something with this."

Hal was given a copy of the song, and he took it home and showed it to his dad. Tim Spencer was as impressed with the song as his son had been. He contacted the author of the words, Stuart Hine, secured the rights to the song, and guided it to become one of the most beloved hymns of the twentieth century.

And that's the story of how the Lord used a Gideon Bible and the godly prayers of a praying wife to transform the author of "Cigarettes, Whiskey, and Wild, Wild Women" into the Christian who helped introduce the world to the hymn "How Great Thou Art."

Then sings my soul,
My Savior God, to Thee,
How great Thou art.
How great Thou art.
Then sings my soul,
My Savior God, to Thee,
How great Thou art.
How great Thou art.

P.S. – Dennis Donnelly has told this story many times at Gideon banquets and missionary functions. Several years ago he was sitting on the front row of the First Presbyterian Church of Hattiesburg, Mississippi, waiting to speak on behalf of the Gideons. Also on the program that day was a missionary from Malawi, East Africa. Since he was scheduled for an upcoming Gideon trip to Malawi, Dennis was eager to hear what the missionary had to say. Nothing could have prepared Dennis for the missionary's closing statement: "I've been a missionary in Malawi telling people about Jesus because my grandpa, Tim Spencer, read a Bible in a hotel room in Hazelton, Pennsylvania, sixty years ago."

The missionary was Dr. Steve Spencer, son of Hal, and grandson of Tim, and he and his family are still serving the Lord faithfully in Malawi with an organization known as African Bible Colleges.

And that's how one Gideon Bible changed the world and gave it a great song . . .

. . . and this book its title!

Up on the Housetop

Benjamin Hanby

Benjamin Hanby

1. Up   on   the house - top   rein - deer pause,   Out jumps good old
2. First comes the stock - ing of   lit - tle   Nell;   Oh, dear   San - ta,
3. Next comes the stock - ing of   lit - tle   Will;   Oh,   just   see what a

San - ta Claus;   Down through the chim - ney with lots   of   toys,
fill   it   well;   Give   her   a   doll - ie that laughs and cries,
glo - rious fill!   Here   is   a   ham - mer and lots   of   tacks,

All   for the lit - tle ones,   Christ - mas   joys.
One   that will o - pen and shut   her   eyes.   Ho,   ho,   ho!
Al - so   a   ball   and a   whip that cracks.

who would-n't go! Ho, ho, ho! who would-n't go!   Up on the house-top

click, click, click,   Down through the chim - ney with Old Saint Nick.

From the Rooftop to the Stall

*H*ere's a Christmas trivia question: Exactly when did Santa Claus begin the risky practice of landing his reindeer and sleigh on rooftops? How long has he been doing that, and who first suggested such a reckless habit? I can tell you on good authority that the first rooftop landing occurred in 1864, in the town of New Paris, Ohio. That's when and where songwriter Benjamin Hanby wrote "Up on the Housetop," our oldest secular Yuletide song and the first popular song to feature the character of Santa Claus.[66]

> *Up on the housetop, reindeer pause,*
> *Out jumps good ol' Santa Claus.*
> *Down through the chimney with lots of toys,*
> *All for the little ones, Christmas joys.*

Benjamin was born in 1833 in Rushville, Ohio. His father, William Hanby, was a bishop with the Church of the United Brethren in Christ, and Bishop Hanby's story is interesting in itself. He'd grown up in a poverty-stricken family in Pennsylvania, but left at age seventeen to apprentice himself to a saddle-maker named Good. The man proved the reverse of his name, and Hanby found himself in virtual slavery. He escaped at age twenty, came to Ohio, and was converted to Christ at age twenty-two. By twenty-three, he was married, licensed in the ministry, and traveling on a preaching circuit through rural Ohio. He had thirty preaching stations to cover each month, which meant a sermon per day, every day and every month. His salary was thirty-five dollars a year. In his first year, he witnessed about a hundred conversions, and it was the beginning of a lifetime of great evangelistic fruitfulness. During William's first year of itinerant ministry, little Benjamin was born on July 22, 1833.[67]

Ben was a precocious child and according to subsequent reports, "blessed with a happy temper and bubbling over with good humor."[68] He grew up listening to his father preach, and very often the sermons touched on the evils of slavery. The Hanbys were heavily involved in the Underground Railroad, and Benjamin drank in every word of his father's abolitionist passion. Ben also sang in the church choir, delighted the congregation with his cheerful attitude, and felt the Lord calling him to follow his father into the ministry.

At the age of sixteen, Ben enrolled in his denominational school, nearby Otterbein College, and he worked his way through school by taking teaching assignments in nearby classrooms. He was popular with children and played with them on the playgrounds and in the surrounding woods. Wanting to use his love of music, he added singing to the curriculum. He also invited his schoolchildren to church, and several families began attending.

At Otterbein, Ben proved to be a diligent student with natural leadership tendencies. He excelled at athletics, especially wrestling and swimming (on one occasion he saved a fellow student from drowning). He wrote a play that was received with acclaim, and he was always involved in the school's musical productions.

It was during this period of his life that Ben was traveling one day by train reading the *Cincinnati Gazette*. He became absorbed in the story of a slave sale in Kentucky, in which a young black woman, Nelly Gray, was sold and forcibly separated from her wailing loved ones. She was dragged away to Georgia with little likelihood of ever seeing her family again.[69] To Ben, the story reinforced all his father's sermons against the evils of slavery. There on the train, Ben started sketching out the words to a song, and when he returned home that night he continued working on it. Finishing the words and music, the young college student sent it on a whim to a music publisher. Time passed, and he assumed it had been tossed in the wastebasket.

Imagine Ben's surprise when he learned "Nelly Gray" had been published and was quickly becoming one of the most popular songs in the nation. Going to Columbus, Ohio, Ben purchased a copy and immediately wrote to the publisher, asking why he hadn't been notified of the acceptance of the manuscript. The publisher, claiming the address had been lost, sent him twelve free copies. Ben submitted a request for royalties and received this reply: "Dear sir: Your favor received. Nelly Gray is sung on both sides of the Atlantic. We have made the money and you the fame— that balances the account."[70]

The music publisher made a small fortune; Ben had twelve copies of the song. But in retrospect, the important thing is the influence "Nelly Gray" had on American society. Coupled with Harriet Beecher Stowe's *Uncle Tom's Cabin*, Ben's song whipped up the winds of antislavery sentiment in the North and greatly accelerated the nation-rupturing collision that was coming. His mournful ballad touched the nation with the sad plight of slaves who were torn from their families and transported to plantations away from one another.

After graduating from Otterbein in 1858, Hanby took a short-term job for the college and traveled as its representative through Pennsylvania, Virginia, and Maryland. He also married one of his classmates, Kate Winter, and the couple settled down in domestic life with Ben writing songs and teaching school. The Civil War was breaking over the nation, and Ben's songs were being popularly sung by Northern soldiers.

But increasingly, Ben felt God's call on him for ministry. His sister later said, "The foremost business of his life, from conversion to the end, was the salvation of souls. One day in church he rose and with pallid face, which none of us can ever forget, calmly said, 'Brethren, God is preparing me either (to die) or for greater service to Him.'"[71]

Soon he and Kate were pastoring a church in the village of Lewisburg, Ohio. He was described as "young, scholarly, and eloquent; kind, genial and optimistic; direct, ingenuous, and sincere; blest with a refined and intelligent face and a poetic soul that found expression in song."[72] The little church adored their young song-writing pastor. His sermons were well prepared but never read from a manuscript. And he took a special interest in the children and youth of the congregation, teaching them drawing, singing, and Bible lessons.

As often happens, Ben Hanby's youthful exuberance, fresh methods, and rapid success created problems for him, especially with his denomination. The more "pious" folks questioned his innovations. A concern arose that Ben had neglected preaching the great doctrines of the faith. The growing chorus of criticism took its toll, and Ben quietly left his pastorate and severed ties with his denominational connection.

A young man with so much talent and personality was as valuable then as now; and soon Ben found employment with John Church Music Company of Cincinnati. Two years later, he took a job with the Root & Cady music house of Chicago. It was during this time he wrote "Up on the Housetop" as a Christmas sing-along for children. It was written in New Paris, Ohio, and published in 1865 by George Root. It was a fun song, but Ben's greater interest was in writing Sunday school songs. His wife later recalled, "He loved to write children's songs because he loved children. Teaching them, singing with them, and writing songs for them was, I think, his real work. He was happier in it than in anything else that he ever did."[73] During this time he composed about sixty melodies and wrote words to about half of them.

Another thing occupied Ben's energy during his early thirties. He was working day and night on a textbook for teaching his system of music. It was original and practical, and he fully expected its publication to be well received and to meet his family's financial needs.

In 1866, he took the nearly completed manuscript with him on a business trip to St. Paul, but en route he became seriously ill and had to return home. The checked trunk containing his manuscript was lost in transport and no trace of it was ever found. His manuscript was gone.

Arriving home, Ben was flushed and having obvious trouble breathing. He was put to bed, but he kept rousing himself to write Sunday school songs and Gospel choruses. One of them was a children's prayer that expressed his own aspiration for the Lord:

Oh, Shepherd, Savior, King,
Come, make this heart Thy throne;
Drive out Thy foes, Thou Mighty One,
And make me all Thine own.

Ben's illness lingered, and though he remained cheerful and sanguine, his wife and friends grew alarmed. Ben was full of plans for the future and talked about the projects he intended to tackle. But he was dying. His illness was diagnosed as tuberculosis and he passed away on March 16, 1867, at the age of thirty-four.

His body was taken to his alma mater where students, professors, and friends moved in silent procession to a little cemetery near a winding stream. If you visit the cemetery today, you'll see a monument in his honor. And if you're visiting Westerville, Ohio, you can stop by and see the Hanby House, which is located on West Main Street and kept open in his honor by the Westerville Historical Society.

Oh, there's one more thing.

Perhaps you're asking: Why in a book about hymns would there be such a long story about the man who wrote "Up on the Housetop"?

It's because Benjamin Hanby—lover of song and lover of children, pastor, musician, composer of America's greatest antislavery ballad and history's first secular song about Santa Claus, a young man who died just as he was becoming a renowned American musician—also gave us one of our greatest Christmas carols, one that follows the life of our Lord Jesus from Bethlehem to Galilee to Jerusalem to Glory, one that gives children and adults the full story of the life of the Christ child—"Who Is He in Yonder Stall?"

Who is He in yonder stall
At whose feet the shepherds fall?
Who is He in deep distress,
Fasting in the wilderness?

Who Is He in Yonder Stall?

Benjamin Russell Hanby

Benjamin Russell Hanby
LOWLINESS

1. Who is He in yon - der stall, At whose feet the shep-herds fall?
2. Who is He the peo - ple bless For His words of gen - tle - ness?
3. Who is He who stands and weeps At the grave where Laz - arus sleeps?
4. Lo! At mid-night who is He Prays in dark Geth-sem - a - ne?
5. Who is He who, from the grave, Comes to heal and help and save?

Who is He in deep dis - tress, Fast - ing in the wil - der - ness?
Who is He to whom they bring All the sick and sor - row - ing?
Who is He the gath -ering throng greet with loud, tri - um-phant song?
Who is He on yon - der tree Dies in grief and ag - o - ny?
Who is He that, from His throne, Rules through all the world a - lone?

'Tis the Lord! O won-drous sto - ry! 'Tis the Lord! The King of glo - ry!

At His feet we hum-bly fall, Crown Him, crown Him Lord of all!

'Tis the Lord! O wondrous story!
'Tis the Lord! The King of Glory!
At His feet we humbly fall,
Crown Him! Crown Him, Lord of all!

Who is He the people bless
For His words of gentleness?
Who is He to whom they bring
All the sick and sorrowing?

Who is He that stands and weeps
At the grave where Lazarus sleeps?
Who is He the gathering throng
Greet with loud triumphant song?

Lo! At midnight, who is He
Prays in dark Gethsemane?
Who is He on yonder tree
Dies in grief and agony?

Who is He that from the grave
Comes to heal and help and save?
Who is He that from His throne
Rules through all the world alone?

'Tis the Lord! O wondrous story!
'Tis the Lord! The King of Glory!
At His feet we humbly fall,
Crown Him! Crown Him, Lord of all!

West Point, Two Women, and the World's Most Famous Children's Hymn

A flat-bottomed rowboat plowed across the Hudson, bobbing on the currents, the oars hoisted and pulled by old Buckner, dressed for the occasion in white shirt and suspenders. Behind him, the austere gray stones of the United States Military Academy at West Point climbed skyward like ramparts of an enormous fortress on a hill. The only sound was the splashing of the oars as they cut the water—that, and the groaning of the breeze through the gorge and the occasional cawing of a crow.

Three hundred yards away on the east bank of the Hudson, a slender elderly woman awaited the passengers. A paisley shawl was draped around her shoulders and a large black ribbon encircled her graying hair, which was parted in the middle and pushed back from a deeply lined face. Pitchers of lemonade sat in her kitchen and the sweet aroma of gingerbread wafted through the house.

Scattered with artistic randomness around the old place were flower gardens, grape arbors, raspberry bushes, and vegetable plots, beyond which the hemlock and pine forest was pot-marked with little pathways disappearing into the thicket.

One by one, the young men disembarked and jaunted up the flowery pathway toward the house, escaping the confinement of their duties for a rare afternoon of refreshment, lemonade, and gingerbread. These sturdy West Point cadets were coming to study the Bible at the feet of the far-famed author of a song they had known from childhood: "Jesus loves me, this I know, for the Bible tells me so."

One More Day's Work for Jesus

Anna B. Warner

Robert Lowry

1. One more day's work for Je - sus, One less of life for
2. One more day's work for Je - sus! How sweet the work has
3. One more day's work for Je - sus! O yes, a wea - ry
4. O bless - ed work for Je - sus! O rest at Je - sus'

me! But heaven is near - er, and Christ is clear - er Than
been, To tell the sto - ry, to show the glo - ry, Where
day; But heaven shines clear - er, and rest comes near - er, At
feet! There toil seems plea-sure, my wants are trea-sure, And

yes - ter-day, to me. His love and light fill all my soul to-night.
Christ's flock en-ters in! How it did shine in this poor heart of mine.
each step of the way; And Christ in all, be - fore His face I fall.
pain for Him is sweet. Lord, if I may, I'll serve an - oth - er day!

One more day's work for Je-sus, One more day's work for Je-sus, One

more day's work for Je - sus, One less of life for me!

This is the remarkable story of Anna Warner and her sister Susan. It's a riches-to-rags tale of poverty and patriotism featuring a cast of characters that included Manhattan publishers, West Point cadets, two peculiar gray-haired women, an American president, a family of Christian heroes, one black sheep, and millions of children around the world.

The Warners were a notable family in American history. Six of them fought in the Revolutionary War alongside George Washington; and after the war the family came into the possession of Gilbert Stuart's famous portrait of Washington, which became their most prized possession. Jason Warner, who fought with distinction in the War of Independence, had four sons, two of which enter our story. The first, Thomas, the oldest sibling, was born in Canaan, in 1784. He became an Episcopal priest; and though his religious passions ran shallow, Thomas managed to be appointed chaplain at West Point Military Academy, a post he filled with debatable distinction for ten years. He wasn't good at following directions or regulations, he was frequently absent, and it's said he often used other people's sermons without giving them credit. Dismissed from his job at West Point in 1838, Thomas returned to Europe where he wandered about sponging off friends until he landed in debtor's prison where he died in 1848. He was buried in a pauper's grave in Paris.

Despite his flaws, Thomas did one very good thing. While at West Point, he persuaded his brother Henry to buy 280 acres of real estate situated just across the Hudson River. It was dubbed Constitution Island. The two brothers dreamed of building a resort there, complete with a castle-themed hotel.

Henry was just the man to undertake such a project. As an attorney in New York City, he had worked in the law offices of Robert Emmet before establishing his own practice in 1814. Three years later, he married Anna Marsh Bartlett, a wealthy socialite. The Warners were rising stars in the city's social and commercial life; and as Henry's income grew, he dabbled in business ventures and real estate. His name was suggested for political office, and his future seemed as bright as a full moon.[74] But Anna died following the birth of the couple's fifth child in 1826. Three of the children also passed away before reaching adulthood. Henry's sister Frances became a mother to the remaining children, two precocious sisters named Susan and Anna.

Henry purchased Constitution Island in 1836. Though it was undeveloped, there was a simple white-framed house, portions of which dated from the American Revolution. Hiring a crew of builders, he quickly expanded the house, intending it to become the servants' quarters for the lavish summer home he planned to build for himself on a nearby plot. He also hired New York architect A. J. Davis to draw up plans for a hotel. He visualized an exclusive resort for the wealthy, and the project was discussed excitedly in the New York papers.

Disaster

The next year Henry's high-flying world collapsed in the financial panic of 1837. The cook, maids, coachman, gardener, and tutors were released.[75] Forced to sell his elegant home on St. Mark's Place in New York City, Henry moved his family in 1838 into his newly renovated "servants' house" on Constitution Island.

Anna was thirteen years old at the time, and Susan was eighteen; and it was a rude awakening. Gone were the servants and most of the silverware. Gone, the bustling streets of New York City. Suddenly the little family found itself on a deserted island in a drafty old house, neck-deep in debt. Henry never fully recovered, either financially or emotionally. He tried farming the island without much success. In his spare time, he tried to practice law and he resumed buying and selling property; but this meant borrowing more money, and his finances went from bad to worse. Eventually, the sheriff seized the family's remaining treasures to be sold at auction, and the Warners were left with a virtually empty house whereupon Anna went out, found some wild flowers, put them in a vase, and suggested everyone try to make the best of it.

Wanting to help, the two sisters worked hard chopping wood and raising vegetables; yet nothing could spoil their childlike love for the island. Their lives were tinged with a certain idyllic color. They rowed on the river, picked wild flowers, planted gardens, tended grapes, studied birds and wildlife, sketched and drew and gazed across the river at the somber bulwarks of West Point. Constitution Island grew sacred to these girls as they explored every square foot of it. Perhaps it was the beauty of the land, or the solemn cliffs of West Point, or the star-spangled skies above their heads; but for whatever reason, the heart of the Warner sisters turned toward God.

Susan and Anna determined to give their lives without reservation to the Lord Jesus Christ; and in 1841, they sealed that commitment by becoming covenanting members of their dad's church, Mercer Street Presbyterian in New York City. Soon they were head over heels in Bible study, first as students and then as teachers. They began distributing Christian literature and speaking of their faith to others. They came to know their Bibles frontward and backward, memorizing large amounts of Scripture.

Rather than subduing the girls, Christianity sent their hearts a'soaring. Susan created fantasy worlds all her own, and she entertained family and friends with stories assembled in the chambers of her mind. She had a keen ability to rattle off vivid spellbinders; and one day in the old dining room as they finished tea, Aunt Fanny collecting the dishes, looked up, and said, "Sue, you love to read so much; I believe you could write a book if you put your mind to it."[76]

Susan made no reply, but the idea struck a cord in her mind.

Soon she put pen to paper and discovered she enjoyed writing very much. Before long, she was head over heels creating a novel, writing much of it in the old house on the island, and other portions while visiting New York. When she read chapters to her family, they ranted and raved, and her father shopped the manuscript around the publishing circles in New York, believing it was the answer to the family's debt. In 1851, *The Wide, Wide World* was published by George P. Putnam.

Within a couple of years, however, *The Wide, Wide World* was in

Jesus Loves Me

Anna B. Warner

William B. Bradbury
CHINA

1. Je - sus loves me! this I know, For the Bi - ble tells me so;
2. Je - sus loves me! He who died Heav-en's gate to o - pen wide;
3. Je - sus loves me! He will stay Close be - side me all the way;

Lit - tle ones to Him be - long, They are weak but He is strong.
He will wash a - way my sin, Let His lit - tle child come in.
Thou has bled and died for me, I will hence-forth live for Thee.

Yes, Je - sus loves me! Yes, Je - sus loves me!

Yes Je - sus loves me! The Bi - ble tells me so.

bookstores everywhere. Thousands of people became Susan Warner fans; and according to contemporary records, her novel became the first book written by an American to sell one million copies. Its popularity during the Civil War era was exceeded only by *Uncle Tom's Cabin*.[77]

While the success of *The Wide, Wide World* enabled the Warners to pay some bills and hang on to their island, Susan never received adequate compensation for her work; nor did Anna. In those days, copyrights were not enforced, and anyone could print and sell copies without benefit to the author. In fact, despite going on to write 106 books between them, the two sisters never fully escaped the ragged nets of poverty. Books were widely pirated at the time; and often because of urgent financial pressure, the sisters sold the rights to their books for immediate cash. This produced incredible pressure on the sisters to keep churning out books. Until her death, Susan published at least one book a year.[78]

The Warner sisters helped pioneer the field of modern Christian fiction, for the truth of Scripture shone through all their plots and pages. Susan's next two-volume novel, *Queechy*, was published in 1852, and afterward came a string of books including *Carl Krinken: His Christmas Stocking* (1854), *The Hills of Shatemuc* (1856), *The Old Helmet* (1863), *Melborne House* (1864), and several others. Her last book, *Diana*, was published by Putnam in 1877.

Meanwhile, Anna was also busy with literary projects. Her first novel was *Dollars and Cents*, published under the pseudonym Amy Lorthrop in 1852. It described the hardships endured by a family who lost their property and all the things dearest to them. She went on to write twenty-five books, including Christian classics, children's books, and various titles dealing with gardening and flowers and homemaking. Some were illustrated with her own line drawings. Her book *Gardening by Myself*, published in 1872, was the first book by an American woman telling women how to grow flowers and vegetables.

It's easy to visualize the two sisters, rising at dawn and meeting in the modest, dimly lit parlor of their old house. Before retiring the night before, they carefully laid out their breakfast items and made sure the kindling basket by the fireplace was filled with wood. Anna generally rose before dawn and started the fire to ward off the morning chill. Afterward, Susan came downstairs for hot tea and a cozy breakfast of bread and butter. The sisters then took their respective seats and began writing. The only sounds heard for the next several hours were the crackling of the flames in the hearth, an occasional coal falling through the grate, and the furious scratching of pens to paper while Stuart's portrait of Washington silently gazed down at them from its central place above the mantel.

By lunch, the sisters generally completed their writing, and the rest of the day was given to chores, errands, entertaining, correspondence, gardening, and a handful of leisure hobbies such as rowing and sketching.

It was a busy life, and not an easy one, especially in the blustery winter seasons when the rivers choked with ice, the temperatures plunged, and deep snows blanketed the little island. The Warners' house wasn't well winterized, so the sisters usually closed it down during the coldest months and traveled to nearby Highland Falls, or they would rent an apartment in New York City or stay in the cottage next to the West Point Hotel.

Jesus Loves Me

In 1860, Susan and Anna coauthored a novel entitled *Say and Seal*. It's an old-fashioned Victorian novel about a romance between a schoolteacher named Endecott Linden and a lovely local girl named Faith Derrick whom he led to faith in Christ. Among the characters in *Say and Seal* is a little fellow named Johnny Fax whose mother was dead. Johnny was smaller than other children and Mr. Linden took a fatherly interest in him. One bitter February day, Johnny fell sick—"no one just knew how; nor just what to do with him—except to send Mr. Linden word by one of the other boys." Mr. Linden fetched the town doctor, but little could be done. Linden, with trembling heart, took Johnny in his arms and paced, calming the child and soothing his fears. On one occasion, Johnny tried to talk, but only one word was understandable: "Sing." Walking back and forth with the torrid little body in his arms, Linden began singing:

> *Jesus loves me—this I know,*
> *For the Bible tells me so:*
> *Little ones to Him belong,—*
> *They are weak, but He is strong.*

Those words soothed the boy, and Mr. Linden placed him in bed. Shortly afterward, he passed away. As people read *Say and Seal*, little Johnny's death touched a nerve, and thousands of people marveled at the beauty of Mr. Linden's deathbed song. But, of course, no one could sing it. Miss Anna had only composed the *words* for the novel, not the music.

One of the readers was William Bradbury, who was arguably America's most prolific hymnist. Bradbury pondered the words, penned a chorus, and created the simple melody that instantly catapulted "Jesus Loves Me" to stardom as the greatest children's song in history.

The fame of the Warner sisters wasn't lost on the leaders across the river at West Point. In 1875 or 1876, a wonderful door opened for the sisters. A group of officers' wives asked Susan to teach a Sunday afternoon Bible class, and many of the students wanted to attend. Susan was cautious. "Do you really think the cadets would like me?" she asked, adding, "It would be a great pleasure to do it."

Anna later described its beginnings: "The first day, there was a very large gathering, curiosity helping on the numbers. After that, it varied from week to week, as must be always, I suppose; especially among Cadets, where guard duty sometimes interferes; and where Sunday is the free day for seeing friends."

During the winter months, the Bible studies were conducted weekly at the old cadet chapel, but the rest of the year they were held on Constitution Island, the cadets arriving by boat. When Susan wasn't well, Anna substituted. It was a sight. Anna had a curl on either side of her face, and the sisters both dressed in old, rustling silk dresses with ruffles at the necks and wrists. These dresses had been cut from the same pattern for forty years, and the sisters looked like displaced characters from one of their own novels. But Susan had a way of telling stories that engrossed the cadets and made her Bible studies very popular, and Anna provided liberal doses of advice and affection.[79] The classes weren't mandatory, but each week large numbers showed up. The boys took their seats in a semicircle around Susan, and she asked each cadet to read a Bible verse. Then she opened the Scripture to them for about a half hour until her strength gave out and she brought the lesson to a close.

One of the cadets recalled, "The visits to Constitution Island were regarded as a great privilege, for not only did they make a break in the severe routine of the daily life, but they enabled the boys to roam further afield than was possible at the Academy, where the restrictions of the cadet limits were pretty irksome to boys accustomed to the free run of the town or country. So the privilege of going to Constitution Island as one of 'Miss Warner's boys' was eagerly sought and highly prized. Every Sunday afternoon during the summer encampment the sisters would send their elderly man. . . . He pulled the old flat-bottomed boat across the river to the West Point dock, where the boys with the coveted permits were waiting for him."[80]

"Her English was the best and purest I have ever heard," recalled another cadet, "and as she went on and her interest grew her eyes shone like stars and her voice became rich and warm. . . . She always gave to the boys the brightest and most optimistic side of the faith she loved so well. When she had finished and lay back pale and weary against her cushions her sister, Miss Anna, came down from the house with the rarest treat of the whole week, tea and homemade ginger-bread. After that the two sisters and the boys talked over the things of the world that seemed so far from that peaceful quiet orchard. The boys confided their aims and ambitions, and the sisters in the simplest, most unostentatious way sought to implant the right ideals and principles. Miss Warner never forgot any of her boys, and up to the time of her death kept up a correspondence with many of them."

In 1885, Anna and Susan boarded up their home for the winter and made the short excursion to Highland Falls where they planned to stay at the cottage of John Bigelow, a friend who spent the winters elsewhere. While there, Susan became ill and passed away. The funeral was held in Highland Falls, and the officials at West Point arranged to bury her in the cemetery at the Academy with full military honors, an unprecedented tribute for a civilian.

Miss Anna later explained, "By special permission of the Secretary of War, she was laid in the government cemetery at West Point; there, where so many of her 'boys' would pass near her; so many at last come back to rest. From almost at her feet the wooded, rocky ground slopes sharply down to the river; and beyond that, on the other shore, is . . . Martelaer's Rock,— with the old Revolutionary house where so much of her work was done."[81]

After Susan's death, Miss Anna continued the Bible classes alone until her own death in 1915. A constant stream of cadets, officers, dignitaries, strangers, reporters, friends, and neighbors paraded up her flower-edged pathway each day. Added to that, bundles of mail arrived each week at the local post office. It added to her burdens, yet some of Anna's greatest blessings were tucked away in those letters and parcels, coming from the hundreds of cadets whose lives had been touched by the sisters through the decades. These "boys" were constantly seeking counsel, requesting prayers, sending gifts, and extending invitations. Anna once wrote, "Some of these boys think they can't get married comfortably unless I look on."[82]

"The winter has gone by like an express train, but loaded as if it had been a freight," Anna said, describing her workload to a friend. "I have been so busy, with two printers at work, and the throng of letters that must not delay. . . . They keep me busy, these gray uniforms."[83]

One of her "boys," Col. James L. Lusk, was later ordered back to West Point. His wife, Mary Lusk, later said: "It is hard to give any idea of the atmosphere Miss Anna created about her. She was strict without harshness, religious without gloom, narrow-minded as the world counts it, but broad-minded in her interest in all branches of study. . . . The love of all that is beautiful was a strong element in her character and . . . She would laughingly say that one of the reasons for the great beauty of the Island was that her family had never had sufficient means to spoil it."[84]

In all, the Warners taught the Bible to cadets at West Point for a span of forty years. One of the men, Col. F. W. Altstaetter, described his experiences with Miss Anna:

When I went to West Point as a cadet in 1893, I was only seventeen years of age and accustomed to living in a large family. For the first three years I was there I practically entered no private house except Miss Warner's . . . . You can imagine what that meant to me . . . . Under date of my first Christmas there I find quite a good bit on the subject, ending as follows: "I do not like West Point very well, but if it were not for Miss Warner, and of one of my classmates, I'd hate the place as long as I stayed here."

My first acquaintance with Miss Warner was when, a bashful, homesick new cadet, feeling very down trodden, I was invited to stay after the regular chapel service on Sunday morning and join her Bible class. She was then a little body, with a wonderfully sweet face crowned with two curls that hung down on each side before her ear. It was one of the saddest faces I ever saw when in repose, but when she smiled it was like a shout of glory with a benediction in it.[85]

Throughout their lives, the Warner sisters realized that the ultimate answer to all their financial needs was literally right under their feet. Constitution Island was an enormous asset, and developers were scurrying to purchase it from the women. But their love for the island and their appreciation for its heritage made such proposals out of the question. They wanted to give the island to West Point to preserve its hallowed history.

In 1908, through the generosity of a friend named Margaret Olivia Sage who offered her one hundred and fifty thousand dollars for her home, Anna was able to bequeath Constitution Island to the West Point Military Academy.

Anna Warner continued living in the simple white-frame-house and remained active for the remainder of her life. Even in her eighties, she was often seen rowing her boat around the edges of her island. Then in the fall of 1914, she packed up her belongings, planning to spend the winter in Highland Falls. She never returned to the house, for like her sister she passed away in Highland Falls during the winter. Her funeral was conducted in the old chapel at West Point, cadets serving as pallbearers. At the cemetery, the entire corps lined up as the bugler played "Taps," after which the coffin was lowered quietly into the ground. Anna and Susan Warner were the only civilians buried in the military cemetery at West Point at that time, and their graves are located in the far corner beside a stone wall that overlooks their beloved Constitution Island.

Their home is now a museum in their honor, preserved and operated by the Constitution Island Association in cooperation with the U.S. Military Academy at West Point. It has changed little since that day when Anna closed the door behind her; and boatloads of tourists show up each summer to walk among Miss Anna's flowers and up and down the little trail from the pier to the house, and to linger in her living room, kitchen, and bedroom. Scattered throughout the house are other gifts, sent from around the world by cadets who never outlived the influence of these two old women who never married but whose sons were legion.[86]

PART 4
HYMNING IN PRIVATE AND IN PUBLIC

In Private: Hymns as Therapy—
Why We Must Draw Strength
from Song

I n 1965, the Fourth of July fell on a Sunday and the official holiday was observed on Monday. Diane Young, a college student, had planned along with her boyfriend to spend the day at the lake with her parents, but the plans fell apart when her folks delayed their departure for the lake. Diane and her boyfriend had to get back to campus for Tuesday classes.

Her parents took off for the lake without them, but the afternoon trip ended horrifically. A terrible car wreck instantly took the life of Diane's mother, age forty-six. Diane's sister-in-law died in the emergency room. Her father, forty-nine, passed away the next morning. And Diane's twelve-year-old brother was unconscious and given little hope for survival. An older brother was also seriously injured and hospitalized.

"At age eighteen," Diane told me, "I was the only family member not in the accident. I ended up planning my parents' funerals, picking out the caskets and grave sites. During the next few roller-coaster days, I faced trials so extreme I could hardly bear them.

"But I grew up among Evangelical Mennonites, and I learned the great hymns of Christianity while a child. In those dark days and in the difficult years since, I've found great strength in singing, 'When peace like a river attendth my way, when sorrows like sea billows roll, whatever my lot Thou hast taught me to say, "It is well, it is well with my soul."'"

Diane's younger brother did survive and her older brother also recovered. Her boyfriend became her husband; and the two of them are now serving the Lord in full-time ministry with the Gideons. Her testimony

Now the Day Is Over

Sabine Baring-Gould   Joseph Barnby

1. Now the day is o - ver,
2. Je - sus, give the wear - y
3. Grant to lit - tle chil - dren
4. Through the long night watch - es
5. When the morn - ing wak - ens,

Night is draw - ing nigh, Shad - ows of the
Calm and sweet re - pose; With Thy ten - derest
Vi - sions bright of Thee; Guard the sail - ors
May Thine an - gels spread Their white wings a -
Then may I a - rise Pure, and fresh, and

eve - ning Steal a - cross the sky.
bless - ing May mine eye - lids close.
toss - ing On the deep, blue sea.
bove me, Watch - ing round my bed.
sin - less In Thy ho - ly eyes.

is: "Through many family trials and sorrows like sea billows that have rolled on for years, and through times when I myself could have died, God has ministered to my soul through this great hymn, 'It Is Well.' It remains one of my favorites today. Because of Jesus, my sins have been nailed to the cross and some day the trumpet will sound. I can say with firm assurance, 'Praise the Lord, it is well with my soul.'"

Hymns are self-medicating therapies good for whatever ails us. From infancy to old age, they're internal medicines that strengthen, heal, and uplift us. They're vitamins for the soul and excellent antidotes against emotional disease and distress. From birth till death, hymns accompany us along life's road. I once received a treasured letter from a woman who read the first volume of *Then Sings My Soul*. She told me of being a hymn-lover all her life. And she came by it naturally, she said. Her mother had sung through the entire Lutheran hymnal while nursing her.

On the other end of life's spectrum, I had a wonderful letter from Vonette Bright who told me that when her husband, legendary Christian leader Bill Bright, was dying, they turned to the hymns in *Then Sings My Soul*, read the stories, and sang one song of praise after another. Dr. Bright ascended to heaven in a cloud of worship. From birth to death, we derive spiritual stamina from the great hymns of the faith.

In 2 Kings 3, three distraught kings visited the prophet Elisha, seeking help. Elisha was none too pleased to see them. To him they were "small potatoes and few in the hill"—but he heard them out, then said, "Bring me a harpist." The Bible says, "While the harpist was playing, the hand of the LORD came upon Elisha and he said, 'This is what the LORD says . . .'"

Elisha provided the message and the miracle they needed, but he did so against the backdrop of a song. According to the old commentator Matthew Henry, Elisha realized that hearing God's praises sweetly sung, as David had appointed, would cheer his spirits, settle his mind, and put him into a right frame of mind for both speaking to the Lord and listening to Him. "Those who desire communion with God must keep their spirits quiet and serene," said Henry. "Elisha being refreshed and having the tumult of his spirits (lessened) by this divine music, the hand of the Lord came upon him."

"I wonder if you feel as I do," missionary Amy Carmichael once wrote a friend, "about the heavenliness of song. I believe truly that Satan cannot endure it, and so slips out of the room—more or less!—when there is true song. It leads to a sort of sweetness too. . . . Prayer rises more easily, more spontaneously, after one has let those wings, words and music, carry one out of oneself into that upper air."[87]

Read the Hymns

You don't always have to even sing the hymns. Simply reading them is dipping into the richest sacred poetry of the ages. So keep a hymnal at your desk or bedside. It may be a little harder to find hymnals now, since most churches project the words of their songs onto screens. But publishers are still publishing hymnbooks (and we've included lots of hymns in the *Then Sings My Soul* series of books). You can also find multiple shelves of old hymnbooks in used bookstores and antique malls. Assemble a small collection and use them during your devotions. I keep a hymnal at my desk and even if a hymn is unfamiliar to me, I enjoy reading its words. Sometimes I try singing them by picking out the notes (I'm not a musician) or I make up my own tunes (hoping no one is listening) or find another hymn tune that fits the meter.

Many hymns have been written for the close of day, and they can serve as a veritable benediction as you fall asleep. I'm inordinately fond of Sabine Baring-Gould's nocturnal hymn "Now the Day Is Over." I've never been able to get my church in Nashville to appreciate it, so I just occasionally sing it myself at the close of a hard day. (And yes, there are still sailors tossing in the deep blue sea.)

Now the day is over, night is drawing nigh,
Shadows of the evening steal across the sky.

Jesus, give the weary calm and sweet repose;
With Thy tenderest blessing may mine eyelids close.

Grant to little children visions bright of Thee;
Guard the sailors tossing on the deep, blue sea.

Through the long night watches may Thine angels spread
Their white wings above me, watching round my bed.

When the morning wakens, then may I arise
Pure, and fresh, and sinless in Thy holy eyes.

Not all the selections in the hymnbook are equally meaningful to me. Some hymns are inferior in quality or antiquated in language. But ferreting out the good ones is a spiritual discipline worth pursuing, and having a hymnbook close at hand is akin to having a Bible nearby.

Memorize the Hymns

In my book *100 Bible Verses Everyone Should Know by Heart*, I present a case for lifelong Scripture memory. Hymn memory is almost as great a blessing.

Hymns are often easier to memorize than Bible verses because they have built-in rhythm and rhyme. Still, it takes some effort. On a car trip to Illinois I recently asked my ten-year-old granddaughter, Christiana, to help me memorize Josiah Conder's hymn "Day by Day the Manna Fell." Not knowing the tune, we memorized it as one would memorize a poem. She retained the words faster than I did, but I've had many occasions to quote it since. Best of all, I think Christiana will remember it all her life. Two of my favorite stanzas say:

God of Grace and God of Glory

Harry Emerson Fosdick

John Hughes
CWM RHONDDA

1. God of grace and God of glo - ry, On Thy peo - ple pour Thy power;
2. Lo! the hosts of e - vil round us Scorn thy Christ, as - sail His ways!
3. Cure thy chil - dren's war - ring mad-ness; Bend our pride to Thy con - trol;
4. Set our feet on loft - y pla - ces; Gird our lives that they may be
5. Save us from weak res - ig - na - tion To the e - vils we de - plore;

Crown thine an - cient church - 's sto - ry; Bring her bud to
From the fears that long have bound us, Free our hearts to
Shame our wan - ton, self - ish glad - ness, Rich in things and
Ar - mored with all Christ - like gra - ces In the fight to
Let the search for Thy sal - va - tion Be our glo - ry

glo - rious flower. Grant us wis - dom, Grant us cour - age,
faith and praise. Grant us wis - dom, Grant us cour - age,
poor in soul. Grant us wis - dom, Grant us cour - age,
set men free. Grant us wis - dom, Grant us cour - age,
ev - er - more. Grant us wis - dom, Grant us cour - age,

For the fac - ing of this hour, For the fac - ing of this hour.
For the liv - ing of these days, For the liv - ing of these days.
Lest we miss Thy king-dom's goal, Lest we miss Thy king-dom's goal.
That we fail not man nor Thee, That we fail not man nor Thee.
Serv - ing Thee whom we a - dore, Serv - ing Thee whom we a - dore.

Day by day the promise reads,
Daily strength for daily needs.
Cast foreboding fear away,
Take the manna of today.

Oh to be exempt from care,
By the energy of prayer.
Strong in faith with mind subdued
And elate with gratitude.

Meditate on the Hymns

In his memoirs, President George W. Bush recounts what happened on September 11, 2011. He was in a schoolroom in Florida when he learned the towers of the World Trade Center had been hit and that America was under attack. As the Secret Service was rushing him down Florida Route 41, he learned a third plane had struck the Pentagon. He sat back in his seat and absorbed the news. By the time he arrived at *Air Force One*, it was clear that the White House was on war footing. Agents carried assault rifles and surrounded the airplane. Bush entered the 747, stepped into the Presidential Cabin, and asked to be alone. He thought of the fear that was seizing the nation. He could see the fear on the faces of the flight attendants onboard the plane. He thought of those who had already been killed in the attacks and of their families.

There alone in that little office, getting ready for the takeoff, Bush prayed for guidance; then he thought of the lyrics of one of his favorite hymns, "God of Grace and God of Glory." The recurring refrain of the hymn says: "Grant us wisdom, grant us courage, for the facing of this hour."[88]

Sometimes we can't sing the hymn, but if we know the words we can let them roll over our minds like a gentle stream, refreshing and renewing our courage.

Play the Hymns

We have two ways of playing the hymns. Some people can play them on musical instruments; the rest of us have to play them on the radio or its modern electronic equivalent. The good news is that hymns have never been more accessible than now. Before we wring our hands too much about the loss of hymns, remember that no generation has enjoyed greater, quicker, more complete and instant access to hymns than ours. You're as close to a beloved hymn as your portable electronic gizmo. Virtually all the hymns are somewhere on the Internet or can be found through an online music provider. We've gone from records to tapes to discs to instant downloads. It's never been easier to listen to your favorite hymns ancient or modern.

We've also got buttons on our radio dials that connect us with Christian stations. Not long ago, I dropped off a rental car and met the lady who tidies the car for the next customer. She told me that as a believer she had found a simple way to witness. "Every time I process a returned car," she said, "I make sure the buttons are preset to Christian stations and that my favorite Christian station is selected first whenever the customer turns on the radio. Who knows when someone will hear a song or sermon and be saved."

I suggest you have Christian music playing as your children come into the kitchen for breakfast in the morning. Listen to Christian music traveling in the car or van. Consider the great hymns as one of the ways of fulfilling Deuteronomy 6:7, which tells us to talk with our children about the Scriptures as we sit at home and as we walk along the way, when we rise up and when we go to bed.

When appropriate, play the great hymns of the faith in sick rooms and hospitals. I recall Ruth Bell Graham telling us that during the final illness of her mother, Virginia Bell, nothing soothed the frail old woman like hearing her favorite hymns. Ruth collected those hymns, playing them often, and later a record producer developed an album based on the selections.

Pray the Hymns

There's something even better than *playing* the hymns, and that's *praying* the hymns. In recent years, a number of books have taught us how to "pray the Scriptures." What a powerful practice! In the same way, we can pray the hymns. Think of how many of our great hymns are written as prayers.

There are prayers of aspiration like "Come, Thou Fount of every blessing, tune my heart to sing Thy praise." There are prayers of reassurance, such as "Great is Thy faithfulness, O God our Father." There are hymns of thanksgiving like "Now Thank We All Our God." Or consider this little-known hymn of thanksgiving by the ailing nineteenth-century English hymnist Jane Fox Crewdson.

> *O Thou, Whose bounty fills my cup*
> *With every blessing meet!*
> *I give Thee thanks for every drop—*
> *The bitter and the sweet.*
>
> *I praise Thee for the desert road,*
> *And for the riverside;*
> *For all Thy goodness hath bestowed,*
> *And all Thy grace denied.*

Using hymns, we can sing prayers of praise: "All glory, laud, and honor, to Thee Redeemer, King. . . ." We can rededicate ourselves to Him by singing, "Have Thine own way, Lord, have Thine own way." We can face the future with Philip Doddridge's great hymn that says, "Tomorrow, Lord, is Thine / Lodged in Thy sovereign hand."

We can also turn the hymns into prayers for others by tweaking them a little, especially in the use of pronouns. Years ago when I was worried about someone I loved, I took the hymn "Teach Me Thy Way, O Lord." I changed it to say, "Teach him Your way, O Lord, teach him Your way. / Your guiding grace afford, teach him Your way. / Help him to walk aright,

Come, Thou Fount of Every Blessing

Robert Robinson

Traditional American Melody

1. Come, Thou fount of ev-ery bless-ing, Tune my heart to sing Thy grace.
2. Here I raise my Eb-e-ne-zer; Hith-er by Thy help I come.
3. Oh, to grace how great a debt-or Dai-ly I'm con-strained to be!

Streams of mer-cy, nev-er ceas-ing, Call for songs of loud-est praise.
And I hope, by Thy good plea-sure, Safe-ly to ar-rive at home.
Let thy grace, Lord, like a fet-ter, Bind my wan-d'ring heart to Thee:

Teach me some me-lo-dious son-net, Sung by flam-ing tongues a-bove.
Je-sus sought me when a stran-ger Wand'ring from the fold of God;
Prone to wan-der, Lord, I feel it, Prone to leave the God I love.

Praise the mount! I'm fixed up-on it, Mount of God's un-chang-ing love.
He, to res-cue me from dan-ger, In-ter-posed His pre-cious blood.
Here's my heart, Lord, take and seal it, Seal it for Thy courts a-bove.

more by faith less by sight. / Lead him with heavenly light. Teach him Your way."

It takes very little effort to turn your hymnbook into a prayerbook. It's made for that.

Sing the Hymns

Obviously we should sing the hymns. At least, it seems obvious to me; but don't just sing them at church. The famous missionary Amy Carmichael once told of a time in her childhood when, during a family vacation on the northern Irish coast, she and her siblings had gone rowing. It wasn't a safe place for children, and their getting in the boat had been foolhardy. The tides were very powerful. The children were caught in the currents and being swept toward the open sea. Her two brothers, straining at the oars, looked up at Amy in alarm and shouted, "Sing!"

"I sang at the top of my voice the first thing that came into my head," she said. It was the hymn:

> *He leadeth me, O blessed thought,*
> *O words with heavenly comfort fraught;*
> *Whate'er I do, where'er I be,*
> *Still 'tis God's hand that leadeth me!*

"It certainly wasn't God's hand that led us out into forbidden water," Amy later wrote, "but it was He who caused the coastguard men to hear that song and row quickly to the rescue; so we weren't swept over the bar."[89]

Recently I received a letter from a man named Roy Swanberg who lives in Princeton, Illinois. In 1962, Mr. Swanberg was stationed with American forces in the countryside of England. On this particular occasion, he had worked hard for several days on a difficult assignment, and he was exhausted. It was almost time for him to go off duty, and just at that moment his sergeant approached him and chewed him out over some small matter not even of his own doing.

Roy was steamed, or as he told me, "spitt'n mad," and as soon as his shift was over he stormed down the road, determined to leave the base and hike off his anger. He forgot that English traffic moves on the opposite side of the road, and just as the sun went down a large truck brushed past him, sending him tumbling into the ditch.

That made matters worse, and Roy decided he didn't care if he was hit or not. He was far from home, exhausted, lonely, and feeling sorry for himself. He said that if some temptation had offered itself to him at that moment, he'd probably have done it, whatever it was. He kept walking through a town or two, and he walked all night in a big circle.

The sun was coming up as he headed back to base. His thoughts turned of home. At five-thirty in the morning in England, his family would still be asleep back in Minnesota. They were proud of their only son, serving in the military. He thought of his sisters and friends and neighborhood and school back in Minneapolis, and of his church. And to his surprise, he started thinking about his childhood Sunday school classes and his childhood teachers.

And he thought of the Sunday school songs he had learned as a child—"The B-I-B-L-E: Yes, that's the book for me." He began to hum the tunes to "Jesus Loves Me," and "Thank You, Lord, For Saving My Soul." He began singing aloud the words of "Heavenly Sunshine," "Blessed Assurance," and "Trust and Obey."

Near the end of his long nocturnal walk, Roy remembered the song that says "I Have the Joy, Joy, Joy, Joy Down in My Heart." It was truly a personal revival. He arrived back at camp, cleaned up, got dressed for a new day, and though he hadn't slept all night, went back to work, greeted his sergeant with a smile, and dove back into his work with the joy of Jesus in his heart.

Some time ago, I saw two verses in Psalm 106 that struck me with the force of their contrast.

- Verse 12 says the Israelites, after their deliverance at the Red Sea, *believed His promises and sang His praise.*
- Verses 24–25 contain these interesting words: *They did not believe His promise. They grumbled in their tents.*

When we believe His promises, we sing; when we don't, we grumble. Both morning and evening, both in public and private, let's sing the hymns, thinking about the words and using the verses to help us sing our great Redeemer's praise.

Proclaim the Hymns

Every Sunday churches around the world sing the great hymns of the faith; but sometimes there's an extra punch in our voice. We're proclaiming, evangelizing, testifying, and even sometimes singing with godly defiance before a hostile world.

In her book *Jungle Harvest*, Ruby Scott told of working among the Tila Chol Indians in southwestern Mexico. On one occasion, the young church there faced a time of humiliating disappointment. The local witch doctor had vowed to completely destroy the Christian influence. The Christians took the threat seriously and began memorizing Scriptures emphasizing the power and authority of Christ.

Among the converts was a former alcoholic named Rosendo, whose testimony had touched many in the area. Once known as the village drunk, he had become a hardworking family man who bore a clear testimony for Christ. Nevertheless, through a diabolical series of events, Rosendo was lured back into a state of public drunkenness and the Christians became the laughingstock of the village. The ridicule was merciless, and the witch doctor delighted in fanning the flames.

The next Sunday, Rosendo made his way to church with his eyes down. Standing before the Christians, he confessed what he had done and quoted a verse about God's forgiveness. "I have not only brought shame to our Lord, but to you, too," he said. "I'm sorry. I don't know if you want to forgive me or not."

Sitting down, he buried his face in his hands.

Suddenly another Christian stood up, a man named Felix. He told of how his young son had fallen facedown into a mud puddle. The boy was muddy, but the splatter had also splashed up on the father. But Felix had not rejected his son; he had held him until he stopped crying and then cleaned him up.

"Friends," he continued, "our brother Rosendo has fallen on his face in the mud. We have a Heavenly Father who loves him, has helped him up, and wiped the mud off him. He will hold him close and love him until the pain and embarrassment goes away. All of us have felt the splat of Rosendo's fall. We have been laughed at—and it hurt. But our Lord suffered a much deeper hurt for the things we have done."

The congregation agreed, and someone stood up and started singing a hymn—"How Great Thou Art." With one accord, the whole church burst into song with great swells of joy. Then came another hymn, followed by another. For a solid hour, the church reverberated with hymns until the pastor stood to preach a spontaneous but powerful sermon tailored to the situation. The church had peace and continued to grow, and Ruby Scott and her coworker Viola Warkentin realized that the Word of God had been translated successfully not only into the Tila language, but into the Tila hearts.[90]

The songs pealing from the little church that day were weapons. Every word was a message and every note a missile. No one in the town missed the point. We may sometimes fall and fail, but we have an infallible God and an unfailing Savior, and there's "Victory in Jesus."

Quote the Hymns

Hymns are as powerful when quoted as when sung. When the British "Prince of Preachers" Charles Spurgeon was a boy, his grandfather offered to pay him a bit of money for every hymn he memorized. Propelled by the bargain, young Charles committed many hymns to memory. Now whenever you read a Spurgeon sermon (they're masterpieces of encouragement), you can't help noticing how virtually every message is punctuated with fragments and phrases from hymns. Spurgeon salted his messages with the quoted verses of hymns.

As a preacher, I've found that nothing is more powerful than moving effortlessly from a preached sentence to a quoted hymn. If preaching from Philippians 3, for example, about suffering the loss of all things for Christ, it's natural and impacting to insert from memory the words . . .

> *When I survey the wondrous cross*
> *On which the Prince of Glory died,*
> *My richest gain I count but loss,*
> *And pour contempt on all my pride.*

When sharing a word of testimony or exalting in God's ability to liberate us from our sins and addictions, I often quote the thrilling fourth verse of Wesley's "And Can It Be?"

> *Long my imprisoned spirit lay*
> *Fast bound in sin and nature's night;*
> *Thine eye diffused a quickening ray—*
> *I woke, the dungeon flamed with light;*
> *My chains fell off, my heart was free,*
> *I rose, went forth, and followed Thee!*
> *Amazing love! How can it be,*
> *That Thou, my God, shouldst die for me?*

How often in sickrooms and hospital corridors have I quoted Cowper's "God Moves in a Mysterious Way" or Gerhardt's "Commit Whatever Grieves Thee." The fourth verse of "How Firm a Foundation" is a metrical paraphrase of one of my favorite Bible verses (Isaiah 41:10) and excellent to quote:

He Leadeth Me

Joseph H. Gilmore

William B. Bradbury

1. He lead-eth me, O bless-ed thought! O words with heaven-ly com-fort fraught!
2. Some-times 'mid scenes of deep-est gloom, Some-times where E-den's bow-ers bloom,
3. Lord, I would clasp Thy hand in mine, Nor ev-er mur-mur nor re-pine;
4. And when my task on earth is done, When by Thy grace the vic-t'ry's won,

What -e'er I do, where-e'er I be, Still 'tis God's hand that lead-eth me.
By wa-ters still, o'er trou-bled sea, Still 'tis His hand that lead-eth me!
Con -tent what-ev-er lot I see, Since 'tis my God that lead-eth me.
E'en death's cold wave I will not flee, Since God through Jor-dan lead-eth me.

He lead-eth me, He lead-eth me, By His own hand He lead-eth me;

His faith-ful fol-lower I would be, For by His hand He lead-eth me.

Fear not, I am with thee, O be not dismayed,
For I am Thy God, I will still give Thee aid.

Memorize the hymns so you can quote them in letters, in conversations, in Bible studies, and from the pulpit.

Lean on the Hymns

As we read, memorize, ponder, play, sing, proclaim, and quote the hymns, we'll find ourselves leaning on them in the process, drawing strength from their rich doctrines, internalizing their biblical theology, and relying upon the Lord whom we're lauding. Paul Creech is a fellow pastor, ten years my junior, who lives in Georgia. We serve together on a missionary board and I have utmost respect for him. Several years ago he battled cancer, and I was greatly impressed by his attitude and spirit. Recently we received the difficult news that his cancer has returned.

I was in Georgia last month on a speaking engagement, and Paul was there. He stood in the meeting to say a few words and to give his testimony. He was frail and using a walker. His young son was with him. Paul read a little poem he had written. It was called "Again," the letters A-G-A-I-N standing for "Almighty God Always Is Near."

Almighty God always is near
With a warm hug, wiping my tear.
His love is strong, driving out my fear;
Almighty God always is near.

Encore, a double dip, or two
That's been my habit, how about you?
Rerun movies seem better the second time around,
A gentle kiss lifts the foot off the ground.

Again, the doctor said, with a forced smile;
My breath trapped in my throat for a while.
Cancer—it's back, oh what dread,
Biopsy confirmed it, was what he said.

Then I heard God's whisper, soft, stead, and sure,
We've done this before, this time is no chore.
Hold My hand and stay near, let go of every fear,
I'm with you AGAIN, I always am near.

And then Paul burst into singing. He didn't have a piano or guitar to accompany him; it was a cappella; and Paul doesn't have a trained voice. But it moved all of us deeply. It was a simple medley. The first verse was from Doug Little's song "He's Been So Good to Me." Then there was a verse of "The Love of God," and then a verse of "Great Is Thy Faithfulness." We sat and listened in poignant silence, for we felt we were on holy ground. In leaning on the hymns, Paul was leaning on his Lord.

Pass the Hymns Down to Your Children

Appreciating the hymns as I've described in this chapter is the best way of passing them down to the next generation. One of the reasons I love the hymns today is because I heard my mother sing hymns like "When They Ring Those Golden Bells for You and Me" as she went about her housework. I recall my dad singing in the choir on Sundays. When my own girls were small, I'd often rock them to sleep singing my favorite hymns or some of the new songs we were learning at that time, such as "Oh, How He Loves You and Me."

Some parents take it a step further.

Dr. David Outlaw and his wife, Angie, are dear friends of mine who love the hymns. David told me just this evening how they have chosen a hymn for each of their five children as a lifelong theme song. It began when their firstborn, Carson, was an infant. They found that he almost always fell asleep at night when they rocked him and sang the old Gospel song "I Know the Master of the Wind." Their next child, Victoria, seemed to fall asleep best with the hymn "O Worship the King."

And then came Conner—early. After a troubled pregnancy, Angie gave birth to a premature little boy who spent the first seven weeks of his life in neonatal intensive care unit. David and Angie stayed by his incubator day and night as he fought for life, and every night they read him Psalm 139 and sang the hymn "I Sing the Mighty Power of God." Conner did just fine, thank you. That became the theme song of his life and solidified the practice of assigning each child a hymn.

By the time Schaeffer arrived, his hymn was already in place: "Holy, Holy, Holy." David told me, "We sang it for the first time in the hospital; and just as we were about to begin, the anesthesiologist walked into the room. Turns out he was a Christian, and so he joined in and sang with us that first time."

Baby Number Five was Elizabeth Grace, who was given the hymn "Grace Greater than All Our Sin," with its wonderful uplifting words: "Grace, Grace, God's Grace . . ."

Every night, David and Angie tuck in each child with the singing of their special hymn.

Oh yes, here's a P.S. to the story. Last year, Schaeffer was hit by a car while riding his bicycle down the street. Angie ran to his side while a passing doctor administered treatment. To calm him down, the family encircled him, held his hand, and sang his hymn—"Holy, Holy, Holy." Conner has recovered from his injuries, but he'll never outlive the memories of God in Three Persons, Blessed Trinity.

Start Each Day with a Hymn

Psalm 92 declares: "It is good to praise the LORD and make music to your name, O Most High, to proclaim your love in the morning and your faithfulness at night" (verses 1–2).

The most important thing about our day is how we begin it. If we get started on the right foot, we'll be ahead of the game all day long. The heroes of Scripture certainly knew this. In the Sinai wilderness, the Israelites went out and gathered manna to eat each morning (Exodus 16:21). When the tabernacle was set up, Aaron was told to burn fragrant incense on the altar every morning when he tended the lamps (Exodus 30:7). The priests were to begin each day with the morning sacrifices (Leviticus 6:12).

When King David established the regular worship patterns in the capital city of Jerusalem, he decreed that each day should begin with the Levitical choirs singing and thanking and praising God (1 Chronicles 23:30).

We're told that Job began the day by offering sacrifices early in the morning for his family (Job 1:5).

The psalmist said, "In the morning, O LORD, you hear my voice; in the morning I lay my requests before you and wait in expectation" (Psalm 5:3).

The author of Psalm 59:16 wrote, "In the morning I will sing of your love; for you are my fortress, my refuge in times of trouble."

In Psalm 88:13, he prayed, "In the morning my prayer comes before you."

Moses prayed in Psalm 90:14, "Satisfy us in the morning with your unfailing love, that we may sing for joy and be glad all our days."

Isaiah said, "In the morning my spirit longs for you. . . . Be our strength every morning . . ." (Isaiah 26:9; 33:2). And later he wrote, "The Sovereign LORD has given me an instructed tongue, to know the word that sustains the weary. He wakens me morning by morning; wakens my ear to listen like one being taught" (Isaiah 50:4).

Jeremiah, the weeping prophet, was encouraged by the knowledge that God's compassions never fail. "They are new every morning," he said, "great is your faithfulness" (Lamentations 3:23).

The prophet Ezekiel said, "In the morning the word of the LORD came to me" (Ezekiel 12:8).

The Bible's greatest example of how to start the day is this simple verse in Mark 1:35: "Very early in the morning, while it was still dark, Jesus got up, left the house and went off to a solitary place, where he prayed." And, of course, the first disciples trekked to the garden tomb and found it empty early on Easter morning. Up from the grave He arose!

Here is my suggestion: Learn to begin each day with an appointment with the Lord during which you read His Word, offer a prayer, seek His agenda for your day, and sing a hymn. End the day the same way. Let the hymns become daylong and lifelong companions, and never be without a song.

As Eliza Hewitt put it in her happy chorus:

Singing I go along life's road,
Praising the Lord, praising the Lord!
Singing I go along life's road,
For Jesus has lifted my load.

In Public: Old New Praise—
Why We Must Embrace
Interwoven Worship

T he Old New Synagogue sits like a gothic treasure chest in the heart of Prague's famed Jewish Quarter. It's a vaulted rectangle of gables, naves and bays, and windows—twelve of them, for the twelve tribes of Israel. As Europe's oldest extant Jewish synagogue, it has become a beacon of survival in a threatening world. Why is it called the "Old New" Synagogue? When first built it was dubbed the New or Great Synagogue. But as newer synagogues were built in Prague, people started calling it the Old New Synagogue. The name stuck.

I'm an advocate of Old New churches too, especially in our worship habits. In the years since we published the first volume of *Then Sings My Soul*, a lot of mail has landed on my desk from fellow hymn-lovers. Some of them have taken a dig at the newer music we're hearing now at church. One man, for example, told me, "Thank you for writing about the great hymns of the faith. I love the hymns. I dislike this new Christian music everyone is singing nowadays."

Well, he actually said "hate," but I think he meant "dislike."

I usually respond to these kinds of letters by saying something like this: "I love the old hymns too, and we want to keep them alive and popular. But it's also important to remember that if there's ever a generation of Christians who don't write its own music, Christianity is dead. Every generation needs to compose its own praises—and those songs written by a younger generation aren't likely to sound exactly like those of prior eras. We should learn to enjoy both."

I want to appeal for this kind of interwoven worship—a style of public

Praise God, from Whom All Blessings Flow

Thomas Ken

att. to Louis Bourgeois

Praise God from whom all bless - ings flow.

Praise Him, all crea - tures here be - low.

Praise Him a - bove, ye heav'n - ly host.

Praise Fa - ther, Son and Ho - ly Ghost. A - men.

praise that incorporates the old hymns and the newer music with seamless joy. There's a sense in which our worship should not be traditional or contemporary but timeless. I believe heaven will ring with songs from all the ages, so why shouldn't we begin now? If worship unites the entire family of God—past, present, and future—isn't it appropriate to intertwine the ancient with the modern? When I sing the Doxology, I'm joining in an exercise of praise known to my grandparents and great-grandparents. When I sing the newest upbeat chorus from a praise-and-worship band, I'm joining voices with my grandkids.

Narrow bands of worship are harmful and consumeristic. I'm an outspoken advocate for integrated, interblended, intermixed worship—the old and the new interwoven. There has never been a generation of Christians that sang only its own music while discarding all the songs of prior epochs.

Blended worship is the standard operating procedure for church history. When the New Testament Christians developed the songs we see in the New Testament, they didn't stop singing the psalms of David. When Ambrose and the early hymnists created new music for their generation, they didn't discard the older hymns from the first and second centuries. When Isaac Watts was writing his newfangled hymns in the early 1700s, the congregations still sang from the Psalter. When Fanny Crosby gave us "Blessed Assurance," the church didn't discard "A Mighty Fortress" or "All Hail the Power." When I was growing up, we sang John W. Peterson's new songs alongside "Holy, Holy, Holy." We added the new music to the old and enjoyed both together. That's generally the way it's been done until now.

I'm troubled at churches that only sing contemporary praise-and-worship songs at the expense of the great classics of Christian history. On the other hand, some churches never sing anything written after 1950. I belong to one particular group that for some reason won't sing anything at its annual meetings that isn't at least a decade old. The participants often criticize praise-and-worship music; but if the dubious chorus is at least ten years old, it gets slipped into the order of service. We're late adopters. On the other hand, I'm tired of going to conferences that treat hymns as if they carried the plague.

While every congregation and Christian group has its unique profile and demographic, I think it's generally unhealthy to veer away from interwoven worship at our public meetings. At one time our church had a traditional service and a separate contemporary service. That approach increasingly troubled me. We were telling people they were consumers to be catered to, not intergenerational worshippers gathering at God's throne. We were saying . . .

- If you want to sing your own music to the exclusion of everyone else's, that's fine. We'll cater to you.
- If you want to enjoy your one small slice of musical preference while rejecting all others, that's fine. We'll cater to you.
- If you want to ignore two thousand years of heritage—or if you want to neglect a whole new generation of young worshippers— not a problem. We'll cater to you.
- If you want to be among the most narrow worshippers in the history of Christianity and only sing the constricted little grouping of songs that you happen to like, fine. We'll cater to you.

A few years ago, we decided to stop catering and start leading. We introduced our church to Old New worship. I was told it would never work, but it has worked and it will continue to work. It only fails among unusually intolerant folks, for Christianity in all its dimensions has always thrived on being anchored to the rock but geared to the times (as Youth for Christ says in its historic slogan).

Younger worshippers need the legacy of the great hymns; and older worshippers need the exuberance of fresh praise. That's the long and short of it. Being seeker-friendly doesn't exclude the great hymns. Modern sinners need to know that Jesus Shall Reign, that Christ the Lord Is Risen Today, and that There Is a Fountain Filled with Blood. They need to realize There Is a Balm in Gilead and Jesus Paid it All.

Disregarding two thousand years of hymnody is irresponsible and, if not corrected, irreversible. I do sense we're in danger of losing the great hymns of the faith. For several years, I've had the privilege of lecturing before graduate-level students at one of the world's leading seminaries for worship leaders. Sitting before me in the classroom are young men and women who have dedicated their lives to the ministry of music. They are the best of the best, and each is sharp, dedicated, earnest, and a lover of worship. But they look at me with blank expressions when I begin discussing some of my favorite old hymns—"If Thou but Suffer God to Guide Thee," "When Morning Gilds the Skies," "Praise the Savior, Ye Who Know Him," "My Faith Looks Up to Thee," "I Heard the Voice of Jesus Say," "In Heavenly Love Abiding," "Jesus, I Am Resting, Resting."

I am astounded that these emerging worship leaders in the graduate program of a conservative evangelical seminary do not know the hymns, except for a handful of the most famous titles. I somehow feel the old hymns are fading away like World War II veterans passing from the scene, a few each day. Soon they'll all be gone. But if we lose the legacy of our past, we have no foundation for the future.

Several years ago, I wrote a book entitled *On This Day in Christian History* because I've been concerned we're becoming an era of Christians with little or no knowledge of the "great cloud of witnesses" who have preceded us. We somehow think we poofed into existence with no trail of blood and valor behind us. Most people won't take the time to read great tomes on Christian history, but I thought a daily glimpse at an event from the past would provide small doses of our rich legacy. *Then Sings My Soul* is the musical companion to *On This Day in Christian History*. The stories and the songs of all the ages comprise a heritage too great to lose.

The good news is that great hymns can be rediscovered, revived, and woven into the mixture of the musical formulas used every Sunday by millions of Christians in hundreds of thousands of churches. We can tell the stories behind the hymns, as I've tried to do in the *Then Sings My Soul* series. We can present them in new musical settings. We can write new melodies to old words, and put new twists onto old tunes.

Praise Ye the Lord, the Almighty

Joachim Neander

Straslund Gesangbuch

1. Praise to the Lord, the Al - might - y, The King of cre - a - tion!
2. Praise to the Lord, Who o'er all things So won-drous-ly reign - eth,
3. Praise to the Lord! O let all that is in me a - dore Him!
4. Praise to the Lord, Who doth pros - per Thy work and de - fend thee;

O my soul, praise Him, For He is thy health and sal - va - tion!
Shel - ters thee un - der His wings, Yes, so gent - ly sus - tain - eth!
All that hath life and breath, Come now with prais - es be - fore Him.
Sure - ly His good - ness and mer - cy Here dail - y at - tend thee.

All ye who hear, Now to His tem - ple draw near;
Hast Thou not seen How all thy long - ings have been
Let the a - men sound from His peo - ple a - gain:
Pon - der a - new what the Al - might - y can do,

Join me in glad ad - o - ra - tion!
Grant - ed in what He or - dain - eth?
Glad - ly for aye we a - dore Him.
If with His love He be - friend thee.

But we cannot afford to lose the hymns.

At the same time, our appreciation for the hymns doesn't preclude us from embracing next-generation praise. I hope I never become too old to sing the newest songs of praise to the Lord. Ecclesiastes 7:10 warns us about living in the past, saying, "Do not say, 'Why were the old days better than these?' For it is not wise to ask such questions."

Last week I had lunch with a man who complained that the music in our church is too loud. I think the word "loud" was a synonym for several sentiments he was feeling. I reminded him that every service contains hymns and Gospel songs, along with some of the newer expressions of praise.

"Yes, but even the hymns are jazzed up," he said.

Well, maybe a little. But I tried to tell him that perhaps his attitude was at least half the problem. "Rather than complaining about the music," I said, "why not rejoice that every Sunday you're surrounded by people of all ages—including tons of young people—exuberantly praising the Lord!"

Yes, we sold the organ at our church. I was not in favor of it. I love the organ, but I didn't get my way on that issue. I'm not going to pout. I just downloaded my favorite organ hymns onto my iPod.

Yes, we have guitars and drums. But remember—in Bible times they liked their strings and cymbals.

Yes, we use projected words. I do miss the hymnals, but I also like the smooth transitions that the screens allow in singing tapestries of praise. And I keep a hymnal at my desk for my devotions, so I haven't really lost it at all. I mark it up like a Bible.

Yes, we do sometimes jazz up the old hymns. But I still recognize them, and the kids behind me enjoy singing them. So I say praise the Lord for that! We very often complain about the very things for which we should be thankful.

And speaking of complaining . . .

Complaining about your church's music may say as much about you or me as about our worship leaders. We certainly have an obligation to offer appropriate input and we can speak up for the old hymns. I do. But beware of a grumbling spirit. Complaining tends by its very nature to run against the spirit of the Bible, which warns about "murmuring in our tents."

I've been in enough churches to recognize the personalities who believe they're the plumb line of opinion. If anything happens they don't like, it's tantamount to the steeple falling or the roof caving in. I'm not going to bedevil my worship leader or my church staff because they don't completely share my tastes. I want to learn from them, and I want to have good relationships with them. That way perhaps one day they'll take a deep breath and include "The God of Abraham Praise" in the order of service.

A related subject that frequently shows up in my correspondence has to do with the quality of praise-and-worship music, or the lack thereof. It's said that much modern hymnody is uneven in the quality of lyrics and melodies. It lacks depth; and many important subjects aren't addressed. Yes, that's true. That was also true for the golden era of English hymns. Untold thousands of songs were written. Charles Wesley wrote over six thousand hymns. Most of them quickly faded into disuse; but not all. And without the large quantity of attempts, we wouldn't have gleaned the ones of enduring value.

In essence, what I'm saying is a reflection of our Lord's law of the kingdom in Matthew 13:52—wise stewards bring out of their storehouses treasures both old and new. The loss of either the old or the new is greater than we can bear. Worship wars are a useless exercise. The same Bible that gives us three-thousand-year-old psalms to sing also tells us to sing a new song unto the Lord.

Let's be Old New worshippers. Support your worship leader. Enjoy the drums. Retain the organ if you can. Learn the new songs, and adapt to them with grace in your heart. And don't let the great hymns of the church fade away.

Epilogue

Hymn Lover Emeritus

I 'd like to close the *Then Sings My Soul* set of books with a brief tribute to a dear friend of Katrina's and mine, Cliff Barrows, Hymn Lover Emeritus. No one has done more than Cliff during the last sixty years to popularize the power of Christian song. His choirs and musicians on Billy Graham's televised evangelistic crusades introduced new songs and reintroduced old ones to the world. He uncovered and popularized such classics as Fanny Crosby's "To God Be the Glory," and the beloved hymn of the ages, "How Great Thou Art." His infectious attitude, constant smile, and uplifting voice brought the history of hymnody into our homes and hearts for two generations.

I first met Cliff when I was a student at Columbia International University in Columbia, South Carolina, where Cliff came to preach for several nights. Having grown up in a family that regularly watched Billy Graham's televised crusades, I had admired his friendly voice and easy smile. But I didn't know he could preach. He delivered wonderful sermons to us during the college chapel services. One day he met me in the student center. I asked, "Mr. Barrows, what would you advise me to do about ministry? I think God may be calling me to preach or pastor, but I'm not sure."

"Robert," he said, "if you can do anything other than preach, do it. But if you find that you're not happy unless you're in the pulpit, than that's what you should do."

Shortly afterward I got a job working with the Billy Graham team as a sort of intern or gofer, serving in the Atlanta and Tidewater crusades. I saw Cliff up close under intense pressure. Though he expected excellence from himself and those around him, he never lost his poise, his smile, or the friendly texture of his voice.

Years passed, and we were together again when Billy and Cliff came to Nashville in 2000 for one of their final crusades. Subsequently, my wife, Katrina, and I have gotten to know him and Ann and we've reveled in his treasure trove of stories, his keen insights, and his frequently quoted stanzas of great hymns and simple poems.

I once had coffee with him when I asked if, during his long years of rigorous ministry and travel, he suffered periods of discouragement. He thought a moment then said, "Rob, I have never known a despondent day." Surprised, I asked him how that could be, to which he replied with heartfelt sincerity, "It's because the joy of the Lord is the strength of my life." He went on to quote to me an old Horatius Bonar hymn that I've since memorized myself and included among the hymn stories in this book:

> *Fill Thou my life, O Lord my God,*
> *In every part with praise,*
> *That my whole being may proclaim*
> *Thy being and Thy ways.*
>
> *Fill every part of me with praise;*
> *Let all my being speak*
> *Of Thee and of Thy love, O Lord,*
> *Poor though I be and weak.*
>
> *So shall each fear, each fret, each care*
> *Be turned into a song,*
> *And every winding of the way*
> *The echo shall prolong.*
>
> *So shall no part of day or night*
> *From sacredness be free;*
> *But all my life, in every step,*
> *Be fellowship with Thee.*

Cliff enjoys telling how in 1944, as a twenty-two-year-old newly married man, he was on his honeymoon with his wife, Billie. In Asheville, North Carolina, a friend took them to hear a young North Carolina preacher named Billy Graham who was speaking at Ben Lippen Conference Center. A crisis arose when there was no song leader for the service. Someone recommended Cliff. According to Cliff's account, Billy said, "Well, we can't be choosy."

Billy and Cliff went on to become the most far-flung evangelistic team in history. I asked Cliff what had happened to the regular music director that evening.

"He got sick," he said laconically.

As much as I appreciate the hymns, Cliff inspires me to love and learn them more than ever. He knows more hymns by heart than anyone I've ever met. You're never with him without his quoting verses to hymns. He struggles now with impaired vision and has trouble seeing the hymnbook. But I was amazed to watch him lead music recently. He led every hymn by heart—with all their verses. He knows hundreds (thousands, I think) of hymns by heart. When I asked him about it, he said with his characteristic enthusiasm: "Rob, the great hymns of the faith are continually flooding my mind. I revel in trying to recall their words."

He began learning hymns early, in childhood, for his mother urged him to memorize the hymnbook. "It will be of great help to you in the future," she said. "It will be a constant source of encouragement in your life and work." She had no idea how much her advice would mean years later when he was leading great crusade choirs of multiplied thousands in the greatest arenas and stadiums on earth.

Cliff's father loved the hymns too, though he wasn't a musically gifted man. The Barrows had a dairy farm, and one day Cliff's father said to him, "It's time you learned to milk old Betsy the cow. Let's go to the barn and I'll show you how it's done and you can start tomorrow." Entering the barn, Mr. Barrows grabbed the milking stool and pail, sat down, cleaned off the working area, and loudly started singing a hymn. His pitch was off and the singing wasn't on key, but he sang hymns the whole time he was milking.

The next morning Cliff went out to assume the work. Positioning the stool, he cleaned off the spigots, sat down with the pail, started into a hymn, and went to work. All went well at first, but suddenly Betsy hauled off and gave Cliff an unexpected kick that overturned both him and the stool, and spilled the milk.

As Cliff tells it, he went running into the house, found his dad, and humorously complained, "Dad, you've been singing off-key so long to that old cow that she doesn't appreciate good singing when she hears it!"

On another occasion, the elder Barrows, who was an avid Gideon, traveled to Rangoon. The area was under an oppressive government, and Gideon Bibles had been removed from the hotel rooms. While there, he attended a meeting of the local Gideons who were trying to get Bibles back into the hotels. During the meeting two men were singing hymns in one end of the room, and the singing was disruptive. Mr. Barrows had trouble following the discussions because the two hymn-singers were going at it a few yards away. Finally he asked, "Why are those men singing while we're trying to have this meeting?"

The local Gideon replied, "Because this room is bugged, and the singing confuses the enemy who is trying to listen to us."

Glancing over to me, Cliff said, "There's a spiritual lesson in that. When we sing, it confuses the enemy and allows the Lord's work to proceed."

I've asked Cliff how he used the hymns in his own personal devotions. "When you were on the road," I asked, "coming back to your hotel at late hours from the crusade services with their tens of thousands and hundreds of thousands of people, how did you unwind and get yourself settled down for bed?"

"I always carried a harmonica with me," he said. "Back in my hotel room, I would pull out my harmonica and play the great hymns of the faith. They would relax my spirit. Bev Shea was often in a room nearby, and he said he could sometimes hear them through the ventilator. Then

I would lay out my Bible, my devotional book, and my harmonica on the desk so they'd be ready the next morning when I rose for my morning devotions."

To my surprise, his wife, Ann, opened his briefcase and there, in its original box wrapped in a rubber band, was his old tried-and-true harmonica. He still carries it with him. "I used to play the trombone," he said, "but I don't have the air for it anymore. My lungs hardly have enough power for the harmonica, but nothing can diminish the sound of the great hymns of the faith as they flood through my thoughts day and night. It is a devotional exercise to endeavor to recall the words of the stanzas."

The last couple of times I've been with Cliff, he's said, "Let me leave you with a little poem." And he has quoted a little verse by Wilbur D. Nesbit that's evidently one of his favorites. It's not a hymn; not even a Gospel song. But it does reflect the life and legacy of a man whose life is fueled by the joy of the Lord and whose trademark smile is legendary. It begins . . .

The thing that goes the furthest to making life worthwhile;
That costs the least and does the most is just a pleasant smile.[91]

Thank you, Cliff Barrows, for your smile, for the friendly lift and lilt of your voice, for your radiant love for our Lord Jesus Christ, and for serving so many of us for so many years as a walking, rejoicing, personified hymnal.

Blessed Assurance, Jesus Is Mine!

For some time, I've been thinking of a special ending for this book. I'd like to take the final pages to invite you to the One who breaks the power of cancelled sin and sets the prisoner free. I long for everyone on earth to be able to say, "It is well with my soul. Jesus is all the world to me."

In the middle of the third verse of the great English hymn "Holy, holy, holy," Reginald Heber wrote some magnificent words:

> *Only Thou art Holy;*
> *There is none beside Thee,*
> *perfect in pow'r,*
> *in love and purity.*

The message of the gospel—the good news!—begins with the holiness of God. He is utterly unique, all glorious above, the Ancient of Days, God in Three Persons, Blessed Trinity. He is immortal, invisible, God only wise.

But another hymn expresses the opposite truth:

> *Prone to wander, Lord, I feel it;*
> *Prone to leave the God I love.*

As the apostle Paul put it in Romans 3:23: "All have sinned and fall short of the glory of God." All our griefs and sorrows are explained in that biblical word "sinned." God is holy, but we aren't. It's a divide greater than the Grand Canyon, greater than the distance between galaxies, greater than the gulf between heaven and hell. But not greater than the love of God.

> *The love of God is greater far*
> *Than tongue or pen can ever tell;*
> *It goes beyond the highest star,*
> *And reaches to the lowest hell.*

That's why God, His Son not sparing, sent Him to die though we scarce can take it in. Our great Redeemer came down upon a midnight clear, an infant holy, infant lowly, now in flesh appearing. In the little town of Bethlehem Jesus came forth to be born of a virgin. He proved His righteousness by living a holy life in a fallen world, and He died on a hill far away on an old rugged cross. It was grace broader than the scope of our transgressions and greater far than all our sin and shame.

Jesus paid it all. Sin had left a crimson stain, but He washed it white as snow. There is power in His blood, and His blood will never lose its power.

> *There is a fountain filled with blood*
> *Drawn from Emmanuel's veins,*
> *And sinners plunged beneath that flood*
> *Lose all their guilty stains.*

The core of gospel truth is this: "The wages of sin is death; but the gift of God is eternal life through Jesus Christ our Lord" (Romans 6:23 KJV).

> *Living He loved me,*
> *Dying He saved me,*
> *Buried He carried my sins far away.*
> *Rising He justified, freely forever,*
> *One day He's coming.*
> *O glorious day!*

The Lord wants to exchange our sin for His salvation, our hurt for His healing, and our hell for His heaven. He wants to give us blessed assurance, the confidence of knowing "I once was lost but now I'm found, was blind but now I see."

You can experience God's grace and the assurance of salvation right now by confessing your sins, trusting Christ as your Savior, and acknowledging Him as Lord. The Savior is waiting to enter your heart, waiting for you to say: "I have decided to follow Jesus. No turning back, no turning back."

If you'd like to receive the Lord Jesus as your Savior, or rededicate your life to His service, or find assurance of your salvation, just pray these simple words and make them your own.

Just as I am without one plea,
But that Thy blood was shed for me,
And that Thou bidst me come to Thee,
O Lamb of God, I come, I come.

Just as I am, and waiting not
To rid my soul of one dark blot,
To Thee whose blood can cleanse each spot,
O Lamb of God, I come, I come.

Just as I am, though tossed about
With many a conflict, many a doubt,
Fightings and fears within, without,
O Lamb of God, I come, I come.

After all, it's not the *hymns* that change our lives, but *Him*! Romans 10:9 says: "If you confess with your mouth, 'Jesus is Lord,' and believe in your heart that God raised him from the dead, you will be saved."

And what a day of rejoicing that will be!

Blessed Assurance

Fanny J. Crosby

Phoebe P. Knapp

1. Bless-ed as - sur - ance, Je - sus is mine! Oh, what a fore-taste of
2. Per - fect sub - mis-sion, per-fect de - light! Vi-sions of rap-ture now
3. Per - fect sub - mis-sion, all is at rest. I in my Sav-ior am

glo - ry di - vine! Heir of sal - va - tion, pur-chase of God,
burst at my sight! An - gels de - scend-ing bring from a - bove
hap-py and blest; Watch-ing and wait - ing, look-ing a - bove,

Born of His Spir - it, washed in His blood! This is my sto - ry,
Ech - oes of mer - cy, whis-pers of love.
Filled with His good-ness, lost in His love.

this is my song, Prais-ing my Sav - ior all the day long. This is my

sto - ry, this is my song, Prais-ing my Sav-ior all the day long.

Notes

1. Robert J. Morgan, *Near to the Heart of God* (Grand Rapids: Revell, 2010), 5.
2. Philip Schaff, *History of the Christian Church: Vol. III, Nicene and Post-Nicene Christianity* (Grand Rapids: Wm. B. Eerdmans Publishing Company, 1910), 576.
3. Frank Fortunato with Paul Neeley and Carol Brinneman, *All the World Is Singing* (Tyrone, GA: Authentic Publishing, 2006), 3–4
4. See my book *The Red Sea Rules* (Nashville: Thomas Nelson, 2001).
5. Paul L. Maier, *Eusebius: The Church History: A New Translation with Commentary* (Grand Rapids: Kregal, 1999), 201.
6. Richard Chenevix Trench, *Sacred Latin Poetry* (London: Macmillan & Co., 1874), 138.
7. Rev. James F. Lambert, *Luther's Hymns* (Philadelphia: General Council Publication House, 1917), 15.
8. Harry Eskew and Hugh T. McElrath, *Sing with Understanding: An Introduction to Christian Hymnology.*
9. Theodore L. Cuyler, who wrote the introduction to Ira Sankey's memoirs, described these Gospel songs as "a peculiar style of popular hymns which are calculated to awaken the careless, to melt the hardened, and to guide inquiring souls to the Lord Jesus Christ . . . powerful revival hymns." In Ira D. Sankey, *My Life and the Story of Gospel Hymns* (Philadelphia: The Sunday School Times, 1906), iii.
10. John Julian, *A Dictionary of Hymnology* (New York: Charles Scribner's Sons, 1892), 308.
11. Adapted from my book *Come Let Us Adore Him* (Nashville: J. Countryman, a division of Thomas Nelson Publishers, 2005), 76–77.

12. Adapted from my book *Come Let Us Adore Him* (Nashville: J. Countryman, a division of Thomas Nelson Publishers, 2005), 72–73.

13. Eleanor A. Towle, *John Mason Neale: A Memoir* (London: Longmans, Green, & Co., 1906), 214.

14. John Mason Neale, Mary Sackville Lawson, *Collected Hymns, Sequences and Carols* (London: Hodder and Stoughton, 1914), v–vi.

15. Thomas Ken, *Morning, Evening, and Midnight Hymns* (London: Daniel Sedgwick, 1864), xii.

16. Ibid., xiii.

17. Charles S. Nutter and Wilber F. Tillett, *The Hymns and Hymn Writers of the Church* (NY: The Methodist Book Connection, 1911), 373.

18. Frederick Arthur Clarke, *Thomas Ken* (London: Methuen & Co., 1905), 3.

19. Adapted from my book *Come Let Us Adore Him* (Nashville: J. Countryman, a division of Thomas Nelson Publishers, 2005), 16–17.

20. Phineas Camp Headley and George Lowell Austin, *The Life and Deeds of Gen. U. S. Grant* (Boston: B.B. Russell, 1885), 114–115.

21. For the story behind "O Happy Day," see *Then Sings My Soul: Book 1*.

22. Information for this segment came from John Stoughton, *Philip Doddridge: His Life and Labors* (London: Jackson and Walford, 1852).

23. Wilber Fisk Crafts, *Trophies of Song* (Boston: D. Lothrop & Co., 1874), 173.

24. J. Hart, *Hymns Composed on Various Subjects: A New Edition* (London: for M. Jones, 1811), xi.

25. Thomas DeWitt Talmage, *Points, or Suggestive Passages, Incidents, and Illustrations* (London: Hodder and Stoughton, 1874), 289.

26. Joseph Ivimey, *History of English Baptists: Vol. IV* (London: Isaac Taylor Hinton, 1830), 590.

27. Edwin McKean Long, *Illustrated History of Hymns and Their Authors* (Philadelphia: P. W. Ziegler & Co., 1876), 280.

28. Ibid, 284.

29. "The Death-Bed of Samuel Medley," *The Earthen Vessel and Christian Record & Review for 1847: Volume III* (London: James Paul, 1847), 49–51.

30. Adapted from my book *Come Let Us Adore Him* (Nashville: J. Countryman, a division of Thomas Nelson Publishers, 2005), 56–57.

31. Frederick Douglas How, *Bishop Walsham How* (London: Isbister and Company, 1899), 173.

32. Ibid., 238.

33. *Notes and Queries: A Medium of Intercommunication for Literary Men, General Readers, Etc., Fourth Series—Volume Tenth, July – December 1872*, London, page 55.

34. Francis Arthur Jones, *Famous Hymns and Their Authors* (London: Hodder and Stoughton, 1902), 63.

35. William Chatterton Dix, *The Pattern Life; or, Lessons for Children from the Life of Our Lord* (London: Griffith, Farran, Okeden, & Welsh, 1885), excerpted from pages 33–60.

36. Frederick Douglas How, *Bishop Walsham How* (London: Isbister and Company, 1899), 110.

37. Caroline M. Nole, *The Name of Jesus and Other Verses for the Sick and Lonely* (London: Hatchards, Piccadilly, 1878), vi.

38. Ibid., 121.

39. William Dorling, *Memoirs of Dora Greenwell* (London: James Clarke & Co, 1885), 144.

40. Dora Greenwell, *Selected Poems from the Writings of Dora Greenwell* (London: H. R. Allenson, 1906), v–vi.

41. D. W. Whittle, *Memoirs of Philip P. Bliss* (Chicago: A. S. Barnes & Company, 1877), 330–331.

42. Fanny Crosby and Samuel Trevena Jackson, *Fanny Crosby's Story of Ninety-Four Years* (New York: Revell, 1915), 137.

43. Fanny Crosby, *Memories of Eighty Years* (Boston: James H. Earle & Co., 1906), 138.

44. *The Continent*, May 22, 1919, 660.

45. "Rev. Dr. Elisha A. Hoffman" in the *New York Times*, November 26, 1929.

46. Harold Begbie, *The Life of General William Booth* (New York: MacMillan Company, 1920), 444.

47. Delilah Leontium Beasley, *The Negro Trail Blazers of California* (Los Angeles: Delilah L. Beasley, 1919), 225.

48. Jack R. Landbom, *Master Painter Warner E. Sallman* (Macon: Mercer University Press, 1999), 52.

49. "Record of Christian Work," Volume 41, by Alexander McConnell, William Revell Moody, and Arthur Percy Fitt, in the section "Selected Thoughts for the Quiet Hour," October 1922.

50. Darlene Deibler Rose, *Evidence Not Seen* (OM Publishing, 1988), 128.

51. Quoted by William J. Reynolds in *Companion to Baptist Hymnal* (Nashville: Broadman, 1976), 116–117.

52. Information for this segment was gleaned from *The Miracle Goes On* by John W. Peterson with Richard Engquist (Grand Rapids: Zondervan, 1976), passim. John's quote about his grandfather is on page 21.

53. Kenneth W. Osbeck, *101 More Hymn Stories* (Grand Rapids: Kregel Publications, 1985), 53–54.

54. John W. Peterson with Richard Engquist, *The Miracle Goes On* (Grand Rapids: Zondervan, 1976), 155–157.

55. Adapted from Bill Gaither and Ken Abraham, *It's More than the Music: Life Lessons on Friends, Faith, and What Matters Most* (New York: Hachette Book Group, 2003).

56. Adapted from Gloria Gaither, *Something Beautiful: The Stores*

Behind a Half-Century of Songs (New York: Hachette Book Group, 2007), the chapter titled "The Longer I Serve Him (The Sweeter He Grows)."

57. Adapted from Gloria Gaither, *Something Beautiful: The Stores Behind a Half-Century of Songs* (New York: Hachette Book Group, 2007), the chapter entitled "Let's Just Praise the Lord."

58. As told on Stuart Townend's website, www.stuarttownend.co.uk/, slightly condensed.

59. Both the story behind "In Christ Alone" and the quote at the end of the segment are from the Gettys' website, www.gettymusic. com.

60. Quoted in Jane Fletcher, *American Priestess: The Extraordinary Story of Anna Spafford and the American Colony in Jerusalem* (New York: Doubleday, 2008), 108–109.

61. "The Americans of Jerusalem" by R. C. Morgan in *The Gospel in All Lands*" by the Methodist Episcopal Church Missionary Society, 1891, 465–466.

62. "The Story of Bertha Vester" by Elias Antar in "Saudi Aramco World, Volume 18, Number 4, July/August 1967, at http://www. saudiaramcoworld.com/issue/196704/the.story.of.bertha.vester. htm, accessed August 11, 2011.

63. From the history of the Spafford Center as documented on its website at http://www.spaffordcenter.org/history, accessed August 11, 2011.

64. Michael Z. Wise, in an article in *Travel + Leisure* at http://www. michaelzwise.com/articleDisplay.php?article_id=113, accessed August 10, 2011.

65. I am indebted to Pastor Bill Shepherd of Friends Community Church in Sturgeon Bay for sending me a copy of a well-researched 1947 booklet written by his predecessor, John H. Baxter, published in 1947, entitled *The Story of the Old Rugged Cross at Sturgeon Bay, Wisconsin*. Much of this chapter is based on Baxter's research. The quotes at the end of the chapter are

from an article in the *Los Angeles Times* on February 1, 1958, "Author of Famed Hymn in Hospital" by Richard Mathison.

66. "Jingle Bells" is older, but it was originally written for Thanksgiving.

67. Daniel Berger, *History of the United Brethren of Christ* (Dayton: The Otterbein Press, 1910), 296. Berger also relates a touching story about the death of Bishop William Hanby. Just before he passed away at his home in Westerville, Ohio, on May 17, 1880, a friend named Joseph Cook came to visit him. Hanby was very gracious, listening with interest to the report of Cook's work, and when he was preparing to leave, the old bishop took Cook's hands and said earnestly, "May the blessing of the Lord God be upon you and your work." Mr. Cook responded, "And may we meet in the city that hath foundations." Bishop Hanby finished the quotation, saying, "Whose builder and maker is God." Cook replied, "Even so may it be." The atmosphere was so tender at this spontaneous Spirit-prompted ritual that it was followed by perfect silence that no one dared break, so the visitors filed out of the room silently. Shortly afterward, Hanby uttered, "I am in the midst of glory!" and passed away.

68. *Ohio History, Volume 14* (Columbus: Ohio Archaeological and Historical Publications, 1905), 183.

69. There are various versions of the story behind "Nelly Gray." Some claim that Ben was traveling through Kentucky and actually witnessed her heartbreaking separation from her family.

70. *Ohio History, Volume 14* (Columbus: Ohio Archaeological and Historical Publications, 1905), 192.

71. Ibid., 200.

72. Ibid., 202.

73. Ibid., 206.

74. Olivia Egleston Phelps Stokes, *Letters and Memories of Susan and Anna Bartlett Warner* (New York: G. P. Putman's Sons, 1925), 13.

75. *At Home with Susan and Anna Warner: Receipts and*

Remembrances from 1836 to 1915, compiled and illustrated by the Constitution Island Association, West Point, NY, 1977, p. 6.

76. Lois Livingston, "West Point, Anna Warner, and 'Jesus Loves Me,'" in *Christian Herald* (date unknown), p. 24. Also Olivia Egleston Phelps Stokes, *Letters and Memories of Susan and Anna Bartlett Warner* (New York: G. P. Putman's Sons, 1925), 137.

77. From a document from the Warner Archives entitled "Warner Family Papers 1800–1916, 18 Boxes," 2.

78. Ibid.

79. Olivia Egleston Phelps Stokes, *Letters and Memories of Susan and Anna Bartlett Warner* (New York: G. P. Putman's Sons, 1925), 43. Also Anna Walker, *The Life and Letters of Susan Warner* (New York: G. P. Putman's Sons, 1909), 492.

80. From a document entitled "Jesus Loves Me: Incidents from the Life of Anna Bartlett Warner," written by Charlotte Snyder and copyrighted 2004 by the Constitution Island Association, Inc.

81. Olivia Egleston Phelps Stokes, *Letters and Memories of Susan and Anna Bartlett Warner* (New York: G. P. Putman's Sons, 1925), 12.

82. Ibid., 74.

83. Ibid., 81.

84. Quoted in *A Warner Compendium*, prepared by the Constitution Island Association, 1975.

85. Ibid.

86. This section is condensed from my book *Jesus Loves Me This I Know: The Remarkable Story Behind the World's Most Beloved Children's Song* (Nashville: J. Countryman, a division of Thomas Nelson Publishers, 2006). I am deeply grateful for the cooperation and assistance of the United States Military Academy at West Point and by the Constitution Island Association, with special gratitude to Faith S. Herbert, archivist for the Warner files for the Constitution Island Association; Richard de Koster, executive director of the

Constitution Island Association whose personal assistance was invaluable; and Colonel and Mrs. Rick McPeak.

87. Frank L. Houghton, *Amy Carmichael of Dohnavur* (Fort Washington, PA: Christian Literature Crusade, 2000), 354.

88. George W. Bush, *Decision Points* (New York: Crown Publishers / Kindle Edition), chapter 5.

89. Frank L. Houghton, *Amy Carmichael of Dohnavur* (Fort Washington, PA: Christian Literature Crusade, 2000), 27.

90. Ruby Scott, *Jungle Harvest* (Conservative Baptist Home Mission Society, 1988), chapter 9.

91. "The Value of a Smile" by Wilbur D. Nesbit, quoted in *The Playground*, September, 1908, 18.

Alphabetical by Title

Author/Songwriter

First Line of Hymn